T0318324

"This basic introduction to Aquinas's theological thought is a great achievement: it succeeds in combining well-informed presentations of selected topics from the *Summa theologiae* with acute discussions of contemporary critiques and debates around his theology."

—**Rudi te Velde**, *Tilburg University, Netherlands*

"An accessible introduction to the theology of Thomas Aquinas, Harkins balances historical contextualization of Aquinas' thought and engagement with modern interpretations and misinterpretations, using illustrative analogies and humor to explain difficult theological concepts in an engaging style."

—**Aaron M. Canty**, *Saint Xavier University, USA*

THOMAS AQUINAS

THE BASICS

Thomas Aquinas: The Basics is an engaging introduction to the theology of arguably the greatest theologian and philosopher of the Middle Ages. The sophistication and complexity of his thought can be daunting for those approaching his work for the first time. Through this lively and accessible book, Harkins provides an entry point to understanding Aquinas's mature theological thought. As well as giving an overview of Aquinas's life and written works, this book examines Aquinas's understanding of:

- the nature and purpose of theology;
- God's nature, existence, and operations;
- the Trinity;
- creation;
- evil;
- the human person, human happiness, and the virtues;
- Christ and salvation; and
- the sacraments.

Including a useful glossary of key terms, this text is ideal for students and interested non-specialists seeking an understanding of the theology of Aquinas.

Franklin T. Harkins is Associate Professor of Historical Theology and Professor Ordinarius at Boston College School of Theology and Ministry, USA.

The Basics

For more information about this series, please visit:
https://www.routledge.com/The-Basics/book-series/B

THOMAS AQUINAS

THE BASICS

Franklin T. Harkins

LONDON AND NEW YORK

First published 2021
by Routledge
2 Park Square, Milton Park, Abingdon, Oxon OX14 4RN

and by Routledge
52 Vanderbilt Avenue, New York, NY 10017

Routledge is an imprint of the Taylor & Francis Group, an informa business

British Library Cataloguing in Publication Data
A catalogue record for this book is available from the British Library

Library of Congress Cataloging-in-Publication Data
Names: Harkins, Franklin T., author.
Title: Thomas Aquinas: the basics / Franklin T. Harkins.
Description: Abingdon, Oxon ; New York : Routledge, 2021. | Includes
bibliographical references and index.
Identifiers: LCCN 2020034939 | ISBN 9780367349912 (hardback) |
ISBN 9780367349868 (paperback) | ISBN 9780429329197 (ebook)
Subjects: LCSH: Thomas, Aquinas, Saint, 1225?-1274.
Classification: LCC B765.T54 H29 2021 | DDC 230/.2092—dc23
LC record available at https://lccn.loc.gov/2020034939

ISBN: 978-0-367-34991-2 (hbk)
ISBN: 978-0-367-34986-8 (pbk)
ISBN: 978-0-429-32919-7 (ebook)

Typeset in Bembo
by Taylor & Francis Books

CONTENTS

ACKNOWLEDGMENTS

It is a pleasure to thank the people and institutions who have, in various ways, supported me in writing this book. I am grateful for a Boston College Faculty Fellowship during the Spring of 2020, which gave me time outside the classroom to read and think and write. The staff of the Theology and Ministry Library at Boston College, especially Steve Dalton and Michael McGrath, very generously enabled me to access books from the collection when the University and the library were closed due to the COVID-19 pandemic. Thanks to the students to whom over the years I have taught the theology of Thomas Aquinas; they made me aware of the need for an accessible introduction to Aquinas the theologian. Many thanks also to Rebecca Shillabeer and Amy Doffegnies at Routledge for their enthusiasm for the project from the beginning and their kind assistance in various ways throughout the process. I am grateful for the anonymous reviewers of the manuscript whose learned comments and suggestions have made this a better book than it would have been otherwise. I must also thank my parents, Bill and Mary Harkins, and my brother, Vernon, for their support and encouragement of all my academic endeavors throughout the years. Finally, I owe the greatest debt to my beloved wife, Angela, and our wonderful son, Joseph: without their constant love, unflagging support, and profound patience, this project would not have come to fruition. I lovingly dedicate the book to them.

INTRODUCTION
AQUINAS THE THEOLOGIAN

WHY STUDY AQUINAS?

In March 2017, John Marenbon delivered the annual Aquinas Lecture at Maynooth University. It was provocatively titled, "Why We Shouldn't Study Aquinas" (Marenbon 2017). Here Marenbon argued that, in an effort to correct the "exaggerated preeminence" that Aquinas has been given by scholars of medieval philosophy and theology particularly since the rise of Neothomism in the late-nineteenth century (see, e.g., McGinn 2014: 163–209; Kerr 2009: 109–113), all specialized study of Aquinas should be suspended and redirected to other medieval thinkers for several decades (Marenbon 2017: 2, 11). For Marenbon, my writing this book on Aquinas's theology and your reading it serve only to reinforce the "Aquinocentrism," as he calls it, that has dominated inquiry into medieval thought for the past 150 years. Both you and I would have been better served if I had produced a book on another significant, though less well-known, medieval thinker, perhaps Boethius, Avicenna, Gersonides, or John Buridan. My writing and your reading such a book would have served the noble task of undoing "Aquinocentrism" rather than advancing it.

Although Marenbon is hardly alone among contemporary scholars in seeking to encourage studies that reflect and exhibit the rich diversity of medieval thought, his lecture dramatically raises the question of why we should study Thomas Aquinas. What value, if any, is there in reading Aquinas, a Catholic theologian who lived some 800 years ago and whose patterns of thinking differ so markedly from our own? Aquinas is generally recognized as the greatest theologian and philosopher of the Middle Ages, and one of the most significant Christian thinkers of all time. But he is not easily accessible to beginning students or general readers of his works today, due to the apparently foreign modes of his discourse and the complexity of his thought. Yves Congar once told young Dominicans that it would take them 15 years to grasp Aquinas (O'Meara 1997: xvi–xvii). Aquinas's discursive format can present a stumbling block even to seasoned scholars. Jan-Heiner Tück, for instance, describes the technical, scholastic Latin in which Aquinas wrote as "formal, impersonal, and without aesthetic appeal" (Tück 2018: 11). Similarly, John Marenbon maintains that the form of the *Summa theologiae* (*ST*) is characterized by a "strangeness and apparent perversity" (Marenbon 2016: 74). For Aquinas and his medieval readers, however, the format of the *ST*—with its parts divided into questions, which are, in turn, divided into articles—was neither strange nor perverse. In fact, its form, a model of rational clarity, was perfectly natural and commonplace in the medieval universities, having grown out of the standard pedagogical practice of disputation (Torrell 1996: 59–69; Noone 2003: 61–63; Bauerschmidt 2005: 22–24). Indeed, Jean-Pierre Torrell has described the *ST* as "the most beautiful specimen" we have in the scholastic genre of the disputed question (Torrell 1996: 63).

Torrell and other scholars who have studied Aquinas carefully for many years have come to understand not only the scholastic modes of discourse in which Aquinas wrote (e.g., disputed questions, *summae*, commentaries on Aristotle), but also—and more significantly—the deep theological and philosophical insights that these modes convey and even clarify. In my view, these profound insights constitute the primary reason why we *should* continue to study Aquinas. When we study a great theologian like Aquinas, we come to see how he saw God, creation, evil, the human person and the purpose of human life, Christ and His saving work, and the sacraments. The twentieth-century Jesuit Bernard Lonergan spent decades probing the massive Thomistic corpus, striving, as he described it, "to reach up to the mind of Aquinas" (quoted in Kenny 2002: v). Additionally, precisely at those points where Aquinas's mind seems most exciting or strange to us, we are (hopefully) led to recognize, examine, and even question our own presuppositions and approaches. In treating Aquinas on evil and suffering, Eleonore Stump puts it this way:

> One of the benefits of [studying] the history of philosophy, especially the history of philosophy from periods such as the Middle Ages whose cultures are so different from our own, is that it helps us to see the otherwise unnoticed and unexamined assumptions we bring to philosophical issues such as the problem of evil.
>
> (Stump 2003: 478)

But neither understanding what Aquinas thought nor becoming more aware of our own assumptions is the ultimate end of studying Aquinas, it seems to me. Rather, both of these intermediate goals aim finally at helping us to see reality anew, with fresh eyes and with greater clarity. Thomas O'Meara notes that Aquinas's writings, through which we gain access to the theologian and his vision, are "guides and witnesses to life," in which, if read rightly, we find "an inspiring access to the real" (O'Meara 1997: xvi). Similarly, Lawrence Dewan observes that we study Aquinas not merely to find out what the medieval Dominican master thought, but to help us in our attempt to see reality (Dewan 2008: 8). This perspective on the objective of reading past thinkers is actually that of Aquinas himself, who, in commenting on Aristotle's *On Heaven and Earth*, explains: "The purpose of the study of philosophy is not that we might know what people have thought, but rather [that we might know] what is the truth about reality" (*In De caelo* I lect. 22 n. 8; Dewan 2008: 480n2). This basic metaphysical realism—which affirms that there is a knowable reality that exists independently of our conceptual frameworks, perceptions, and linguistic practices—is a foundational element of Aquinas's thought, as we will see throughout this book. It may also be precisely where Aquinas proves most challenging to our customary postmodern assumptions and thought-patterns, and thus ultimately most helpful in leading us to a different vantage point from which to see God, ourselves, and all that is.

Anyone who has tried to introduce others to the thought of Thomas Aquinas—whether through classroom teaching, public lectures, casual conversation, or writing a book—knows well its difficulties and dangers. As O'Meara says, "The wrong introduction renders a theological genius dry and tedious and turns intellectual excitement into boredom" (O'Meara 1997: xvi). Furthermore, the vast majority of recently published introductory volumes on Aquinas either focus on his philosophical thought rather than on his theology, or, if they do primarily treat Aquinas's theology, they are lengthy, conceptually and formally sophisticated, and intended for specialists. This volume, then, aims to provide a basic intro- duction to Aquinas's mature theological thought specifically for students and general readers who are relative newcomers to the medieval master. I hope it proves interesting and helpful to more advanced readers of Aquinas as well. My general method is two- fold. First, I provide close readings and concise analyses of select topics and particular questions in the *ST*, though I also regularly invoke his other works in an effort to highlight Aquinas's theolo- gical assumptions and working method. As more experienced readers of Aquinas will doubtless notice, many aspects of his thought and teaching—sometimes significant ones—have, of necessity, been omitted. Second, in order to demonstrate the continuing relevance of Aquinas for theology today, I engage some of the more influential modern and postmodern readings and cri- tiques of his thought. My hope, through this dual approach, is to introduce Aquinas the theologian in an accessible and lively way so as to deepen understanding and appreciation of his teaching on its own terms.

LIFE AND WORKS

Published treatments of Aquinas's life, works, and Dominican and scholastic contexts—whether concise overviews or more extended studies—abound. Some particularly useful ones in English, on which the following sketch depends, include Weisheipl (1974), Torrell (1996, 2005: 1–16), O'Meara (1997), Tugwell and Boyle (1988), McInerny (1998: x–xxi), Chenu (2002), Wawrykow (2005b: vii–ix), Kerr (2009: 1–30), Mulchahey (1998), and Noone (2003).

Thomas Aquinas was born c. 1225 at the family castle of Roc- casecca, located about midway between Rome and Naples in what was then the Southern Italian county of Aquino. His parents, Landolfo and Theodora, had nine children—four boys and five girls—and Thomas was the youngest son. Around 1230, when Thomas was about five years old, his parents entrusted him as an oblate to the ancient Benedictine monastery of Monte Cassino, where he received his elementary education and exposure to monastic life. In 1239, around age 14, Thomas was sent to Naples for more advanced study in the liberal arts and philosophy. Here the young Aquinas seems to have been first exposed to Aristotle's natural philosophy and metaphysics by his teacher, Peter of Ireland. In Naples too Aquinas became acquainted with the Dominican Order, the Order of Preachers, a relatively new mendicant ("begging") order founded by St. Dominic in 1215 in southern France with the express purpose of saving souls through learned preaching.

Aquinas took the Dominican habit in the spring of 1244, against his family's wishes, and the Order sent him to Paris the following year to continue his studies in philosophy and theology under Albert the Great. When, in summer 1248, Albert left Paris to begin teaching at the newly established Dominican *studium generale* in Cologne, Aquinas followed him. Over the next four years, from 1248 to 1252, Aquinas would be deeply influenced by Master Albert, whom he heard lecture on Peter Lombard's *Sentences*, Dionysius's *On the Divine Names*, and Aristotle's *Nicomachean Ethics*. Aquinas was, most likely, ordained a priest during his sojourn in Cologne, and seems to have delivered cursory lectures on Isaiah, Jeremiah, and Lamentations toward the end of the Cologne period. These biblical commentaries constitute Aquinas's first theological works.

On Albert's recommendation, the Dominican Order appointed Aquinas, beginning in September of 1252, a *baccalarius Sententiarum* at Paris, in which capacity he lectured on the Lombard's *Sentences*, "the standard theological textbook" on which every aspiring master of theology in the high and late Middle Ages was required to comment (Rosemann 2004: 3). His lectures, delivered over the next four years, have come down to us as the *Scriptum on the Sentences*, a massive commentary whose modern Latin edition runs to 6,000 pages! In February 1256, around age 31, still several years shy of the minimum age requirement of 35, Aquinas was awarded the *Licentia docendi*, the license to teach as a Master of Theology, at the University of Paris. From 1256 until 1259 (commonly designated the "first Paris regency"), he occupied one of the two Dominican chairs in theology at Paris, where his primary tasks were to lecture on Sacred Scripture, to hold private and public disputations on various questions arising from the biblical text and its patristic commentary, and to preach to his colleagues and students on special occasions.

Aquinas departed Paris in 1259, having been called back to Italy to serve the educational needs of his Order. For the next decade he taught his religious confreres in Dominican priories in Naples (1259–1261), Orvieto (1261–1265), and Rome (1265–1268), where he was commissioned by the Roman province, "for the remissions of his sins," to found a *studium* at Santa Sabina. By the time he left Paris, Aquinas had already produced a number of significant works, including the *Scriptum on the Sentences*, the *Disputed Questions On Truth, On Being and Essence, On the Principles of Nature*, and the *Exposition on Boethius's On the Trinity*. His impressive productivity continued during the Italian period, when he completed the *Summa contra Gentiles* and penned the *Literal Exposition on Job, The Golden Chain* (a Gospels commentary drawing on patristic quotations), the *Commentary on Aristotle's On the Soul*, the first part of the *Compendium of Theology*, and various disputed questions. In 1268, Aquinas returned to the University of Paris for a second teaching stint as regent master of theology, which lasted until 1272. During this "second Paris regency," Aquinas continued writing his *magnum opus*, the *Summa theologiae*, which he had begun in 1266 while in Rome. In this same period, he was busy lecturing on the Gospels of Matthew and John, composing various disputed questions (*On Evil, On the Virtues*, and *On the Union of the Incarnate Word*), and commenting on such works of Aristotle as *On Sense, Physics, Meteorology, Politics, On Interpretation, Posterior Analytics, Ethics*, and *Metaphysics*.

In spring of 1272, Aquinas again left Paris and returned to Italy, this time having been tasked by the Roman province of his Order to organize a *studium generale* of theology in the location of his choice. He chose Naples, where he appears to have lectured on the Pauline epistles for a second time (the first having been at Rome from 1265–1268) and on the Psalms. Aquinas also continued working on the *Compendium of Theology* and the Third

Part of the *Summa theologiae*, both of which remained unfinished at his death.

After composing a total of approximately 90 theological, philosophical, exegetical, polemical, liturgical, and occasional works—consisting of more than eight million words—Aquinas's prolific writing career came to an abrupt end in late 1273 (see Gilson 1994: 381–428 for a catalogue of his works). While saying Mass on the morning of Wednesday, December 6—the Feast of St. Nicholas—Aquinas was suddenly struck by something that profoundly affected him. After this extraordinary experience, he never wrote or dictated another word. When his *socius*, Reginald of Piperno, encouraged him to continue working on the *Summa*, Aquinas famously replied, "I cannot do any more. Everything I have written seems to me as straw in comparison with what I have seen" (quoted in Torrell 1996: 289). Although we cannot know with certainty what exactly Aquinas experienced on December 6, the historical and biographical evidence points to some sort of mystical vision or special divine revelation. Of the event, Simon Tugwell and Leonard Boyle write: "It looks as if Thomas had at last simply been overwhelmed by the Mass, to which he had so long been devoted and in which he had been so easily and deeply absorbed" (Tugwell and Boyle 1988: 266). Aquinas was never the same after this experience. In February 1274, while traveling northward from Naples to attend the Second Council of Lyons, he fell ill and was taken to the Cistercian Abbey of Fossanova. There, in the early morning hours of Wednesday, March 7, 1274, Thomas Aquinas died. He was not yet fifty years old. Aquinas was canonized in 1323, less than fifty years after his death, and declared a Doctor of the Church in 1567.

SUMMA THEOLOGIAE

Aquinas's greatest and most well-known work is his mature 'summary of theology,' the *Summa theologiae* (*ST*). Indeed, Aquinas's *ST* is unquestionably one of the most profound and influential works of Christian theology ever written (Davies 2014: xiii; Bauerschmidt 2005: 11; Torrell 2005: ix). Over 1,000 commentaries have been written on the *ST*: the only works of Christian literature that have been commented upon more frequently, to my knowledge, are

Scripture and the *Sentences* of Peter Lombard (McGinn 2014: 2; Rosemann 2004: 3). And even now, long after the heyday of Neothomism, countless books and articles on Aquinas's most significant work are published every year (McGinn 2014: 3). The secondary literature is vast and daunting. When I mentioned to a fellow medievalist at a conference some time ago that I was planning to write an introduction to the theology of Thomas Aquinas, he responded, "You are brave, and you have a lot of reading to do!" I have indeed read much, but the studies that remain unread are even more numerous.

Students today are more likely to encounter Aquinas and his *ST* in philosophy courses than in theological studies, and—for a variety of reasons which need not detain us here—the Dominican master is usually thought of as a philosopher rather than a theologian. In general, Aquinas's Five Ways (*ST* I.2.3) have been of far greater interest to modern readers than, for instance, his treatment of the mode of the hypostatic union (*ST* III.2). So the question is often asked whether Aquinas was (primarily) a philosopher or a theologian, with scholars of each discipline wishing to claim him as their own. As I hope the following chapters will make clear, Aquinas was principally a theologian, concerned chiefly with understanding and teaching those truths revealed to us by God. But because he assumes that some of what has been divinely revealed is knowable by natural reason and that none of what has been revealed is contrary to reason, Aquinas thinks it necessary to bring philosophy to bear on the theological enterprise. Aquinas was indeed a Christian theologian, but, as Brian Davies puts it, "one anxious to think philosophically about some key religious beliefs, especially ones about the existence and nature of God" (Davies 2016b: 7; Bauerschmidt 2005: 21–22). He expected theology, like the universe itself, to make sense (O'Meara 1997: 38). Indeed, Aquinas's most important and enduring intellectual contribution may well be his showing that faith and reason are complementary modes of apprehending reality and thus that theology must be wed to philosophy (Davies 2002: 181–94; McCosker and Turner 2016: 1–2).

If Leonard Boyle is correct about the setting of the *ST*, Aquinas composed his great work precisely in an effort to broaden the intellectual horizon of his Dominican students at Santa Sabina and generally to counterbalance the "lopsided system of theological education in the Order" (Boyle 1982: 30). Having been tasked by his province in 1265 with establishing a *studium* in Rome, Aquinas appears to have been free to develop his own curriculum for his particular students. He chose to situate the practical or moral theology that hitherto had dominated Dominican education within a broader and richer theological and philosophical frame. The *Summa*, which Aquinas began composing at Santa Sabina in 1266, is the product of his personal pedagogical project. When he discloses his intention to treat whatever belongs to the Christian religion in a way that is suitable "for the instruction of beginners" (*ST* I.prologue [hereafter prol.]), Aquinas seems to have in view his own young, run-of-the-mill Dominican students, who were likely beginners in their mendicant way of life as much as in theological study (Boyle 1982: 15–17). Aquinas's aim of contextualizing traditional moral instruction within a wider body of 'systematic theology' is evident in the basic tripartite structure of the *ST*.

The *ST* is an imposing work, running to over 1.5 million words. Its three major parts consist of 512 questions and no fewer than 2,668 articles (McGinn 2014: 2; Kerr 2009: ix). The First Part (or *Prima pars*, abbreviated "I"), consisting of 119 questions, treats God and the procession of creatures from God. The Second Part (*Secunda pars*), which is the largest (comprising 303 questions), concerns the human person as the image of God, "according to which he too is the principle of his own actions" (*ST* I-II.prol.). This massive moral part is divided into two. In the First Part of the Second Part (*Prima secundae*, abbreviated "I-II"), Aquinas considers happiness, the ultimate end of human life, as well as human acts and their principles, both intrinsic and extrinsic. The Second Part of the Second Part (*Secunda secundae*, abbreviated "II-II") concerns those particular habits or intrinsic principles of human actions that are the virtues. Finally, the Third Part (*Tertia pars*, abbreviated "III") treats Christ, "the Savior of all," and the benefits bestowed by Him on the human race. This part remains unfinished, as Aquinas stopped writing at q. 90 (on penance) on December 6, 1273.

Modern readers of the *ST* have wondered whether there is a more general plan or organizing principle underlying the work's tripartite division, an architectonic key of sorts that might unlock Aquinas's overarching purpose. In 1939 Marie-Dominique Chenu first proposed the Neoplatonic scheme of *exitus* and *reditus*, the creaturely emanation from and return to God, as this plan (Chenu 1939). Chenu explains how *exitus-reditus* maps onto and accounts for the *ST*'s structure:

> This is the nature of the *Summa*'s construction and the shape of the movement that it describes. The *Prima pars* (First Part) treats the emanation of reality from God as from its principle; the *Secunda Pars* (Second Part) treats reality's return to God as its destiny and goal. And because in fact according to God's free and gratuitous choice (as salvation history reveals to us) this return is achieved through Christ the man-God, a *Tertia Pars* (Third Part) examines the "Christian" conditions of this return.
>
> (Chenu 2002: 137–138)

Chenu's *exitus-reditus* proposal has gained wide—indeed, nearly unanimous—acceptance among Thomists today as having, in Bernard McGinn's words, "a good textual foundation in the *Summa*" and a high degree of explanatory power (see, e.g., McGinn 2014: 68–78; Torrell 2005: 49–50; Wawrykow 2005b: 53–54; Torrell 1996: 150–153; Jordan 2016; Coakley 2016: 222–223; Pope 2002: 30).

A few scholars, however, have identified fundamental problems with *exitus-reditus* and suggested alternate architectonic schemes. For instance, Albert Patfoort and Rudi te Velde have noted—rightly, in my view—that *exitus-reditus* is too simple to account for the structural complexities of the *ST* (Patfoort 1963; Te Velde 2006: 11–18). The movement of *exitus* cannot be strictly or easily identified with the *Prima pars*, for example, as already here Aquinas treats aspects of the *reditus* of creatures to God as final cause (e.g., divine government in qq. 103–119). And, indeed, he introduces the notion of God as humankind's end as early as q. 1 a. 1, well before he begins discussing creaturely procession from God in q. 44. Secondly, because the *reditus* that begins, according to Chenu, in the *Secunda pars* continues into the *Tertia pars*, the traditional *exitus-reditus* scheme fails to explain why Aquinas devotes a separate part of his *Summa* to Christology, particularly after he has treated the "new law" of the Gospel and grace as means of salvation in I-II qq. 106–114 (Te Velde 2006: 15–16). Thirdly, the common assumption that the language of the *ST* itself attests to the *exitus-reditus* structure is simply mistaken. Rudi te Velde is correct, on my reading, in affirming that "[n]o textual evidence in the *Summa* can be found in support of the hypothesis that Thomas intended the three parts to be organized according to the scheme of *exitus-reditus*" (Te Velde 2006: 12).

Te Velde maintains, by contrast, that the programmatic statements of Aquinas's various prologues point to the organization of the *ST* according to three agents, namely God, the human, and Christ (Te Velde 2006: 17–18; *ST* I.2.prol). The *Prima pars* treats God and His work of creation (I.2.prol.). The *Secunda pars* takes up the rational human person, the very image of God, and his work of freedom (I-II.prol.). Finally, the *Tertia pars* deals with Christ and His work of salvation (III.prol.). In my view, Te Velde's 'agentic model' is preferable to Chenu's *exitus-reditus* proposal in that it resolves the key difficulties presented by the latter: it has greater explanatory power when mapped onto the *ST*'s tripartite structure, it accounts for why Aquinas treats Christ in a separate part of the work, and, perhaps most significantly, it is grounded in Aquinas's own descriptions of his procedure.

Finally, a brief orientation to the format of the articles that constitute the questions of the *ST* may prove helpful for new readers. Although the number of articles varies from question to question, each article has the following structure:

- *Objections* (abbreviated in citations below as "obj. 1, 2, 3" etc.). Here Aquinas offers several brief arguments against the position that he himself will take in the *corpus* or body of the article. Each objection may cite one or more authorities (e.g., scriptural, patristic, philosophical).
- *Sed contra* ("On the contrary"; abbreviated "s.c."). The *sed contra* states an argument and/or authority generally opposed to that of the objections. Aquinas will make effective use of this argument and/or authority in developing his solution to the question and responding to the objections.
- *Corpus* (abbreviated "co."). Aquinas provides his response or answer to the question here, in the "body" of the article. He aims to reconcile the authorities of the *sed contra* with those of the objections, often by having recourse to grammatical, logical, philosophical, and/or theological distinctions.

- *Replies to the objections* (abbreviated "ad 1, 2, 3" etc.). Here Aquinas brings to completion the scholastic work of reconciling divergent authorities and positions, explaining specifically how his answer in the corpus serves to address each objection.

In the following chapters, I will cite the *ST* according to part, question, article, and section of article as illustrated by these examples: *ST* I.2.3 co.; *ST* I-II.111.3 obj. 1; *ST* II-II.175.6 s.c.; *ST* III.50.2 ad 2.

2

SACRED DOCTRINE

One of Aquinas's fundamental assumptions, which has profound implications for his entire theological project, is that we, as humans, have been created for a purpose that is beyond our natural capacity, namely to know God perfectly, to see God as He is (1 Jn 3:2). By means of our intellectual souls, which distinguish us from other corporeal creatures, we are naturally ordered to a supernatural end: the beatific vision of God (see Ch. 7 below). For all of us ordinary humans (which Aquinas calls "pure humans"), however, this perfect knowledge of God is not possible in this earthly life; rather, beatific vision is a gift of that glorified life enjoyed only by the saints in heaven. "It must be said that God cannot be seen in His essence by a pure human being [*ab homine puro*]," Aquinas explains, "unless he is separated from this mortal life" (*ST* I.12.11 co.). As we will see in Ch. 8, the one notable exception appears to be Jesus Christ, whom Aquinas understands to have enjoyed the beatific vision in his human soul from the moment of conception and throughout His earthly life (*ST* III.10, 34; Christ is not really an exception to the above rule at all because, according to Aquinas, Christ is *not* a "pure human"). But for the rest of us, how is it that we come to know God in this life? By what means does God teach us in the here and now? How can we apprehend any truths whatsoever about God, particularly those that are necessary for final salvation? This is the basic line of inquiry with which Aquinas opens his *Summa theologiae*. The first question of the First Part, on the nature and extent of what Aquinas calls "sacred doctrine" (*sacra doctrina*), provides important answers to these critical questions; indeed, it has been described as "the greatest contribution to theological method that the greatest theologian of the Middle Ages has to offer" (Baglow 2004: 1).

Before we examine *ST* I.1, let us briefly consider what Aquinas takes to be the human person's "threefold knowledge [*triplex cognitio*] of divine realities" (*Summa contra Gentiles* [hereafter *ScG*] IV.1). This scheme of how the human variously knows God and the things of God provides an important epistemological backdrop to *ST* I.1. At the outset of *ScG* IV, Aquinas explains that the human—on account of his intellectual and embodied nature—takes his knowledge of whatever object he knows from sensible realities. Where God is the object to be known, however, our natural knowing runs into an immense, seemingly insurmountable, problem: it cannot 'see' or otherwise sense the divine substance in itself because God's substance, in Aquinas's own words, "disproportionately transcends all sensible things, indeed all other existing things [*omnia alia entia*]" (*ScG* IV.1). As we will see in Ch. 3, God is not, according to Aquinas, a being who can be observed and studied empirically; indeed, God is not *a* being among beings in the universe at all. And yet, Aquinas insists that "the perfect good of the human is that he should know God in whatever way [*quoquo modo*]" (*ScG* IV.1). But again, how is knowing God possible for us? The operative phrase here is *quoquo modo*, "in whatever way." Aquinas understands well that whatever degree of understanding of divine realities we might attain to in this life pales in comparison to the perfect vision of God enjoyed by the blessed in the next.

And so there is a "threefold knowledge of divine realities." Aquinas explains:

> The first is that whereby the human, by the natural light of reason, ascends through creatures to the knowledge of God. The second is that whereby divine truth, exceeding human understanding, descends to us according to the mode of revelation, not however as something demonstrated to be seen, but as set forth in words to be believed. The third is that whereby the human mind will be lifted up to gaze perfectly upon the things that have been revealed.
>
> (*ScG* IV.1)

This third mode of knowledge ordinarily obtains only in the life of the world to come, whereas the first two pertain to this present life. The philosophical mode, which proceeds according to natural reason, aims at scientific *demonstration* or proof, and so the conclusions reached are clearly 'seen.' By contrast, the properly theological mode, which proceeds according to divine revelation, aims at *belief* in realities that cannot be proven or 'seen' this side of heaven. Following Heb. 11:1 (*Faith is the evidence of things unseen*), Aquinas takes seriously that the object of faith is always something that the believer does not know demonstratively or scientifically, although he recognizes that one person may know scientifically the same truth that another person holds by faith (*ST* II-II.1.4, 5). Thus, what is 'seen' by one remains 'unseen' by the other.

With these preliminaries in view, let us turn to a consideration of Aquinas's understanding of the necessity, nature, and mode of sacred doctrine.

THE NECESSITY OF SACRED DOCTRINE

Strikingly, Aquinas opens q. 1 of the *Prima pars*—and the entire *Summa*—by treating the necessity of sacred doctrine (*sacra doctrina*); even before he has established what *sacra doctrina* is and how it proceeds (aa. 2–10), he asks whether it is necessary (a. 1). It would seem, the objections explain, that we humans need no other doctrine (*doctrina*) besides the "philosophical disciplines" because whatever truths are within the grasp of reason—and indeed all things whatsoever that are true and that are (i.e., that exist)—are adequately treated in the philosophical disciplines. This is true even of God Himself, as there is a branch of philosophy called "theology" or "the divine science" (*theologia sive scientia divina*), as Aristotle shows in *Metaphysics* VI (*ST* I.1.1 obj. 2). Following Aristotle, Aquinas understands this *theologia*, also called Metaphysics or First Philosophy, to be the highest philosophical discipline and indeed speculative wisdom itself by virtue of the fact that it studies what is most causal (viz., God as the highest cause), most universal (viz., being in general [*ens commune*]), and most immaterial (viz., subsistent immaterial realities like angels and the soul) (*In Metaph.*, prooem.). In the previous century, Hugh of St. Victor too had identified "theology" (*theologia*) as the first theoretical or speculative philosophical science, which treats God and spiritual creatures (*Didasc.* II.2). This explains why Aquinas uses the term *sacra doctrina* here rather than *theologia*. The "teaching" (*doctrina*) with which he is concerned diverges in significant ways from that of the philosophical science of "theology." Aquinas himself puts it this way: "The theology that pertains to sacred doctrine differs in kind [*secundum genus*] from that theology that is part of philosophy" (I.1.1 ad 2).

What distinguishes sacred doctrine from what may properly be called 'philosophical theology' or 'natural theology' is related to the twofold meaning of the Latin word *doctrina* (and its English equivalents, "doctrine" or "teaching"). *Doctrina* refers both to the *content* of what is taught—as we intend its English equivalent when we use such phrases as 'Christian doctrine' or 'the doctrine of God'—and to the *mode* by which instructional content is conveyed, that is, the manner of content delivery—as when we say of a professor, 'Her classroom teaching is excellent.' For Aquinas, 'sacred doctrine' signifies both *what* God teaches (i.e., the particular content) and *how* He teaches it (i.e., the pedagogical mode). Concerning content, sacred doctrine differs in part from philosophical theology, as we will soon see. But what distinguishes this "holy teaching" from that of the philosophical disciplines more fundamentally is its pedagogical mode, the manner according to which God delivers certain truths to humankind. Whereas the objections in a. 1 focus on content—noting that whatever can be known rationally about any subject, including divine realities, is taught by the philosophical sciences—Aquinas's solution emphasizes the mode of sacred doctrine, namely divine revelation.

It is sacred doctrine's revelatory mode, in fact, that accounts first and foremost for its necessity. Aquinas begins his response thus: "It must be said that it was necessary for human salvation that—besides the philosophical disciplines, which are investigated by human reason—there be a certain teaching according to divine revelation [*doctrinam quandam secundum revelationem divinam*]." Some translators infelicitously render Aquinas's *doctrinam* here (and more generally) in English as "knowledge," which is, in fact, an appropriate translation of the Latin term *scientia*. As we will see, Aquinas understands sacred doctrine to be a *scientia* as well. But *doctrina* and *scientia* should not be confused or conflated. Whereas *doctrina* properly signifies teaching (both a body of truths taught and how it is taught), *scientia* denotes knowledge or "science" (indicating both a body of truths known and how it is known). What is taught and what is known are often related, of course, but they are not identical. For example, a six-grade math teacher—let's call her Mrs. Hall—never teaches any of her students everything about math that she herself knows. Alternatively, a particular student, Max, even after sitting in Mrs. Hall's class for a year, may know very little of what she did convey to the class, whether her teaching came through verbal instruction, working out practice problems on the board, or textbook chapters assigned for weekly reading and review. Furthermore, when presented with the equation, $7554838925 \div 3 = x$, different students arrive at the correct value of x in different ways. Charlotte uses her calculator to discover quickly that $x = 2518279642.67$. Sophia, however, comes to *know* that $x = 2518279642$ rem. 2 by accurately doing the long division with pencil and paper. And Oliver, who does not yet understand how to 'work out' such problems using mathematical reasoning, simply *believes* that this is the value of x because Mrs. Hall tells him so. We will return to this example as an analogy of the preambles of faith, one of the two types of truth found in sacred doctrine.

Logically prior, however, to the twofold content of God's sacred teaching is its revelatory mode, which Aquinas understands as necessary for human salvation. Divine revelation is soteriologically necessary firstly because, according to Aquinas, "the human is ordered [*ordinatur*] to God as to a certain end that exceeds the comprehension of reason," and this final end must be known beforehand by humans, who "ought to order [*ordinare*] their intentions and actions" to it (I.1.1 co.). For Aquinas, God has ordered or directed us, both naturally and supernaturally, to Himself; and we, being thus ordered, are in turn obliged to order our thoughts and activities to God. But how can we begin to do this when God, our final end, exceeds our rational capacity? This epistemological problem has its roots in a profound ontological disparity between God and all other existents, as *ScG* IV.1 makes clear. In the opening question of the *Scriptum on the Sentences* also Aquinas notes that there is an infinite ontological distance or disproportionality between the Creator, as First Cause, and His creaturely effects, such that all notions derived from creatures (by way of the philosophical disciplines) are finally insufficient for knowing God in this life (*Scriptum* I q. 1 a. 1 s.c. 2). Here, in language similar to that of *ST* I.1 co., Aquinas explains: "Therefore, it is necessary that there be another, higher teaching [*aliam doctrinam ... altiorem*], which proceeds by way of revelation; and it should make good the defect of philosophy [*philosophiae defectum suppleat*]" (*Scriptum* I q. 1 a. 1 s.c. 2). The purpose, then, of God setting forth the "higher teaching" of sacred doctrine by means of revelation is to supply what is lacking in philosophy, to make up for its defect, in order that we humans might know enough about God as end to direct our lives in this world toward Him so as finally to arrive at the beatific vision.

It is clear from *ST* I.1.1 that Aquinas understands "the defect of philosophy" in terms of the twofold content of sacred doctrine. The two kinds of truth that constitute sacred doctrine, both of which God teaches by way of revelation, are what Aquinas calls the "articles of faith" and the "preambles of faith." The articles of faith are those truths about God—such as the Trinity, Incarnation, and bodily resurrection—that exceed human reason. These articles are among the truths known perfectly by God, of course, but no human is capable of arriving at them through rational investigation. Simply stated, the philosophical disciplines alone can provide no access to the articles of faith; in this way philosophy is fundamentally defective. Thus, any human apprehension whatsoever of the articles absolutely requires God's having revealed them. It also requires the additional supernatural gift of faith, an infused theological virtue that elevates our rational capacity beyond its nature such that it can grasp unseen realities (*ST* I.1.1 ad 1; II-II.4.1, 5; II-II.6.1).

The preambles of faith constitute the second type of truth found in sacred doctrine. In contrast to the articles, the preambles of faith are truths about God that "can be investigated by human reason" (I.1.1 co.) and are presupposed by the articles of faith. Precisely as 'preambles,' they 'walk before' (*pre* + *ambulo*) the articles of faith. That God exists, that God is one, that God is good, and that the human soul is incorruptible are among the preambles of faith, in Aquinas's view (Wawrykow 2005b: 115). It is easy to see, for example, how the Trinity, an article of faith, presupposes such preambles as God's existence and oneness. Similarly, the Christian belief in resurrection presupposes the incorruptibility of the soul (Te Velde 2006: 28). Although the preambles *can* be demonstrated by rational investigation, and indeed the very best philosophers have arrived at them by natural reason alone, Aquinas teaches that "it was necessary that the human be instructed [*instrui*] by divine revelation" concerning them (I.1.1 co.). Note Aquinas's emphasis here on sacred doctrine as a pedagogical *mode*: God instructs us in those same truths (i.e., the same *content*) at which natural reason can arrive. And it was imperative that God teach us humans even concerning the preambles because without divine revelation the truth about God, based on rational investigation alone, would be known only "by a few, and after a long time, and with the mingling of many errors" (I.1.1 co.). This, then, is the second defect of philosophy, according to Aquinas: that it can lead us humans only *imperfectly* to the knowledge of those divine truths that are, in fact, rationally demonstrable.

The fundamental problem underlying such imperfect knowledge is, as we have seen, soteriological. Indeed, Aquinas affirms: "The entire salvation of the human, which is in God, depends on the knowledge of the truth [concerning God]" (I.1.1 co.). With this salvific end in view, Aquinas concludes the corpus of a. 1 thus:

> Therefore, in order that salvation might come about for humans both more fittingly and more certainly [*et convenientius et certius*], it was necessary that they be instructed [*instruantur*] concerning divine realities by means of divine revelation. Accordingly, it was necessary that, besides the philosophical disciplines, which are investigated by means of reason, they have a sacred teaching by means of revelation [*sacram doctrinam per revelationem*].

Here I have rendered *sacram doctrinam* as "sacred teaching" in an effort to capture as clearly as possible Aquinas's point: that because our natural mode of knowing in this life—by rational investigation via the philosophical disciplines—provides knowledge of God insufficient for the salvific end to which we are ordered, God teaches us through His own revelation so as to aid our movement toward final beatitude. We see here at the outset of the *Summa* what we will discover in various ways throughout, namely that, as Bruce Marshall has observed, for Aquinas "*sacra doctrina* always has a soteriological purpose" (Marshall 2005: 5). We should not suppose—as many of his modern readers unfortunately have—that, on account of a technical, scholastic style that may seem unfamiliar to us, Aquinas understands or practices sacred doctrine as an abstract, esoteric endeavor of purely theoretical or academic interest. In fact, as I hope this book will show, Aquinas's teaching on and practice of sacred doctrine point in the opposite direction. "He could not have imagined the study of theology as a merely intellectual exercise," as Timothy Radcliffe rightly remarks (Radcliffe 2016: 23).

Having established the necessity of sacred doctrine both with regard to the articles and preambles of faith, Aquinas concludes the opening article of q. 1 by explaining that nothing prevents different people from knowing the preambles of faith in different ways. That is, although there is a part of philosophy that treats divine realities (I.1.1 obj. 2), the presence of this *theologia* among the scientific disciplines in no way precludes *sacra doctrina* or even renders it superfluous. And this is because, as we have already seen, "the theology that pertains to sacred doctrine differs in kind [*secundum genus*] from that theology that is part of philosophy," in Aquinas's view (I.1.1 ad 2). Lest his reader imagine that such 'generic' difference among sciences treating the same subject is unique to the study of God, Aquinas points out that, in fact, "different methods of knowing establish a diversity of sciences" (ad 2). Different modes of examining and apprehending can lead practitioners of distinct sciences to the same conclusion concerning the same subject. Aquinas provides the example of an astronomer and a physicist, both of whom, using the particular approach of his science, demonstrate that the earth is round. The astronomer arrives at this conclusion by means of mathematics, that is, by abstracting from matter, whereas the physicist does so by carefully examining matter itself. Based on this mundane example, Aquinas concludes:

> Hence nothing prevents another science [*aliam scientiam*] also from treating, insofar as they are known by the light of divine revelation, those same realities that the philosophical disciplines treat insofar as they are knowable by the light of natural reason.
>
> (*ST* I.1.1 ad 2)

Two particularly noteworthy points must be highlighted here. First, Aquinas explicitly identifies sacred doctrine as a "science," which provides an apt segue to a. 2, where he specifically takes up the question whether *sacra doctrina* is a *scientia*. Second, in line with the reality of a *scientia*, Aquinas emphasizes that philosophical theology and sacred doctrine are distinguished, where the preambles of faith are concerned, by the different methods or modes whereby these shared truths are known. On his account, whereas an expert philosopher like Aristotle may arrive by natural reason at the conclusions that God exists and is one, most people who adhere to these truths do so on the basis of divine revelation and faith. Christians throughout the world profess in the Nicene Creed, "I *believe* in one God...," rather than "I *know* one God ..." In sacred doctrine, divine revelation is the mode of teaching (*doctrina*) and apprehension by faith is the mode of human knowing (*scientia*) that corresponds to it in this life. God's own knowledge (*scientia*), from which He reveals the truths of His "holy teaching," is quite different, of course. Like Mrs. Hall with her sixth-grade math students in our analogy above, God does not reveal to humankind everything that He Himself knows. But based on what God has revealed, Christians believe both the preambles, which can be known by reason, and the articles, which cannot. Believers engage in that same mode of apprehension as did Oliver, who simply could not reason his way to the value of x where $7554838925 \div 3 = x$. Sophia, by contrast, provides the analogue for philosophers who access the preambles by rational investigation: she grasped that $x = 2518279642$ rem. 2 not because Mrs. Hall revealed it to the class and she believed it, but rather because she worked out the long division problem, that is, she came to 'see' the correct answer "by the light of natural reason." Sophia and Oliver arrived at the same conclusion, but they did so by different methods or ways of knowing.

THE NATURE OF SACRED DOCTRINE

Having established the necessity of *sacra doctrina* in a. 1, Aquinas treats the nature and mode of this "holy teaching" in the subsequent articles. In discussing its nature, Aquinas is concerned to show that sacred doctrine is a single science in the Aristotelian sense (aa. 2–3), it is principally speculative (a. 4), it is nobler than other sciences (a. 5) and indeed is wisdom in the highest degree (a. 6), and its subject is God (a. 7). Let us consider each of these aspects of the nature of *sacra doctrina* before turning to its mode.

The primary purpose of sacred doctrine, according to Aquinas, is "to hand on the knowledge of God" (*Dei cognitionem tradere*; I.2. prol.). As discussed above, sacred doctrine is a particular body of knowledge that is handed on by revelation and apprehended by faith. Before examining Aquinas on whether this body of knowledge constitutes a "science" according to the Aristotelian concept, it may prove helpful to consider, at a more basic level, its essential nature. What is *sacra doctrina*? Of what precisely does it consist? Some recent scholars have read Aquinas as straightforwardly identifying sacred doctrine with Sacred Scripture. Brian Davies, for example, affirms that "Aquinas takes [*sacra doctrina*] to be equivalent to divine revelation as provided in the Bible" (Davies 2014: 18). Although Sacred Scripture is foundational to its revelatory mode, sacred doctrine encompasses significantly more for Aquinas. Thomas Prügl explains:

> 'Sacred doctrine' ... was not restricted to any one of the theological specializations familiar to us today. Rather, it was seen more broadly, as the process of transmission of saving knowledge having its origin in God and reaching humankind through church doctrine, Scripture, and theology.
>
> (Prügl 2005: 386)

Sacred Scripture and sacred doctrine, then, are not strictly identical for Aquinas. They are, however, profoundly unified, as, in the words of Christopher Baglow, "phases of a broader dynamism of revelation" (Baglow 2004: 2). Similarly, Joseph Wawrykow notes the essential role of human mediation—past, present, and future—in Aquinas's understanding:

> Human beings enter into sacred doctrine as agents of God in passing on the truths necessary for salvation, through the writing of the Scripture in which God's saving truth is proclaimed and, subsequently, in the ongoing interpretation of scriptural teaching and application of its lessons to the contemporary scene.
>
> (Wawrykow 2005b: 132)

Although Aquinas fails to include contemporary theologians among the authorities used in sacred doctrine—which include scriptural writers, doctors of the Church, and philosophers (I.1.8 ad 2)—we may well understand our scholastic theologian himself as participating in the handing on of the knowledge of God that is the principal aim of sacred doctrine. Indeed, as Bruce Marshall observes, "from beginning to end the *Summa* is an exercise in *sacra doctrina*" (Marshall 2005: 3).

Aquinas asks in I.1.2 whether this sacred doctrine is, in fact, a "science" (*scientia*). According to the Aristotelian understanding, which Aquinas and other medieval scholastic theologians inherited, a "science" is an ordered body of knowledge in which self-evident or necessary first principles lead by deductive reasoning to all the truths concerning a particular subject. In his commentary on Boethius's *On the Trinity*, Aquinas writes: "The notion of science [*ratio scientiae*] consists in this, that from certain things that are known conclusions concerning other things are derived of necessity" (*Super De Trin.* I q. 2 a. 2 co.). Scientific knowledge, then, is deductive and demonstrative: what is known scientifically is what can be derive from first principles that require no proof or demonstration themselves. This Aristotelian notion differs essentially from our modern understanding of "science" as a system of knowledge concerning the operation of general laws in the physical universe obtained systematically by formulating problems, collecting data through observation and experimentation, and formulating and testing hypotheses. Because God is not a member of the physical universe and so cannot be studied empirically (more on this in Chapter 3), sacred doctrine as understood by Aquinas could hardly be considered a "science" by modern standards. But might it qualify as a *scientia* in the Aristotelian sense?

At first glance, it seems that both the mode of its teaching (viz., revelation) and its requisite method of knowing (viz., faith) disqualify sacred doctrine as an Aristotelian "science." After all, the first principles from which sacred doctrine proceeds are the articles of faith, which are not self-evident or known through themselves (*per se nota*). They must be revealed by God in order to be apprehended at all. Furthermore, once they are divinely revealed, they are not granted by all, as revelation itself makes clear: *Not all humans have faith* (2 Thess. 3:2; I.1.2 obj. 1). On the contrary, Augustine (in *On the Trinity* XIV.1) describes theology as a "science" whereby "the most salubrious faith is begotten, nourished, defended, and strengthened" (I.1.2 s.c.). On the authority of Augustine, then, sacred doctrine must be a science, Aquinas reasons. But how? And what kind of science is it?

Aquinas explains that even among the philosophical disciplines there are two kinds of science. Those of the first kind proceed from principles known per se "by the natural light of the intellect" (I.1.2 co.). Such sciences include arithmetic and geometry. Although Aquinas offers no examples of self-evident first principles in these sciences, they are not difficult to imagine. In geometry, for example, 'a whole is greater than a part,' and 'a triangle has three sides and three angles.' Such first principles need not, and indeed cannot, be demonstrated by the science itself, as they are simply known per se if they are known at all. One who knows what a whole is—something that has all its proper parts—knows immediately that it is greater than any particular part of which it consists. Sciences of the second kind proceed not from self-evident first principles, but rather from principles "known by the light of a higher science" (I.1.2 co.). These sciences are thus 'under another' science, and so Aquinas calls them "subalternate sciences" (*Scriptum* III d. 24 q. 1 a. 2 qc. 2 ad 3; *De ver.* q. 15 a. 2 ad 15). He provides the examples of perspective, which proceeds from principles known by geometry, and music, which takes its principles from arithmetic. Further examples abound: architecture is subalternate to geometry (among other sciences), aerospace engineering is subalternate to physics (among others), and pharmacy is subalternate to chemistry (among others). That pharmacy proceeds from principles known by chemistry explains why present-day pharmacy schools generally require applicants to have successfully completed one year each of general chemistry and organic chemistry at the undergraduate level.

Aquinas teaches that, although sacred doctrine is clearly not the first sort of science, it is a subalternate science. It proceeds from first principles known by a higher science, which Aquinas identifies as "the science of God and the blessed" (*scientia Dei et beatorum*; I.1.2 co.). "Hence, just as music believes [*credit*] the principles handed over [*tradita*] to it by arithmetic, so sacred doctrine believes [*credit*] the principles revealed [*revelata*] to it by God," Aquinas affirms (I.1.2 co.). Note how the relationship between sacred doctrine and divine knowledge closely parallels that between music and arithmetic, lest we imagine that *sacra doctrina* is utterly different from any of the philosophical sciences. In the same way that sacred doctrine must believe what has been revealed by God, music must believe what arithmetic has passed on to it. Theologians who practice sacred doctrine are by no means unique among scientists in the faith that is required of them.

But what is this "science of God," from which sacred doctrine receives its first principles? *Scientia* means knowledge, so what Aquinas intends here by *scientia Dei* is the knowledge that God has of Himself. According to Aquinas, God understands Himself per se or self-evidently (*ST* I.14.2 co.), the same way that first principles are known by human practitioners of sciences of the first kind. Furthermore, God knows all the things He has made—that is, His creaturely effects—by the same knowledge (*scientia*) whereby He knows Himself because these effects eternally preexist in God (I.1.4 co.; I.14.5 co.). Significantly for Aquinas, these features of God's knowledge account for both the unity and the speculative nature of sacred doctrine, as we will soon see (I.1.3 ad 2; a. 4 co.).

Here, though, we might ask just how analogous the relationship between sacred doctrine and God's knowledge (*scientia Dei*) is to that between a subalternate philosophical science and its higher science. After all, although the musician may not know self-evidently the principles she receives from the mathematician, it is possible that—by studying arithmetic—she *could* come to know them per se, just as the mathematician does. By contrast, no theologian—indeed, no human at all—can investigate God's own self-knowledge such that he comes to 'see' the first principles of sacred doctrine (viz., the articles of faith). It seems that God alone knows them and knows them per se, by knowing Himself. Aquinas suggests a response to this critique when he identifies the science to which sacred doctrine is subalternate as "the science of God and the blessed" (*scientia Dei et beatorum*; I.1.2 co.). God's own self-knowledge is also shared—to the most profound degree possible for ordinary humans—with the blessed in heaven by the grace that Aquinas calls the "light of glory." This light "establishes the intellect in a certain deiformity" such that the beatified human can see or know God perfectly, according to 1 Jn 3:2: *When He shall appear, we will be like Him, and we will see Him as He is* (*ST* I.12.5 co., a. 6 co.). Thus, the blessed see clearly those divine truths that

God has revealed to us in the here and now as the articles of faith. So we ordinary humans can, in fact, know them—just not yet. Aquinas makes clear, however, that the gift of faith elevates the intellect above its natural capacity, enabling even in this life an anticipation of the beatific vision (see Chapter 7). Indeed, faith is "a habit of the mind, whereby eternal life is begun in us, that causes the intellect to assent to things unseen" (*ST* II-II.4.1 co.). Aquinas can aptly describe sacred doctrine, then, as "a certain impression of the divine knowledge [*quaedam impressio divinae scientiae*]" in the believer (I.1.3 ad 2).

Just as God knows Himself per se or through His own essence, likewise He knows all created things not by seeing them in themselves (i.e., as effects actually existing outside of Himself), but rather by seeing them in Himself, since His essence contains the similitude of all things other than Himself (*ST* I.14.5 co.). Aquinas teaches, then, that God's essence is the "sufficient principle" of His knowing all things made by Him, "not only in the universal, but also in the singular" (I.14.11 co.). And because God's essence is one and simple (I.11, 3), so too is His knowledge (*scientia*) of all individual things (I.1.3 ad 2). By extension—because sacred doctrine is "a certain impression of the divine knowledge" (I.1.3 ad 2)—*sacra doctrina* is one science, even though it treats a variety of subjects, including the Creator and creation, angels, corporeal creatures, and human morality (I.1.3 obj. 1, 2). The single science of sacred doctrine considers such varied subjects according to their formal basis in divine revelation, that is, precisely as they have been revealed by God (I.1.3 co.). Aquinas explains:

> It must be said that sacred doctrine, ... being one, extends to things that belong to different philosophical sciences on account of the formal basis [*propter rationem formalem*] to which it attends among diverse things, namely as they are knowable by the divine light.
>
> (*ST* I.1.4 co.)

Relatedly, on the question of sacred doctrine's subject matter, Aquinas teaches that all things considered in the science are treated "under the aspect of God" (*sub ratione Dei*; I.1.7 co.). Because the theologian deals with God Himself and all other things as they are ordered to God as their beginning and end, God can properly be called the subject of this science (I.1.7 co.; I.1.3 ad 1; I.2.prol.). Thus, *sacra doctrina* treats primarily God and secondarily other topics in relation to God. As its principle subject, however, God is necessarily handled differently from that of other sciences. Whereas, according to Aristotle, the nature or essence (*quid est*: literally, the 'what it is') of the subject is presupposed in any science, we cannot naturally know or say what God is (I.1.7 obj. 1). "For, concerning God, what He is not [*quid non est*] is more manifest to us than what He is [*quid est*]," Aquinas teaches (I.1.9 ad 3; I.3.prol.). Thus, instead of a definition of God, the First Cause, sacred doctrine uses His effects, either of nature or grace, when treating the topics it considers (I.1.7 ad 1). Aquinas is quick to note that even certain philosophical sciences demonstrate something about a cause from its effect "by taking the effect in place of a definition of the cause" (I.1.7 ad 1).

By virtue of the fact that sacred doctrine considers "absolutely [*simpliciter*] the highest cause of the entire universe, which is God," Aquinas understands this science to be "wisdom in the highest degree" (I.1.6 co.). According to Aristotle, the wise person (*sapiens*) is the one who orders things in a particular genus rightly and governs them well (*ScG* I.1); as such, he must consider the highest cause of things in the genus or order in which he works. In the order of building, for instance, the architect, who plans the form of a house, is called wise in comparison to the skilled workers below him who chop the wood and prepare the stones (*ST* I.1.6 co.). Whereas the architect is called wise in a particular domain of activity, the one who is wise simply is she who considers the highest cause of all, the beginning and end of the universe (*ScG* I.1). She may be a metaphysician or 'natural theologian,' studying the universal cause through creatures according to human reason; alternatively, she may be a practitioner of sacred doctrine, studying this same cause by way of divine revelation. It is principally this revelatory mode that elevates sacred doctrine beyond all the philosophical sciences, including metaphysics. Aquinas explains:

> But sacred doctrine most properly investigates God according to which He is the highest cause, not only insofar as He is knowable through creatures (as the philosophers known Him, as is said in Rom. 1[:19]: *what is known of God is manifest in them*), but also insofar

as He is known to Himself alone from Himself and communicated to others through revelation [*notum est sibi soli de seipso, et aliis per revelationem communicatum*].

(*ST* I.1.6 co.)

Significantly, sacred doctrine uses the philosophical sciences and embraces what they can rationally discover about God as the highest cause. But it also goes further, in receiving and probing the very self-knowledge that this divine cause of the universe has deigned to share with humanity.

Because sacred doctrine treats a wide range of subjects—some belonging to speculative philosophical disciplines and others to practical ones—Aquinas asks whether the single science of *sacra doctrina* is practical or speculative. It is noteworthy that his renowned teacher, Albertus Magnus, understood theology as fundamentally practical, a "science according to piety" whose perfection is found "in particular works and in those working in particular ways" toward their beatifying end (Albert, *ST* I tr. 1 q. 2 sol., q. 1 ad 1; see Harkins 2019: 8–15). Aquinas, however, takes a different tack. He recognizes that sacred doctrine includes both the speculative and the practical, "in the same way that God also knows, by the same knowledge (*scientia*), Himself and the things He has made" (*ST* I.1.4 co.). Notice here again how sacred doctrine reflects God's own knowledge. But sacred doctrine is more speculative than practical, in Aquinas's view, because it treats divine realities more principally than human acts. This is so because the human is ordered by particular acts to "the perfect knowledge of God, in which eternal beatitude consists" (I.1.4 co.). Such knowledge or 'speculation' (*speculatio*: examination, consideration, contemplation) of God is, of course, a human act, albeit one perfected by divine grace. Significantly, it is the beatific end of human life, which is our ultimate *practical* aim, that accounts for the chiefly *speculative* or contemplative nature of sacred doctrine for Aquinas. This may seem counterintuitive to us, but we must bear in mind that for Aquinas the practical and the speculative are neither mutually incompatible nor in competition with one another. Rather, as Bruce Marshall observes, "Aquinas' point is that the saving aim of *sacra doctrina*, God seen and contemplated by human beings, gives the whole of this teaching its basic character"

(Marshall 2005: 5). In short, because the *Summa* is an exercise in sacred doctrine, it is also an act of divine contemplation and an exhortation to it (Radcliffe 2016: 23).

Given his understanding that sacred doctrine is wisdom itself (I.1.6), Aquinas's teaching that it is superior to all other sciences (I.1.5) should not be surprising. On the face of it, however, it seems that *sacra doctrina* is an inferior, less noble science for two reasons. First, it is not the most certain science, as its first principles—the articles of faith—are susceptible to doubt (I.1.5 obj. 1). Second, sacred doctrine depends on the philosophical sciences, just as music depends on the higher science of arithmetic (obj. 2). Aquinas answers by explaining that sacred doctrine, which is partly speculative and partly practical, "transcends all others," both speculative and practical (I.1.5 co.). It is superior to all speculative philosophical sciences on account of its greater certitude and the higher dignity of its subject matter. Regarding certitude, Aquinas observes: "Other sciences have certitude from the natural light of human reason, which can err, but this one has certitude from the light of divine knowledge [*ex lumine divinae scientiae*], which cannot be misled" (I.1.5 co.). On account of the weakness of our intellect, which leads some humans to doubt the articles of faith, theologians necessarily rely on God's own 'science' of Himself for apprehending truths that are, in fact, "more certain according to nature" than all others (I.1.5 ad 1). Aquinas offers an arresting analogy: our intellect is dazzled by those truths that are "manifest in the highest degree according to their own nature" just as the eye of the night owl is dazzled by the bright light of the sun; the night owl cannot see the intense daylight, although "obscure realities" are easily visible to it (*In II Metaph.* lect. 1 no. 10; *ST* I.1.5 ad 1). Relatedly, sacred doctrine surpasses other speculative sciences also on account of the greater dignity of its subject matter: whereas the others consider only those subjects that reason can grasp, *sacra doctrina* treats principally those that transcend reason (I.1.5 co.). Furthermore, to the extent that it is practical, sacred doctrine is superior to other practical sciences as well. This is so because the dignity of a practical science is a function of the worth of its end or purpose. And the end to which sacred doctrine is directed is, as Aquinas teaches, "eternal beatitude, to which as to an ultimate end all other ends of the practical sciences are ordered" (I.1.5 co.).

To the objection that sacred doctrine depends on the philosophical sciences and thus appears inferior to them, as music is subalternate to arithmetic, Aquinas responds that *sacra doctrina* receives its first principles not from other sciences, but "immediately from God by means of revelation" (I.1.5 ad 2). That it, this science is subalternate and inferior to God's own self-knowledge, but not, in fact, to any of the philosophical sciences (I.1.6 ad 1). Rather, sacred doctrine utilizes the philosophical sciences "as inferiors and handmaidens," as, for example, politics uses military science (I.1.5 ad 2). And it does so not because of any inherent insufficiency, but rather "because of the defect of our intellect," which "is more easily led by the hand [*facilius manuducitur*] from those things that are known by natural reason ... to those that are above reason" (I.1.5 ad 2).

THE MODE OF SACRED DOCTRINE

Given the supernatural end to which we humans have been ordained, sacred doctrine necessarily proceeds according to the mode of divine revelation, on the formal basis of which it considers God and other things in relation to God. This mode of "holy teaching" distinguishes this science from the philosophical disciplines, of course. On the other hand, Aquinas is intent on showing that the special mode of *sacra doctrina* does not render it altogether different from the philosophical sciences and so disqualify it as a real *scientia*. Quite to the contrary, in fact, Aquinas's view is that its revelatory mode, together with its treating principally the first cause of the universe, establishes sacred doctrine as the highest of all sciences. He takes this general approach again when he asks whether sacred doctrine is "argumentative" (*argumentativa*) (I.1.8): that is, does it proceed, as the philosophical sciences do, by rational argumentation? Alternatively, does the faith that sacred doctrine requires override or otherwise replace reason? And if not, how are faith and reason related in *sacra doctrina*?

If sacred doctrine is "argumentative," it argues either from authority or from reason. It is objected, however, that neither mode of argument seems 'fitting' for this science. Argumentation from authority seems unfitting given the dignity of sacred doctrine, since argument from authority is the weakest form of argument. Likewise, argumentation from reason seems unfitting for its end, since faith is not meritorious if reason provides proof of what is believed (I.1.8 obj. 2). In answering this important question, Aquinas once more highlights the similarities between sacred doctrine and other sciences, aiming to show that sacred science proceeds according to the method of 'faith seeking understanding.' He teaches that just as other sciences do not—indeed, cannot—argue in proof of their first principles, but instead argue from these principles to other conclusions, so too sacred doctrine does not and cannot argue in proof of the articles of faith, but rather proceeds from these articles to prove other truths. In 1 Cor. 15, for example, St. Paul argues from the resurrection of Christ in proof of the general resurrection (I.1.8 co.). According to Aquinas, the articles of faith—such as Christ's resurrection—are above reason, but they are not contrary to it; in other words, they are suprarational rather than irrational. Although the articles cannot be demonstrated by reason alone, once they have been revealed by God and apprehended by faith, we humans can reason about them in various ways. When sacred doctrine uses the philosophical disciplines "as inferiors and handmaidens" (I.1.5 ad 2), the human reasoning that is proper to them is brought to bear in order to elucidate what God has revealed (I.1.8 ad 2). This mode of rationally investigating the truths of faith, which Aquinas's own teaching and writing exemplify so well, is grounded in what is perhaps the most fundamental principle of his theological vision, namely that grace perfects nature. Aquinas affirms: "Indeed, since grace does not destroy nature, but perfects it, it is right that natural reason should serve faith, just as the natural inclination of the will submits to charity" (I.1.8 ad 2).

Just as grace perfects nature, divinely revealed truths about God perfect naturally knowable truths about God. Likewise, the supernatural gift of faith, whereby believers apprehend divinely revealed truths, perfects natural reason. Thus, Aquinas affirms that, although the argument from authority based on human reason is the weakest type, argumentation from authority based on divine revelation is "the most efficacious" (I.1.8 ad 2). This is so because "faith rests on infallible truth," namely the perfect truth of God's own self-knowledge (I.1.8 ad 2). And what is contrary to the truth can never be demonstrated. What this means is that arguments mounted against the Catholic faith cannot be demonstrative proofs.

Thus, while it is true that the articles of faith cannot be proven, neither can they be disproven. Rather, arguments against faith are merely difficulties that the theologian (i.e., practitioner of sacred doctrine) must attempt to answer (I.1.8 ad 2; *ScG* I.2). He can debate with opponents by means of Scripture itself if the opponents accept Scripture's authority and some of its truths, "as we can dispute with the Jews by means of the Old Testament, and with heretics by means of the New," Aquinas explains (*ScG* I.2; *ST* I.1.8 co.). But if the opponents do not accept scriptural authority, the theologian must answer their objections by having recourse to natural reason, "to which all are compelled to assent" (*ScG* I.2; *ST* I.1.8 co.). On the other hand, as we have seen, reason is finally "deficient regarding divine realities" (*ScG* I.2).

In light of this understanding of the "argumentative" nature of sacred doctrine, Aquinas sets forth in *ST* I.1.8 ad 2 what scholars have recognized as a 'hierarchy of authorities' used in this science. At the apex of this hierarchy is Sacred Scripture, or, more precisely, God Himself, who is the author of Scripture. The canonical Scriptures have an authority that is intrinsic to sacred doctrine and absolutely certain because it is God's own perfect knowledge that has been revealed to and conveyed through their human writers. "Our faith rests on the revelation made to the apostles and prophets who have written (*scripserunt*) the canonical books," Aquinas teaches (I.1.8 ad 2). Although our tendency—shaped as we are by modern historical-critical approaches to the Bible—is to identify the apostles, prophets, and other producers of its books as "human authors" (see Wawrykow 2005b: 14, 39), Aquinas very rarely calls the human producers of Scripture "authors" (*auctores*) (*De pot.* q. 4 a. 1 co.); rather, in line with ancient and medieval Christian practice, he usually calls them "sacred writers" (*sacri scriptores*). Though the scriptural writers properly share in the authority of the divine revelation that they transmit, Scripture has but one principal "author." "It must be said that the author [*auctor*] of Sacred Scripture is God," Aquinas affirms (*ST* I.1.10 co.; cf. *De pot.* q. 4 a. 1 co.).

Second to the authority of Scripture itself is that of the "doctors of the Church." Here Aquinas appears to have in view primarily Church Fathers such as Augustine, Ambrose, Cyril, John Chrysostom, Gregory the Great, and John Damascene, on whose writings he draws extensively throughout his theology. Their authority

is also intrinsic to sacred doctrine, as they were concerned principally to explicate the saving truths revealed by God in Scripture.
The authority of the doctors differs from that of Scripture itself in
that it is not certain, but rather merely probable. That is, they
could have been—and sometimes were—mistaken in their interpretations of divine revelation. Lowest on Aquinas's hierarchy are
the philosophers, of whose authority sacred doctrine makes use
"where they were able to know the truth by means of natural
reason" (I.1.8 ad 2). Like that of the doctors, the philosophers'
authority is merely probable: even great philosophers like Aristotle
could, and sometimes did, err. And in contradistinction to both its
scriptural and patristic counterparts, philosophical authority is
extrinsic to sacred doctrine. Because philosophers are not concerned with explicating Christian revelation, they stand outside the
purpose and mode of sacred doctrine. Yet, as we have seen, their
insights, gained through natural human reason, can be profitably
brought into the theological enterprise.

Aquinas draws *ST* I.1 to a close by considering how Sacred
Scripture, the font of sacred doctrine, signifies and therefore how
it should be read and understood (aa. 9–10). His primary aim is to
show how Scripture—because its sole author is God and because
God signifies His will otherwise than we humans do—differs
from other texts and perhaps from our expectation as well. In line
with traditional Christian understanding, Aquinas makes two
major points in this regard: that Scripture should and does use
metaphors (I.1.9), and that God signifies using multiple senses
(I.1.10). First, Aquinas teaches that—perhaps contrary to expectation for sacred doctrine, the highest of all sciences—it is "fitting" (*conveniens*) for Sacred Scripture to convey divine and
spiritual truths by means of metaphors or similitudes of corporeal
things. Aquinas explains:

> For God provides for all things according to what comports with their
> nature. But it is natural to the human to come to intelligible realities
> through sensible objects, because all of our knowledge has its begin-
> ning from sense perception. Hence, in Sacred Scripture spiritual
> truths are fittingly [*convenienter*] conveyed to us under metaphors of
> corporeal things.

> (*ST* I.1.9 co.)

To paraphrase Madonna's 1984 hit single "Material Girl": "We are living in a material world and we are material girls [and boys]." Therefore, according to Aquinas, God has graciously accommodated His supernatural revelation to our material and sensible mode of understanding. Scripture sets forth spiritual truths under metaphors of corporeal things so that even the simple-minded (*rudes*), who are otherwise incapable of grasping intelligible realities, might be able to understand them (I.1.9 co.). For Aquinas, then, just as grace perfects nature, so too divine revelation accords with and perfects our natural knowing. Scriptural metaphors lead us by the hand, as it were, from sensible objects to spiritual realities.

But what sorts of sensible objects are most appropriate or effective in this regard? Whereas we might expect Scripture to prefer metaphors taken from higher creatures, which are more similar to the divine likeness, we often find the lowest creatures used as similitudes in the sacred text (I.1.9 obj. 3). Following Dionysius, Aquinas teaches that it is actually "more fitting" that Scripture conveys divine realities under the figures of common or lowly material bodies rather than of higher ones. He offers three reasons (I.1.9 ad 3). First, using metaphors taken from common bodies better preserves the human mind from error, because it knows more easily that such lowly realities do not properly describe divine realities. When we read, for example, *The Lord is my rock* (2 Sam. 22:2), it is, or should be, clear to us that God is not literally a rock! Second, this mode of signification is more appropriate to the way we know God in this life. "For, concerning God, what He is not [*quid non est*] is more manifest to us than what He is [*quid est*], and therefore similitudes of those things that are farther removed from God give us a truer sense that God is beyond [*supra*] whatever we say or think about Him," Aquinas affirms (I.1.9 ad 3). Third, divine truths are better hidden from the unworthy by this type of common metaphorical teaching.

Finally, Aquinas teaches that God signifies in Sacred Scripture by means of multiple senses (I.1.10). Again, it may seem that a particular scriptural text (*littera*) should not have many senses, as this could produce confusion and deceit and "destroy the strength of argument," which must be founded on a single meaning

(I.1.10 obj. 1). With the hermeneutical theory of Augustine and the long tradition of the fourfold sense in the background (see Levy 2018: 19–26), Aquinas explains that God signifies His will differently than we humans do. Indeed, Scripture's divine author has the power to signify not only by words (which are particular signs of things), as we do, but also by things themselves. Thus, whereas every other science only signifies things by words, "this science has the property that the things themselves signified by words also signify something else" (I.1.10 co.). The first mode of signification, whereby words signify things, pertains to the literal or historical sense (*sensus historicus vel litteralis*) of Scripture. The second mode, whereby the things signified at the literal level in turn signify other things, is the spiritual sense (*sensus spiritualis*). Following the most common medieval classification, Aquinas divides the spiritual sense into the allegorical, the moral or tropological, and the anagogical. The allegorical sense is that according to which "the things of the Old Law signify the things of the New Law" (I.1.10 co.). For Aquinas, as for premodern exegetes generally, Christological interpretations of the Old Testament fall within the ambit of the allegorical. The moral sense is that whereby "the things done in Christ or in those things that signify Christ," including Old Testament events, point to what we ought to do (I.1.10 co.). Finally, the anagogical sense is that according to which these things having been done in the Old and New Testaments signify "those things that are in eternal glory" (I.1.10 co.).

On Aquinas's account, these several senses neither cause confusion nor undermine argumentation since all of the spiritual senses are established on the literal sense, the only one from which arguments can be derived (I.1.10 ad 1). The literal sense is not wholly singular, however, since it includes both the proper and figurative signification of words; thus, the metaphorical sense is contained within the literal, in Aquinas's view (I.1.10 ad 3). Furthermore, it is not the figure itself that constitutes the literal sense, but rather what is figured. Aquinas explains, for example, that when Scripture speaks of the arm of God, the literal sense is not such a corporeal member that belongs to the deity, but rather the operative power of which the arm is a figure (I.1.10 ad 3). Significantly, Aquinas understands this polysemous literal sense to be a consequence of the nature of God's own knowledge, from which scriptural revelation comes. He teaches:

> Because, in truth, the literal sense is what the author intends, and because the author of Sacred Scripture is God, who comprehends all things at once by His intellect, it is not unfitting ... if even according to the literal sense there are several senses in one text of Scripture.
>
> (*ST* I.1.10 co.)

Having been introduced to sacred doctrine, let us now turn to a consideration of God's nature, existence, and operations according to Aquinas.

3

GOD'S NATURE, EXISTENCE, AND OPERATIONS

Since the mid-twentieth century, it has become fashionable for theologians to criticize Aquinas's ordering and division of topics in the *ST* (Muller 1995: 673; LaCugna 1991: 145–152). Some question Aquinas's starting point—the unity of the divine essence (I qq. 2–26)—and his treatment of it apart from the Trinitarian persons (qq. 27–43). Catherine LaCugna, for example, claims: "This is a clear departure from the Bible, early creeds, liturgy, and Greek patristic theology, all of which begin with the Unoriginate Father who comes to us in salvation history in the person of Christ" (LaCugna 1991: 147–148). Others similarly wonder why Aquinas postpones treating Christ until the end of his work. The Trinity seems marginalized, and the Incarnation appears as an afterthought appended to a predominantly natural theology.

Careful readers of Aquinas might respond to such critiques in any number of salutary ways. But two general points concerning his approach in the *ST* should suffice here. First, Aquinas's self-professed aim is "to treat the things that pertain to the Christian religion in a way that is fitting for the instruction of beginners" (I.prol.). The principal subject of sacred doctrine, which is identical to neither Scripture nor early creedal statements, is God in Himself, as we have seen. It seems altogether appropriate, then, that Aquinas should treat what pertains to the divine essence at the outset of his teaching. And because sacred doctrine is subalternate to God's own *scientia*—being "a certain impression of the divine knowledge" (I.1.3 ad 2) in the theologian—beginners ought to begin by considering such immanent operations of God in Himself as knowing and willing. Second, in treating God's existence and essence prior to the Trinity and Incarnation, Aquinas illustrates how, in terms of our knowing, the preambles 'walk before' the articles of faith. He teaches,

> It must be said that the existence of God and other truths of this sort about God that can be known by natural reason, as is said in Rom. 1, are not articles of faith, but preambles to the articles; for faith presupposes natural knowledge, just as grace presupposes nature, and as perfection presupposes something perfectible.
>
> (*ST* I.2.2 ad 1)

For Aquinas, because the articles of faith, which are above reason but not contrary to it, necessarily 'build on' and perfect the preambles, which can be arrived at by natural reason, these preambles must be proposed and considered before one can profitably advance to the articles. Before coming to the Trinity (Ch. 4), then, this chapter aims to provide a basic orientation to Aquinas's thought on *what* God is (not), *that* God is, *how* God is (not), and God's operations of knowing and willing.

WHAT IS GOD? NO IDEA!

As a young child, Thomas often asked those around him, "What is God?" (Radcliffe 2016: 29; Tugwell and Boyle 1988: 202–103). As he grew older, this basic question would profoundly shape his life and ministry as a Dominican theologian and teacher. After all, in order to proceed in sacred doctrine, its practitioner must know whether its subject, namely God, exists and what its subject is (Te Velde 2006: 37). Furthermore, for Aquinas, "What is God?" stands as the fundamental question to which all human life and thought has been ordered. And yet, we cannot naturally know what God is. Any positive answer to this question eludes us. Aquinas insists that what God is *not* is more manifest to us than what God is (*ST* I.1.9 ad 3). Throughout our consideration of Aquinas's theology, we will see just how seriously he takes this apophatic or negative approach to God. Because (1) we ascend by natural reason through creatures to the knowledge of God, and because (2) God utterly transcends every created reality, and because (3) even by divine revelation and faith we cannot 'see' God in this life, for Aquinas "the whole enterprise of theology is shot through with unresolvable mystery" (McCosker and Turner 2016: 5). We simply cannot know what God is.

If asked, then, 'What is Aquinas's basic notion or idea of God?', we could rightly respond, 'He has no idea.' It may seem strange, even impossible, that one of the most profound and influential theologians in Christian history has no idea what God is—but it is true. Furthermore, in Aquinas's view, no human does or can have a positive, quidditative concept of God; rather, all we have is a *use* for the word 'God.' Herbert McCabe explains:

> Aquinas holds that we know how to use the word 'God' not because of any idea we have, even a hazy one, of what *God* is, but because of what we know about *other* things. In other words, we use the word 'God' not because we have noticed God but because we have noticed something about the world. What we have noticed, according to Aquinas, is its radical questionableness.
>
> (McCabe 2016a: 103)

The universe raises many questions for us. Why do dogs bark and cats meow? Why do we dream? What's at the bottom of the ocean? How did the universe begin? Theoretically at least, modern science, which studies things within the universe itself, can provide answers to all such questions, even if it has not yet done so. But the universe raises a question more fundamental than any of these, namely: Why does the universe exist at all? That is, why is there anything rather than nothing? In Aquinas's view, although the universe raises this radical existence-question, nothing in the universe can provide an answer to it. Rather, the answer, albeit an ineluctably mysterious one, is 'God,' whom Aquinas takes to be the cause of all things. As the universal cause, God Himself is *not* an existing thing in or alongside the universe. If we were to do some 'ontological addition' or 'metaphysical math,' it is manifest that my wife and I add up to two things in the world. My wife, our son, and I add up to three things. My wife, our son, our dog, and I clearly make four. But, for Aquinas, my wife, our son, our puppy, and God do not and cannot add up to five (Davies 2002: 185; McCabe 2000: 199).

This too may strike us as strange. Aquinas's apophatic and inferential approach to God differs dramatically from that of many modern theologians, philosophers, and ordinary believers who assume that God's existence and nature can be deduced from the very idea of God. Such 'character-theists,' as they are sometimes called, imagine God kataphatically according to certain characteristics, such as power, knowledge, goodness, and love (Moonan 2000). They begin with notions of human or creaturely power, knowledge, goodness, etc., and then envisage God as the being who exists at the farthest extreme of each continuum, who possesses these attributes in the highest degree. Indeed, as Brian Davies has observed, many theologians and philosophers of religion today take God to be essentially what René Descartes understood a human to be, namely "a person without a body who invisibly thinks and wills and lives a life as our contemporary" (Davies 2002: 185). Consider the analytic philosopher Richard Swinburne, who, in rejecting divine eternality, affirms: "We continue to think of God as a person doing now this, now that, as a person existing in time" (Swinburne 1977: 174). Furthermore, many contemporary thinkers understand this kataphatic, 'personal' Cartesian concept of God as precisely what Scripture and Christian tradition propose for belief. The 'openness of God' theologian Clark H. Pinnock, for example, maintains: "Far from a totally unchanging and all-determining absolute Being, the Bible presents God as a personal agent who creates and acts, wills and plans, loves and values ..." (Pinnock 2001: 25). Similarly, John Thiel writes:

> Christians believe ... that God is a person and so possesses a character. The character of God, the sort of person God is, can be described through certain qualities ... God, for example, is creative, and extraordinarily so ... God is good, and extraordinarily so ... God is merciful, and extraordinarily so ... And God is loving, and extraordinarily so ... The [Christian] tradition does claim and teach with authority that God's character is of a certain sort.
>
> (Thiel 2002: 9–10)

Whereas Aquinas recognizes that truths about God that exceed natural reason have been revealed by God and that such terms as "person" (*ST* I.29), "goodness" (q. 6), and "love" (q. 20) can be attributed to God, he insists that these terms are predicated analogically, not univocally, of God and creatures, and that as regards what they signify they are predicated first of God rather than of creatures (I.13.5, 6). Furthermore, Aquinas understands well—with the Christian tradition he inherits—that God is not "a person" in the Cartesian sense at all, but rather is three persons (I.30.1, 2).

If, as we have suggested, many modern theologians and believers conceive of God otherwise than does Aquinas, likewise modern atheists seem to gainsay an altogether different deity. With his usual sagacious wit, McCabe explains:

> Very frequently the man who sees himself as an atheist is not denying the existence of some answer to the mystery of how come there is anything instead of nothing; he is denying what he thinks or has been told is a *religious* answer to this question. He thinks or has been told that religious people, and especially Christians, claim to have discovered what the answer is, that there is some grand architect of the universe who designed it, just like Basil Spence only bigger and less visible, that there is a Top Person in the universe who issues arbitrary decrees for the rest of the persons and enforces them because he is the most powerful being around. Now if denying this claim makes you an atheist, then I and Thomas Aquinas and a whole Christian tradition are atheistic too.
>
> (McCabe 2000: 200)

The popular self-proclaimed atheist Richard Dawkins illustrates McCabe's point well when he observes that Christians believe, quite irrationally, that God is "the Great Policeman in the Sky," constantly surveying human actions to ensure morally upright behavior (Dawkins 2019: 96–99). Although many today may find it surprising, traditional Christian theology does not, in fact, take God to be either "the Great Policeman in the Sky" or the "Top Person in the universe." And Aquinas certainly has no such anthropomorphic notions of God. Aquinas's God is not "some grand architect of the universe" who, from within the cosmos itself, designed all (other) things, in the way that Basil Spence drew up blueprints for Coventry Cathedral, the New Zealand Parliament "Beehive," and Trawsfynydd Nuclear Power Station. It has been claimed, in fact, that one of Aquinas's greatest intellectual contributions is the powerful antidote he provides to such idolatrous understandings of God (Davies 2002: 184–186). For Aquinas, as we have seen, by natural reason alone we can have no positive idea whatsoever of what God is; in other words, we can have no quidditative knowledge of God. Rather, whatever knowledge of God we might possess is arrived at only indirectly and by causal inference (Davies 2016a: 87). Aquinas's famous Five Ways provide such inferential 'roads' whereby we can come to know that God exists.

DEMONSTRATING THAT GOD IS: THE FIVE WAYS

The "five ways" (*quinque viae*) of proving the existence of God in *ST* I.2.3 have captured the imagination of modern interpreters more than anything else Aquinas wrote. Although these demonstrations constitute a tiny portion of the *Summa* (indeed, fewer than 775 words in the original Latin), and although Aquinas never intended them as definitive philosophical arguments that would provide rational certainty for faith in God's existence, the Five Ways have given rise to a vast body of secondary literature and popular commentary (Pawl 2012: 115; Feser 2009: 62–63; Te Velde 2006: 38–39). Indeed, they may well be "the most famous set of arguments for God's existence ever written" (Feser 2009: 62). The Five Ways, as Aquinas presents them, are: (1) the proof from motion; (2) the proof from efficient causality; (3) the proof from contingency and necessity; (4) the proof from gradation of being; and (5) the proof from the governance of things.

Despite the modern fascination with the Five Ways, it is all too easy for us to misunderstand Aquinas's arguments. One reason is that the modern epistemological context of arguments for divine existence is altogether different from that of medieval theology. "For Thomas natural reason functions within an intellective search for the truth of being," Rudi te Velde explains, "while modern reason tends to dismiss any metaphysical claim with regard to the intrinsic knowability of reality" (Te Velde 2006: 38). Our tendency, then, may be to understand Aquinas's terminology ("motion," "first mover," "order of efficient causes," etc.) differently than he intended (Copleston 1955: 122). Richard Dawkins provides a dramatic example of this modern tendency toward misconstrual. Dawkins boldly maintains:

> The five 'proofs' asserted by Thomas Aquinas ... don't prove anything, and are easily—though I hesitate to say so, given his eminence—exposed as vacuous. The first three ... involve an infinite regress—the

answer to a question raises a prior question, and so on *ad infinitum* ... All three of these arguments rely upon the idea of a regress and invoke God to terminate it. They make the entirely unwarranted assumption that God himself is immune to the regress. Even if we allow the dubious luxury of arbitrarily conjuring up a terminator to an infinite regress and giving it a name, simply because we need one, there is absolutely no reason to endow that terminator with any of the properties normally ascribed to God: omnipotence, omniscience, goodness, creativity of design, to say nothing of such human attributes as listening to prayers, forgiving sins and reading innermost thoughts.

(Dawkins 2006: 77)

We will return to this line of critique below. Suffice it here to note that Dawkins's objections are based on what Edward Feser calls "egregious misunderstandings" of Aquinas's arguments (Feser 2009: 64). Of Dawkins, David Bentley Hart says:

He devoted several pages of *The God Delusion* to a discussion of the 'Five Ways' of Thomas Aquinas but never thought to avail himself of the services of some scholar of ancient and mediaeval thought who might have explained them to him ... As a result, he not only mistook the Five Ways for Thomas's comprehensive statement on why we should believe in God, which they most definitely are not, but ended up completely misrepresenting the logic of every single one of them, and at the most basic levels. ... The Five Ways, if properly understood, are far richer and more interesting than Dawkins grasps.

(Hart 2013: 21–22)

The Five Ways are firmly established on Aquinas's assumption that sustained metaphysical reflection on familiar, observable features of the world provides ample evidence for God's existence (Copleston 1955: 114). On the other hand, Aquinas knew well that not everyone is capable of such sustained metaphysical reflection, as Dawkins unfortunately appears to attest. Essential to a proper understanding of the Five Ways is recognizing that, although they take various sensible features of the world as their starting-points, they seek to prove something that is not and cannot be scientifically observable, namely divine existence. Thus, they are not scientific proofs. Rather, Aquinas intends them to show, as Brian Davies puts it, "that things with which we are familiar ought to lead us to suppose that there is something that is quite distinct from the world considered as something to be explored scientifically" (Davies 2014: 36). In other words, the Five Ways variously suggest that nothing in the world itself is sufficient finally to account for the bare fact that certain observable phenomena occur. As such, they are meta-physical or meta-scientific hypotheses.

Aquinas undertakes to demonstrate that God exists precisely because he understands that God's existence is not self-evident or known *per se* to us (*ST* I.2.1 co.). Significantly, Timothy Radcliffe has observed that the Five Ways "are less opposed to atheism than to those who think God's existence is obvious" (Radcliffe 2016: 28). In Aquinas's view, Anselm of Canterbury (c. 1033–1109) assumed that God's existence is readily apparent to all, even the "fool" of the Psalms who says in his heart, "There is no God" (Ps. 13:1; 52:1). Anselm opens his famous 'ontological argument' (*Proslogion* ch. 2) by defining God as "a certain thing than which nothing greater can be thought [*aliquid quo maius nihil cogitari potest*]." For Anselm, unlike for Aquinas, God is an *aliquid*, a certain thing or particular being. And this "certain thing than which nothing greater can be thought" exists in the intellect or understanding (*in intellectu*) of all who think of 'God', even of those who deny the existence of such a supreme thing. Anselm argues that God must exist in reality (*in re*) as well as in the intellect if He is, in fact, "a certain thing than which nothing greater can be thought," because it is greater, ontologically speaking, to exist in reality than in the intellect alone (*Pros.* 2).

Aquinas responds by maintaining that, although a particular person might understand 'God' according to Anselm's definition, it does not therefore follow that God exists "in the nature of things" (*ST* I.2.1 obj. 2). What prevents the proposition 'God exists' (*Deus est*) from being self-evident to us is that we do not know what God is (*quid est*) and so cannot know that 'existence' (*esse*), the predicate, is included in the very quiddity (*quid est*) of the subject, 'God' (*Deus*) (I.2.1 co.). But 'God exists' is self-evident in itself (*secundum se*), according to Aquinas, because "God is His own existence [*suum esse*]" (I.2.1 co.; I.3.4 co.). Here *esse* may also be rendered "being" or "to-be," as Aquinas uses the term to denote

God's act of being or of existence (I.3.4 ad 2; Wippel 2000: 24–25, 522). Because God is "subsistent being itself [*ipsum esse subsistens*]" (e.g., I.4.2 co.; I.11.4 co.) and "being itself through His own essence [*ipsum esse per suam essentiam*]" (I.8.1 co.), God cannot not be. For Aquinas, as David Burrell puts it, "to be God is to be to-be" (Burrell 1979: 24). But to affirm this truth is to say something we do not understand, something of which we have no positive idea. Such statements, then, do not constitute proofs of God's existence. Rather, that God exists must be demonstrated through things that are more known to us (I.2.1 co.).

We must note that, in setting forth the Five Ways and in treating God's existence and operations more generally in *ST* I.2–26, Aquinas is not offering a pure natural theology entirely divorced from divine revelation. On the contrary, as we have indicated, he proceeds as a practitioner of sacred doctrine who understands that "faith presupposes natural knowledge" (I.2.2 ad 1). "Aquinas was a Christian before he became a metaphysician," F. C. Copleston rightly observes. "And he did not come to believe in God simply as a result of his own metaphysical arguments" (Copleston 1955: 111). Surely neither did his Dominican students, beginners in theology (I.prol.), arrive at faith in God's existence only after encountering the Five Ways. If faith presupposes natural knowledge, there is also for Aquinas a sense in which, conversely, natural theology presupposes divine revelation. After all, Aquinas takes a key assumption underlying the Five Ways—namely that God's existence can and must be demonstrated through things that are more known to us (I.2.1 co.)—directly from Sacred Scripture. He notes that the words of Rom. 1:20, *The invisible things of God are clearly seen, having been understood through the things that have been made*, would not be true unless divine existence could be proven from reflection on created realities (I.2.2 s.c.). Furthermore, in *ST* I.2.3, immediately prior to setting forth the Five Ways, Aquinas offers God's own self-revelation to Moses in Exod. 3:14, *I am who am* (*ego sum qui sum*), as his key authority for divine existence (s.c.). For Aquinas, then, both that God exists (as subsistent 'being' itself) and that we can demonstrate this truth by reflecting on the world around us have been revealed to us by God.

Aquinas's First Way of demonstrating God's existence is the argument from motion (*motus*). Because Aquinas gives this way primacy of place, describing it as "more manifest" than the others, and because it has received the most critical scholarly attention, we will consider it in some detail. The argument from motion begins with a simple observation: "It is certain and evident to sense perception that some things in this world are moved [*moveri*]" (I.2.3 co.). And, Aquinas continues, everything that is moved (*movetur*) is moved (*movetur*) by another. His repeated use of passive-voice forms of the verb *moveo* intends to make this clear: everything that "is moved" passively requires something else, a "mover", to act upon it. Motion, as understood here, is not limited to local or spatial motion, as some readers have imagined. Rather, Aquinas takes motion (*motus*) in a broader Aristotelian sense to signify any change—in quality, quantity, or place—characterized by the reduction of something from a state of potentiality to a state of actuality (I.2.3 co.; Wippel 2002: 161–162). And he assumes that only something that is currently in a state of actuality with regard to X can reduce something that is potentially X to being actually X. Aquinas provides the example of fire heating wood: "Something actually hot [*calidum in actu*], such as fire, makes wood, which is potentially hot [*calidum in potentia*], to be actually hot [*actu calidum*], and by this moves and changes it" (I.2.3 co.). This example illustrates Aquinas's earlier point that whatever is moved must be moved by another, namely because it is impossible that the same thing be simultaneously in act and in potential in the same respect. The fire, which is actually hot, cannot at the same time be actually cold; it can only be potentially cold. That is, it cannot lack the same degree of heat that it possesses at the same time that it possesses it. Conversely, the wood, when it is actually cold, cannot at the same time be actually hot. And so, the wood, when it is potentially hot, cannot move itself to a state of actuality with regard to heat: it cannot be both mover and moved at the same time and in the same way.

So everything that is moved must be moved by another: Thing A, for example, must be moved by Thing B. And if Thing B, which moves Thing A, is itself moved, it too must be moved by another—let's call it Thing C. And if Thing C is moved, it must be moved by yet another, Thing D. And so on. But Aquinas claims that such a chain of moved movers cannot proceed to infinity. His reason is straightforward: otherwise there would be no "prime mover" (*primum movens*) and consequently no other movers, since "secondary movers [*moventia secunda*] do not move unless they are moved by the prime mover" (I.2.3. co.). A stick does not move, for example, unless it is moved by the hand. Thus, it is necessary to arrive at some first mover, which is moved by no other. "And this everyone understands to be God," Aquinas concludes (I.2.3 co.).

Commentators, both medieval and modern, have raised various objections to the First Way. The most common and significant of these concern Aquinas's two major premises: (1) that everything that is moved must be moved by another; and (2) that there can be no infinite regress of moved movers. It does not seem universally true, critics have claimed, that everything that is moved requires something else to move it. Two putative counterexamples are often cited: human free will and Newton's law of inertia.

First, already in the late-thirteenth century, Henry of Ghent (c. 1217–1293) held that the free will of a human can move itself, reducing the person from a state of non-action to a state of action (Wippel 2002: 163). Relatedly, many people today have a Kantian understanding of human action as in competition with divine activity in a kind of zero-sum game: 'If I am freely acting, God cannot also be acting or moving me,' the argument runs. What it means to be a human is to be free, and what it means to be free, many today assume, is to will autonomously, that is, wholly apart from God and His omniscience concerning what we are going to do. So God must somehow limit Himself by withdrawing from us when we act freely (Davies 2016a: 99). Richard Swinburne, for example, claims that God "continually limits himself" in order to allow human beings "to determine their own destiny" (Swinburne 1977: 176, 178). Similarly, Clark Pinnock affirms: "God, who is always greater, was willing to limit his own scope of activity in order to make room for the significant other, humanity" (Pinnock 2001: 8). To Aquinas, however, such correlative notions of human freedom and divine self-limitation would have seemed outlandish—indeed, ontologically impossible. "It must be that God is in all things, and intimately [*intime*]," Aquinas teaches, as an agent is present to that on which it works immediately and touches it by its own power (I.8.1 co.). And an agent that acts immediately must act simultaneously with that on which it acts, as Aristotle proves in *Physics* Book VII (I.8.1 co.).

In commenting on the *Physics*, Aquinas puts it this way, invoking the same example from the First Way:

> It is clear that when something moves on account of what is moved, the mover and the movable thing itself are moved simultaneously—just as if the hand, by its own motion, moves a stick, the hand and the stick are moved simultaneously.
>
> (*In Phys.* VII.2.2)

For Aquinas, then, God, who is being itself (*ipsum esse*), is present to every creature and acts in it according to its own natural mode of being (I.8.1 co.). Because it is natural to the human to will particular goods, the human will is moved by external objects that it wills; but only God, the universal good, moves the will "sufficiently and efficaciously" as its object (I.105.4 co.). In Aquinas's view, the external object willed constitutes 'another' reality that moves the human will, as does God Himself. Furthermore, the very power of the human to will is caused and preserved in being by God alone (I.105.4, 5 co.). To the objection that what is moved by another is not free and so it seems that humans do not have free choice of the will, Aquinas maintains that God, as the "first cause" (*prima causa*), moves both natural and voluntary (secondary) causes in such a way that His moving them does not prevent their acts from being natural and voluntary, respectively (I.83.1 ad 3). Thus, far from somehow obstructing our free will, God's act of moving our wills actually *causes* them to move freely. On Aquinas's account, then, human free will is certainly no exception to the rule that everything moved must be moved by another.

A second counterexample to this premise seems to some commentators to have been provided by the influential English scientist Isaac Newton (1642–1726/7). Newton's first law of motion, the law of inertia, states that an object remains at rest or in uniform motion in a straight line unless acted upon by an external force. According to Anthony Kenny, "Newton's law wrecks the argument of the First Way." He explains: "For at any given time, the rectilinear uniform motion of a body can be explained by the principle of inertia in terms of the body's own previous motion without appeal to any other agent" (Kenny 1969: 28). Barring the interference of some physical obstacle, friction, or some other unbalanced force, an object in uniform motion will continue its motion indefinitely. Neither a moved mover nor, by extension, an unmoved mover is required to account for such motion, it would seem. In truth, however, Newtonian inertial motion is altogether different from the Aristotelian *motus* for which Aquinas's First Way seeks to account: the former is *stasis*, a state of balance or equilibrium, whereas the latter is *change*, the reduction of potentiality to actuality. So it seems that Aquinas would not have understood Newton's inertial motion as motion at all (Davies 2016b: 51). Relatedly, whereas observable changes in the world serve as the starting point of Aquinas's argument, inertial motion never naturally occurs anywhere in the universe, which contains no perfect vacuums. W. A. Wallace explains:

> The first law as stated by Newton is neither self-evident nor demonstrable, and as such is not certainly verifiable of physical phenomena in the real world. ... Rather it gives an idealized account of local motion that abstracts from extrinsic factors present in the real world and affecting such motion.
>
> (Wallace 1956: 180)

Newton himself knew well that any local motion in the real world could be explained only by having recourse to some external principle. Indeed, in Book III of his *Optics*, Newton writes:

> The *vis inertiae* [force of inertia] is a passive principle by which bodies persist in their motion or rest , ... By this principle alone there never could be any motion in the world. Some other principle was necessary for putting bodies into motion; and now [that] they are in motion, some other principle is necessary for conserving the motion.
>
> (Newton 1730: 372–373)

Thus, critics of the First Way who imagine that inertial motion disproves Aquinas's first premise appear to be reading the first Newtonian law of motion contrary to Newton himself.

The second major premise of Aquinas's argument from motion—that there can be no infinite regress of moved movers—has also garnered considerable scholarly criticism and misunderstanding. As indicated above, for example, Richard Dawkins suggests that Aquinas arbitrarily conjures up a terminator to an otherwise infinite regress and gives it the name 'God' simply because he needs to prove God's existence (Dawkins 2006: 77). This part of the First Way, then, is logically circular, and so the proof fails. Instead of invoking God as prime mover, Dawkins claims that "it is more parsimonious to conjure up, say, a 'big bang singularity', or some other physical concept as yet unknown" (Dawkins 2006: 78). Others have seen no reason why a series of movers (or efficient causes, in the case of the Second Way) could not go backwards indefinitely, particularly given Aquinas's conviction that the world's temporal beginning cannot be demonstrated from the world itself (I.46.2 co.; Kenny 1969: 33). When Aquinas claims that there cannot be an infinite regress of moved movers, however, he is not denying this possibility absolutely. Rather, he is noting that such an infinite regress would fail to explain *why* there is any motion or change at all. If there were no prime mover, there would be no secondary or intermediate movers, and thus no motion in need of explanation.

Critics of the First and Second Way often misunderstand what sort of order of movers or efficient causes Aquinas has in mind. Perhaps because they imagine Aquinas as intending to propose strictly scientific proofs, they take him as seeking to account for motion or causality in the world by having recourse to some *temporally* first mover or cause in the world itself—hence Dawkins's preference for "a 'big bang singularity'" or "some other physical concept" over God. The chain of movers imagined is a 'horizontal' one, in which the prime mover is the first in time and exists on the same plane as all the others. A series of falling dominos provides an apt analogy: the first falls into and thus moves the second, the second falls into and moves the third, the third the fourth, and so on down the line. Here, as Deism would have it, to identify God as the prime mover is to conceive of Him as the first domino in the series, the one who sets the world in motion (Van Nieuwenhove 2012: 180–181). Aquinas describes this type of series as ordered *per accidens* or accidentally. He provides the example of a series of fathers and sons generating and being generated in a line of descent: "It is accidental to a particular man, inasmuch as he generates, that he was generated by another, for he generates as a man and not as the son of another man" (I.46.2 ad 7). Consider, more specifically, the Old

Testament ancestral line of Abraham, Isaac, Jacob, and Joseph. Abraham's generation of Isaac was purely accidental to Isaac's generation of Jacob, which was accidental to Jacob's generation of Joseph. To put it in the Aristotelian language of the First Way, Abraham was not required to be, nor in fact was he, "in act" as generator when Jacob or Joseph were generated. In fact, when Joseph was born, Abraham was not even alive, although he lived to the ripe old age of 175 (Gen. 25:7–8)! It is not impossible, according to Aquinas, for one man to be generated by another to infinity in this accidental or 'horizontal' way (I.46.2 ad 7).

But, Aquinas teaches, an infinite regress "would be impossible if the generation of this man depended on this man, and on an elementary body, and on the sun, and so on to infinity" (I.46.2 ad 7). Here the series of movers or causes is ordered *per se* or essentially rather than *per accidens*. In such a series, the activity of the first mover (or first efficient cause) moves through a nexus of things moved (or effects), all of which depend equally on the activity of the prime mover (or first efficient cause) (Davies 2014: 35–36). Any movement or change in the series depends on the prime mover acting *here and now*. Thus, the series of movers and things moved is 'vertical' rather than 'horizontal,' the prime mover is 'first' ontologically rather than temporally, and the term 'hierarchy' may better describe the nexus than 'series' (Copleston 1955: 122–123).

If we return to our falling-dominos example and consider it from the perspective of a hierarchy of essentially ordered movers, God would not be the first domino in the series to fall, thereby moving the others. Rather, God would be the table on which all the dominos stand and fall in temporal series. At any given time, each domino is either in potentiality or in actuality with respect to standing or falling because they are 'held up' by the table, which is always 'in act' as a support for the entire series of dominos. And yet, the table is 'unmoved,' of course, that is, its potentiality to fall is never reduced to actuality (hopefully!). Rik Van Nieuwenhove has suggested that, in this same analogy, God is "the One who puts all the dominos there in the first place" (Van Nieuwenhove 2012: 180–181). Although the person who arranges the dominos in series is certainly of primary significance in enabling their standing and falling, imagining God in this way vis-à-vis motion in the world ultimately misses the mark. This is so because the initial disposer of

the dominos need not be—and indeed cannot be—'in act' as disposer in the here and now as the series of dominos falls. But, as an
explanation for any movement within the series, the table is and
must be 'in act' as ontological prime mover—and, furthermore, as
unmoved—at the same time that each domino falls. Without
something outside the series of moved movers, namely the table, it
is impossible to account for any movement within the series.

For obvious reasons, falling dominos on a table may not provide
the clearest illustration of Aquinas's conviction, central to the First
Way, that "what is moved instrumentally cannot move unless
there is something that moves principally" (*ScG* I.13). In setting
forth the First Way, Aquinas provides the example of a stick in
someone's hand: the stick, as an instrument of the person who
wields it, does not move unless the person's hand moves it (*ST*
I.2.3 co.). And, as we have seen, the hand and the stick are moved
simultaneously (*In Phys.* VII.2.2). At a deeper ontological level,
what moves the hand? One might respond: 'The arm does.' And
what moves the arm? 'The brain,' we might answer. Aquinas
would say that the rational soul or free will moves the arm, which
moves the hand, which moves the stick. And what moves the soul
or will of the human who holds the stick? For Aquinas, the ultimate answer is God, as we have seen. Many today disagree, of
course, and might say instead that the oxygen in the atmosphere,
on the one hand, and the glucose, vitamins, minerals, and other
essential chemicals in the brain, on the other, move the human
brain, which moves the arm, which moves the hand, which moves
the stick. At a still deeper ontological level, these people might
note that the sun, by its heat and light, enables plants to grow,
which plants, in turn, produce oxygen for us to breathe and constitute nutrient-rich food for us to eat—both of which are necessary for proper brain functioning. And what causes the sun to exist
and to produce energy?

Scientists and others may be perfectly content to stop asking
these sorts of questions at any particular level of the hierarchy of
essentially ordered movers or causes. But this analogy, I hope,
makes clear Aquinas's point: such a series of moved movers cannot
proceed to infinity. Richard Dawkins appears to understand this
well when, rejecting God as prime mover, he proposes "a 'big
bang singularity', or some other physical concept as yet unknown"

(Dawkins 2006: 78). What he fails to see, however, is that the ultimate *why* question—in this case, 'Why is there any motion in the universe?', or, more generally, 'Why is there a universe at all?'—is not a scientific question and so has no answer within the universe itself. For Aquinas, *everything* within the universe raises this question, but *nothing* within the universe can answer it. If, with Dawkins, we were to propose some 'big bang singularity' as the first mover, Aquinas would surely remind us that what we apparently seek to explain is the temporal beginning of an accidentally ordered series of movers, not the ontological foundation of the "more manifest" changes ordered *per se* with which his First Way is concerned.

HOW GOD IS NOT

Many commentators take Aquinas to be propounding a 'doctrine of God' in *ST* I.3–11, where he considers the manner of God's existence. If, however, we expect a doctrine of God to explain positively and definitively what God is like, Aquinas clearly offers no such doctrine, nor does he intend to (Burrell 1979: 13). He could not set forth such a doctrine if he wanted to—he simply has no idea what God is. But to recognize that Aquinas has no positive concept of the divine quiddity is not to say that he is an absolute agnostic concerning the 'what' and 'how' of God. David Burrell explains Aquinas's mode of proceeding in considering the manner of divine existence:

> What God is like is treated in the most indirect fashion possible, and the only one available to an inquiry by one of his creatures. Aquinas shows under one rubric after another how it is that our discourse fails to represent God. It fails not merely by falling short but by lacking the structural isomorphism requisite to any statement which purports to refer to its object.
>
> (Burrell 1979: 13–14)

Aquinas makes explicit in introducing q. 3, on divine simplicity, that because we cannot know what God is (*quid est*), neither can we know how God is (*quomodo est*), that is, His manner of existing; rather, we can consider only how God is *not* (*quomodo non est*)

(I.3.prol.). Again, we can know the 'how' of God only indirectly and by remotion—in Aquinas's words, "by removing from Him the things that are not fitting [*non conveniunt*] for Him, namely composition, motion, and other things of this sort" (I.3.prol.).

Eleonore Stump has rightly observed that the doctrine of divine simplicity is "perhaps the most difficult and controversial piece of medieval philosophical theology but also one of the most important" (Stump 2003: 92). As I have intimated already and as I hope to make clearer throughout this book, divine simplicity is central to Aquinas's theological vision and thus to his treatment of virtually every topic in the study of God. The fundamental assumption underlying the doctrine of simplicity is that we know how creatures exist and what they are by understanding them as composite beings. In Aquinas's view, which is deeply indebted both to Aristotle and to various Christian writers, to be a creature is to be composed in various ways: in terms of body and soul, matter and form, nature and supposit (i.e., an individual instantiation of a nature), essence and existence, genus and species, and substance and accidents (namely, quantity, quality, relation, place, time, situation, condition, action, and passion). If, for example, we wished to understand and describe me as distinct from granite, we might begin to do so, in Aristotelian and Thomistic terms, as follows. Whereas both granite and I are destructible mobile substances, I have a human body animated by a rational soul. Granite, by contrast, is inanimate, which means it has no soul or life-giving principle at all; rather, it is a solid mass of minerals, particularly quartz and feldspar, formed by the solidification of magma, thus a type of igneous rock. In terms of its qualities, granite is significantly harder and more durable than my human body, which explains why granite is often used as construction material whereas I am not (thankfully)! Although granite and I differ in these and other compositional ways, in both of us essence is distinct from existence: that is, *what* we are is different from *that* we are. To be granite is not to be absolutely. If the granite that currently forms the foundation of my house did not exist, we could still know what granite is—though we couldn't discuss it in my house! Likewise, to be me is not to be to-be.

As we have seen, however, to be God is precisely to be to-be. Thus, God differs radically from granite and from me and from all other creatures in the universe. Whereas these various categories of composition must be applied to creatures in order to understand them, they must be altogether denied of God. Aquinas opens q. 3 by teaching that it must be denied that God is a body, and thus a body-soul composite (I.3.1 co.). Whereas various scriptural passages suggest that God has dimensionality, physical form, corporeal parts, posture, and place (I.3.1 obj. 1–5), Aquinas takes Jn. 4:24, *God is spirit*, as the key authority to the contrary (I.3.1 s.c.). He also introduces philosophical points established by the Five Ways to argue against God's corporality. First, because no body that is not moved can move another and because God is the unmoved prime mover, "it is manifest that God is not a body" (I.3.1 co.). Second, Aquinas teaches that "it is impossible that God is a body" on the grounds that: (1) the first being (*primum ens*) must necessarily be in act and in no way in potential; (2) God is *primum ens* and thus pure actuality, in whom nothing is in potential; and (3) every body is in potential, as, for instance, the human body vis-à-vis the soul that animates it (I.3.1 co.). Building on these points, Aquinas proceeds to show that God also cannot be composed of matter and form (I.3.2), nature and supposit (I.3.3), essence (*essentia*) and existence (*esse*) (I.3.4), genus and species (I.3.5), or substance and accidents (I.3.6). "It is manifest that God is in no way composite, but is entirely simple," Aquinas concludes (I.3.7 co.).

A crucial problem with God's utter simplicity seems to arise, however. Namely, if God is the cause of all creatures and if all creatures are composite, must not God also be composite? Otherwise, the divine cause apparently would fail to be reflected in its creaturely effects (I.3.7 obj. 1). Aquinas responds that things that are from God resemble Him in the way that things caused resemble the first cause, but notes that what it means that something is caused is that it is "in some way composite, because at least its existence [*esse*] is other than what it is [*quid est*]" (I.3.7 ad 1). Creatures do not resemble God in the same way that effects produced by a cause in their own genus or species do. Aquinas is clear, after all, that God cannot be a species of any genus (I.3.5 co.). Creatures resemble God "more distantly" and "according to some sort of analogy," according to Aquinas; namely, insofar as they are beings (*entia*), they are similar to God, "the first and universal principle of all being [*totius esse*]" (I.4.3 co.). But creatures also differ radically from God in that they are caused: they cannot be the sufficient causes of their own existence (*esse*), and so their existence (*esse*) is other than their essence (*essentia*) (I.3.4 co.). Because God is the first efficient cause, however, Aquinas affirms: "It is impossible, therefore, that in God existence [*esse*] is one thing and His essence [*essentia*] another" (I.3.4 co.). We arrive, then, at the heart of Aquinas's doctrine of simplicity: the claim that to be God is simply to be (Burrell 1979: 7). God cannot be qualified or classified or studied scientifically as if He were some object in or alongside the universe of creatures.

GOD'S KNOWLEDGE AND WILL

After treating what belongs to the divine substance, Aquinas begins in *ST* I.14 to consider the things that pertain to God's operation. Knowledge and will constitute operations that remain in the operator (that is, the one who knows and wills), whereas power is the principle of operation proceeding to external effects (I.14. prol.). Here we will briefly consider Aquinas's understanding of divine knowing (q. 14) and willing (q. 19), highlighting several of the more significant elements of his teaching.

First, Aquinas argues that God must possess knowledge "most perfectly" because He is immaterial in the highest degree. This is so because a thing's immateriality is the reason for its ability to know, and its mode of immateriality determines its mode of knowledge (I.14.1 co.). An intelligent thing differs from a non-intelligent thing in that the latter possesses its own form alone, whereas the former can naturally have the forms of other things within it. This, in fact, is what it means to know: that an intelligent thing has within itself the forms of all the realities that are known. "Everything known is in the knower," as Aquinas often says, according to the mode in which the knower knows (I.14.prol.; I.12.4 co.; I.14.6 ad 1; I.16.2 co.; I.43.3 co.). Matter is in potentiality to many forms before it receives a particular form, after which matter contracts the form (I.3.2 co.; I.7.1 co.). When something is known in a knower, therefore, its form exists in the knower without being confined or limited by matter. For instance, the form of the magnolia tree is limited in any particular magnolia tree (i.e., this or that southern or Chinese or kobus magnolia) by its own matter; but when I know the magnolia tree, its form exists in my intellect in a more expansive way, unlimited by matter. What I know—namely the magnolia tree—is a material thing, but my knowledge of it is altogether immaterial. Actual knowing or understanding, then, is form without matter. Furthermore, because God Himself *is* form without matter (I.3.2) and pure actuality (I.3.1), He *is* knowing-in-act or "intelligibility actualized" (Davies 2014: 73). As pure actuality, God is also perfect (I.4.1, 2) and thus He is perfect-knowing-in-act.

Recognizing divine simplicity—according to which God *is* whatever is attributed to Him—we can affirm, according to our ordinary manner of speaking, that God *has* knowledge perfectly. In doing so, however, we must not lose sight of how very different God's knowing is from our own. Indeed, divine knowing, as treated in q. 14, illustrates well Aquinas's basic assumption that we can know something of God by knowing how He is *not*—here, by knowing what is *not* the mode of God's knowing. God's knowing, for example, is not discursive; his understanding is not like that of a scientist, proceeding from principles to conclusions over time (I.14.7 co.). Because God is eternal, completely outside of time, His knowing embraces all time. "The present glance of God extends over all time," Aquinas explains, "and to all things that exist at any time whatsoever, as objects in the present to Him" (I.14.9 co.). Whereas we humans know sensible realities—trees, chairs, and sharks, for instance—by observing them in the world around us, and whereas we come naturally to know God by knowing created things (I.12.12), God knows both Himself and all creatures by understanding Himself, in whom, as first cause, all of his effects preexist (I.14.2, 5). God "sees," for example, sharks—all 500+ species known to us, and all others as well—not by visually examining them in themselves, but rather by knowing Himself, "inasmuch as His essence contains the similitude of things other than Himself" (I.14.5 co.). In God, unlike in us, the intellect, the object understood, the intelligible species, and the very act of understanding are entirely one and the same (I.14.4 co.). They are, in fact, God's substance or essence, which is His existence. Thus, just as to be God is to be, so too to be God is to know. "It is necessary to say," Aquinas teaches, "that the act of God's understanding [*intelligere*] is His substance [*substantia*]" (I.14.4 co.).

Another significant way in which God's knowledge differs from ours, according to Aquinas, concerns its causal nature. Whereas we know things because they exist, the reverse is true in the case of God's knowledge: things exist because God knows them (I.14.8 s. c.). Our knowledge of the whale shark and the dwarf lantern shark—the largest and smallest of shark species, respectively—depends on their actual existence: they must *be* in the world for us to observe and understand them. But our knowing these sharks does nothing to bring them into being, of course. With God's knowledge, things are quite different. God knows the whale shark and the dwarf lantern shark in Himself eternally, since all of God's effects preexist in His understanding. In Aquinas's view, just as an artist's knowledge is the cause of the art that he produces when he works through his understanding, so too God's knowledge is the cause of all creatures (I.14.8 co.). Consider the model or intelligible form of the sculpture *David* in the mind of Michelangelo prior to his sculpting it from 1501–04. By virtue of this intelligible form, Michelangelo knew *David* before he brought him to life out of Carrara marble. In order for *David* to exist materially, however, it was necessary that Michelangelo also will to produce the statue whose form he understood. Without the will, the intelligible form in the agent's mind fails to denote a principle of action (I.14.8 co.). Applying this artist-analogy to God, Aquinas affirms:

> It is manifest, moreover, that God causes things through His understanding, since His being is His act of understanding. Hence, it is necessary that His knowledge is the cause of things insofar as it has the will conjoined [to it]. Hence, the knowledge of God, insofar as it is the cause of things, is customarily called approving knowledge [*scientia approbationis*].
>
> (*ST* I.14.8 co.)

Given the necessary connection between knowledge and will vis-à-vis causation, Aquinas maintains that God's will is also the cause of created things (I.19.4 co.).

A troubling set of questions arises here, however. Since God's approving knowledge is the cause of all creatures, and since God's knowledge is eternal, are creatures therefore also eternal? If they are not—and they seem not to be—how is their temporality and contingency to be explained? Aquinas responds by noting that God's knowledge is the cause of things according to the way in which they exist in His knowledge, but that creatures should exist from eternity was not in God's knowledge. He concludes: "Hence, although God's knowledge is eternal, nevertheless it does not follow that creatures exist from eternity" (I.14.8 ad 2). Similarly, since God's knowledge (which is His essence and existence) is the necessary cause of all created things, we might suppose that all things are therefore necessary and that nothing is contingent (I.14.13 obj. 1). For Aquinas, however, this is not the case at all. In fact, it is precisely because God's knowledge is eternal that He knows future contingents and knows them certainly. What this means is that realities that are both future and contingent from our vantage point as temporal creatures are neither 'future' nor 'contingent' to God. Aquinas explains:

> Although contingent things become actual successively, nevertheless God knows contingent things not successively, as they are in their own being, as we do, but simultaneously. This is because His knowledge is measured by eternity, as is also His being [*esse*]; and eternity, being complete simultaneously, embraces all time ... Hence, all things that exist in time are present to God from eternity ... because His glance extends from eternity over all things as they exist in His own presentness [*sua praesentialitate*]. Hence, it is manifest that contingent things are known infallibly [*infallibiliter*] by God, inasmuch as they are subject to the divine sight according to its own presentness; and nevertheless they are future contingent things with respect to their own causes.
>
> (*ST* I.14.13 co.)

Whereas God's knowledge, as the first cause of future contingents, is necessary, the actual existence of future contingents as future contingents depends on their own secondary or proximate causes. The process philosopher David Ray Griffin seems to miss this crucial point when, of Aquinas's teaching, he says: "The idea that events which are eternally and therefore necessarily known can in themselves be contingent is nonsensical" (Griffin 1976: 77). For Aquinas, however, this idea is perfectly sensible, as his analogy of plant germination aims to show. Although the sun is always causally present in a primary way, the sprouting and development of a plant at this or that time is dependent on such proximate contingent causes as water, oxygen, good soil, and a suitable temperature (I.14.13 ad 1). I cannot know exactly when the peony in my backyard will sprout. But my sprouting peony is present to God from eternity, existing in the "presentness" of His universal vision; thus He knows with absolute certainty the very day, hour, and minute it will sprout. His knowledge and will, in fact, constitute the necessary and supreme cause of my peony and of its sprouting.

Although Aquinas understands the will of God to be, of necessity, always fulfilled and "entirely immutable" (I.19.6, 7 co.), he denies that it imposes necessity on all things that are willed. God wills some things, such as His own goodness, necessarily, of course (I.19.3 co.). But because Aquinas takes God's goodness to be perfect in itself and therefore in need of no creature, he teaches that God's willing things apart from Himself is not absolutely necessary (I.19.3 co.). Rather, God wills these things voluntarily and they happen contingently. And neither His will nor His providence imposes necessity on these contingent realities, according to Aquinas (I.19.8; I.22.4). That is, God's will does not determine particular contingent effects by 'overriding' or 'interfering with' contingent secondary causes that otherwise might have acted differently. For example, ordinarily—that is, barring a miracle—God does not determine that my peony will sprout today instead of four months from now if none of the proximate causes is now present to it. Rather, God's will actually *causes* contingent secondary causes to be, and thus to cause contingently. Aquinas is clear that the divine will is causally primary, whether the things willed are necessary or contingent. In other words, my peony will sprout 126 days, three hours, and seven minutes from now not principally because of the ideal convergence of proximate causes at that moment; rather, it is because God wills my peony to sprout at that moment that He causes the contingent causes—water, oxygen, soil, etc.—to concur toward this particular temporal effect (I.19.8 co.).

If God's will does not ordinarily 'override' contingent secondary causes, we might ask, conversely, whether contingent causes can 'override' the divine will. That is, is God's will always fulfilled, or can it be thwarted by creaturely causes? For Aquinas and other scholastic theologians, human salvation provided the test-case for this significant question (Harkins 2014a, 2014b). Although, according to 1 Tim. 2:4, *God wills that all humans should be saved*, it is clear—according to the exegetical and theological tradition received by Aquinas—that not all humans actually arrive at final salvation. Thus, some people, acting by their own free wills, seem to frustrate what appears to be the divine will for universal salvation (I.19.6 obj. 1). Aquinas responds by reading 1 Tim. 2:4 through the lens of John Damascene's famous distinction between God's antecedent and consequent will concerning salvation. Although in itself God's will is singular and eternal, it may be considered by us, according to Damascene, either as antecedent to any human willing and action regarding salvation, on the one hand, or as consequent to such human willing and action, on the other (Harkins 2014b: 38). Similarly, Aquinas makes clear that the antecedent-consequent will distinction applies not to the divine will itself, but rather to things willed (I.19.6 co.). According to Aquinas, whereas antecedently or absolutely God wills that all humans should be saved, "consequently He wills that some should be damned, according to the exigencies of His justice" (I.19.6 co.). In light of particular circumstances of human willing and action— finally refusing to cooperate with grace to produce meritorious actions, for example—God's will for justice demands that unrepentant sinners be barred from heavenly beatitude. Aquinas offers the analogy of a just judge, who antecedently wills that all humans should live, but consequently wills that a murderer should be hanged (I.19.6 co.).

For Aquinas, God does not temporally observe intractable sinners and change His mind concerning them, deciding now to damn them when before He had determined to save them. Rather, given His eternality and simplicity, God's immutable will, whereby He desires both mercifully to save all humans and justly to punish sinners, is identical with His perfect knowledge, whereby He 'sees' all temporal and contingent human willing and action "as they exist in His own presentness" (I.14.13 co.). His singular will regarding salvation 'takes into account,' as it were, the contingencies of human freedom and action. In fact, God's will actually *causes* the human to will freely and, through grace, to act as a proximate, meritorious cause of glory, the final effect of predestination (I.23.5 co.). Furthermore, Aquinas teaches that just as predestination includes God's will to confer the effects of grace and glory, so reprobation includes "the will to permit someone to fall into sin, and to impose the punishment of damnation for sin" (I.23.3 co.). Significantly, the punishment of the sinner is the very example Aquinas provides in I.19.6 as evidence that God's will cannot be thwarted by creaturely causes:

> Since, therefore, the will of God is the universal cause of all things, it is impossible that the divine will should not achieve its effect. Hence, what seems to withdraw from the divine will in one order falls back into it in another—as the sinner, who withdraws from the divine will inasmuch as he is able by sinning, falls back into the order of the divine will when he is punished by its justice.
>
> (I.19.6 co.)

Aquinas makes clear that, although particular humans can contravene God's will that all should be saved, they cannot prevent the fulfillment of the divine will generally. We see, then, based on his interpretation of 1 Tim. 2:4, that Aquinas understands universal salvation as undermining the freedom of the human such that she is neither an active participant in her own salvation nor therefore truly human. In Aquinas's view, perhaps contrary to modern assumptions concerning the doctrine, divine predestination actually safeguards human freedom and ensures that salvation is both an eternal, divine reality and a temporal, human one (Harkins 2014a).

THE TRINITY

SETTING THE RECORD STRAIGHT

Contemporary theologians often charge classical theology with rendering the doctrine of the Trinity irrelevant to Christian faith and life. Furthermore, they often attribute this regrettable decline of the Trinity into theological oblivion to Thomas Aquinas and his manner of proceeding in the *ST* (Rikhof 2005: 36–37). The basic lines of critique are exemplified by the twentieth-century German Jesuit, Karl Rahner. First, Rahner charges Aquinas with introducing the fundamental structural division between the One God (*de Deo uno*) and the Triune God (*de Deo trino*) that became standard in Catholic theology manuals of the nineteenth and twentieth centuries. Rahner explains:

> [T]his separation took place for the first time in St. Thomas, for reasons which have not yet been fully explained. Here the first topic under study is not God the Father as the unoriginate origin of divinity and reality, but as the essence common to all three persons. ... Thus the treatise of the Trinity locks itself in even more splendid isolation, with the ensuing danger that the religious mind finds it devoid of interest.
>
> (Rahner 1970: 16–17)

Relatedly, Rahner critiques Aquinas's "encapsulation and isolation" of the Trinity from divine unity as overly "philosophical and abstract" and contrary to the order in which God is "experienced in salvation history in his free relations to his creatures" (Rahner 1970: 20, 17–18). Scripture first reveals God the Father as "unoriginate person in his relation to the world," Rahner maintains, after which it discloses Him as the origin of intra-divine life (Rahner 1970: 20n15). The ultimate concern of Rahner and other critics is that Aquinas divorces the Trinity from the doctrines of creation and salvation, thereby losing sight of the truth that God is, before all else, Father, Son, and Holy Spirit "for us" (LaCugna 1991).

A central assumption of this critique is that Aquinas establishes his doctrine of the Trinity on abstract, philosophical concepts such as procession and relations rather than on the more intuitive language of Father, Son, and Holy Spirit that Scripture provides. Such an unbiblical, philosophical beginning leads only, according to Rahner, to "a Trinity which is absolutely locked within itself—one which is not, in its reality, open to anything distinct from it; one, further, from which we are excluded" (Rahner 1970: 18). Here Rahner has in view what Catherine LaCugna has identified as "one of the shibboleths" of Aquinas's theology, namely his teaching that there is no real relation in God to creatures (ST I.13.7 co.; I.28.1 ad 3; I.28.4 co.; I.45.3 ad 1; LaCugna 1985: 649–650). We will return to this controversial doctrine in due course. Suffice it here to note that its modern critics maintain that Aquinas's God is the distant, static, unconcerned God of philosophy rather than the personal, relational, loving God of the Bible (see LaCugna 1985; Pinnock 2001; Wolterstorff 1988). Nicholas Wolterstorff, for example, claims that Aquinas "struggled most intensely" to make sense of the scriptural teaching concerning God's suffering love in light of his philosophical presupposition that God remains completely unmoved by evil in the world. Aquinas's God does not have a suffering awareness of His creatures, Wolterstorff affirms, because He "does not have an awareness of the world at all" (Wolterstorff 1988: 218, 223). Much like Rahner and other critics, Wolterstorff presumes that Aquinas's basic methodological approach to God is 'philosophy first, Scripture second.' They assume that Aquinas begins with a traditional philosophical understanding of God, into which—if he attends to Scripture at all—he tries to accommodate aspects of the biblical portrait. Rahner, for instance, describes Aquinas's attempt to understand the divine processions on the analogy of knowing and loving as a case of "artificial 'eisegesis'" that "makes all of his marvelous profundity look so utterly vacuous." His fundamental error, in Rahner's view, is that "he begins from a human philosophical concept of knowledge and love," which he then applies to the Trinity (Rahner 1970: 19). If only Aquinas had eschewed philosophical "speculation about God's inner being" (LaCugna 1985: 650) and focused instead on the economy of Father, Son, and Holy Spirit as revealed in Scripture and experienced throughout salvation history, the Trinity would not have been consigned to theological and pastoral irrelevance (Rahner 1970: 15–21). But, given Aquinas's actual approach, Catherine LaCugna concludes: "It must be acknowledged that one of the fruits of Thomas's theology was the marginalization of the doctrine of the Trinity" (LaCugna 1991: 167).

The present chapter aims to expound the basics of Aquinas's trinitarian theology in light of this contemporary critique. More specifically, I seek to set the record straight concerning Aquinas's mature Trinitarian theology by carefully considering how he proceeds in the *ST* and why he proceeds as he does. Several preliminary points should serve to highlight how the contemporary critique is predicated on a superficial and anachronistic reading of Aquinas. First, it must be said that the Trinity, far from being a marginalized doctrine, is absolutely central to Aquinas's theology and to his understanding of Christian faith and life. "The Christian faith consists principally in confessing the holy Trinity," Aquinas affirms (*De rationibus fidei*, ch. 1; Emery 2012: 418). Faith believes what we cannot see in this life, but in heavenly glory faith gives way to perfect knowledge and we will see God as He is (1 Jn 3:2). For Aquinas, apprehension of the Trinity anticipates this beatific end and orients our lives even now to the God whom we will finally see face to face (1 Cor 13:12; *ST* I.1.1 co.). Near the beginning of his *Scriptum on the Sentences*, Aquinas teaches: "Indeed, knowledge of the Trinity in unity is the enjoyment and goal (*fructus et finis*) of our entire life" (*Scriptum* I d. 2 q. 1 a. 5 expos.)

Second, Aquinas understands the Trinity, unlike preambles of faith such as divine existence and unity, as an article of faith. Thus, whereas the preambles can be known by natural reason, our knowledge of the Trinity depends entirely on divine revelation. "It must be said," Aquinas insists, "that it is impossible to arrive at the knowledge of the Trinity of divine persons by natural reason" (*ST* I.32.1 co.). This is so because we can naturally know God only from creatures, which lead us to God as effects lead to their cause. By natural reason, then, we can know only what pertains to God as the principle of all things. And because the creative power of God is common to the whole Trinity, it belongs to God's oneness and not to His threeness. Thus, Aquinas concludes: "By natural reason, therefore, we can know concerning God the things that pertain to the unity of essence, but not the things that pertain to the distinction of persons" (I.32.1 co.). We will return to this fundamental distinction, which structures the treatment of God in the *ST*. Let us note here, however, that the Trinity's status as an article of faith gives rise to two necessities: first, that God has revealed it to us (otherwise we would not apprehend it at all); and, second, that Aquinas's consideration of it necessarily depends on the authority of Scripture. Over against the contemporary critique, we will see how thoroughly scriptural Aquinas's mature treatment of the Trinity is, from beginning to end. Indeed, Herwi Rikhof has noted that Aquinas's Trinitarian theology differs from modern treatments of God's threeness precisely in that it presupposes knowledge of Scripture (Rikhof 2005: 55).

Third, in identifying Aquinas as the originator of the "separation" between the treatise on the One God and the treatise on the Triune God in the Catholic manualist tradition, Karl Rahner is simply mistaken. He anachronistically confuses Aquinas's *distinction* between "the things that pertain to the unity of the divine essence" and "the things that pertain to the Trinity of persons in God" (*ST* I.27 prol.; I.2 prol.; I.32.1 co.) with the *formal separation* of the treatment of God's oneness and threeness in neo-scholastic theology manuals produced more than 500 years later (see, e.g., Wilhelm and Scannell 1909). Although Aquinas's distinction does determine the order of his own consideration of God in the *Prima pars*—with qq. 2–26 addressing what pertains to the essential unity and qq. 27–43 what concerns the personal plurality—all of these questions have as their subject the same Triune God. It is not the case, as some have imagined, that in qq. 2–26 Aquinas treats the One God of the philosophers as naturally knowable, after which he turns in qq. 27–43 to the Christian God—Father, Son, and Holy Spirit—as revealed in the Bible. Aquinas's distinction is neither between this God and that, nor between this epistemological approach and that. Rather, it is a fundamental theological distinction, inherited from the early Church, between what is *common* to the three divine persons and what is *proper* to each (Emery 2004:

50–51). All that Aquinas treats in I.2–26—God's existence, simplicity, perfection, goodness, infinity, immutability, eternity, unity, knowledge, truth, life, will, love, justice and mercy, providence, predestination, power, and beatitude—is common to the Trinitarian persons and is addressed as such. In I.27–43, on the other hand, Aquinas takes up procession, relations, persons, properties, notional acts, and missions, all of which pertain to what is proper to the Father, Son, and Holy Spirit. Furthermore, as we will see, his treatment of what is proper assumes and variously depends on his teaching concerning what is common.

But should Aquinas have reversed this order, as Rahner suggests, and treated "God the Father as the unoriginate origin" and all else that is proper before he considered what is common to the divine essence (Rahner 1970: 16)? Would this not have been a more experiential and intuitive approach given the scriptural data? Aquinas himself thought not, and held just the opposite, in fact: to address the proper before the common would violate the natural order of human understanding. In terms of human thinking, what is common is naturally prior to what is proper; as such, the common is included in our understanding of the proper. The example Aquinas provides, as if anticipating Rahner's critique, is that of the divine Father: "God is included in our understanding of the person of the Father, but not the reverse" (ST I.33.3 ad 1). By extension, when we understand any of the divine persons—and indeed, the very notion 'divine person'—included therein is the divine essence, its existence, simplicity, perfection, goodness, etc. (Emery 2004: 50–51). Thus, just as the preambles of faith are, according to Aquinas, rightly considered before the articles since "faith presupposes natural knowledge" (I.2.2 ad 1), similarly what pertains to the divine essence is preliminary to what concerns the Trinity of persons because the proper naturally includes and presupposes the common.

Finally, the criticism that the *ST* presents a purely immanent Trinity that is isolated from salvation history and "absolutely locked within itself" (Rahner 1970: 18) bespeaks a surprising inattention to Aquinas's work and to the integrated nature of his mature theology. As a careful reading of the *ST* reveals, Aquinas understands well that the mystery of the Trinity has profound implications for both creation and salvation. In fact, in reply to the objection that a Trinitarian doctrine seems superfluous since God's threeness cannot be known by natural reason, Aquinas teaches:

> It must be said that knowledge of the divine persons was necessary for us in two ways. In one way, [it was necessary] for thinking rightly about the creation of things. Indeed, the fact that we say that God made all things by His Word excludes the error of those who propose that God produced things by the necessity of [His] nature. Moreover, the fact that we locate a procession of love in Him shows that God produced creatures not because of some need, nor because of any other extrinsic reason, but because of the love of His own goodness. ... In another way, and principally, [it was necessary] for thinking rightly about the salvation of the human race, which is accomplished through the Incarnate Son and through the gift of the Holy Spirit.
>
> (ST I.32.1 ad 3)

For Aquinas, our thinking correctly about both creation and salvation demands not only that God has revealed Himself as a Trinity, but also that this great mystery, once revealed, be apprehended by us (with the supernatural aid of faith, of course). Here we must clearly distinguish between what is necessary *for our knowing God* and what is necessary *for God*. Whereas, in Aquinas's view, Trinitarian doctrine is absolutely necessary for us to know creation and salvation rightly, it was not absolutely necessary for God, who is necessarily a Trinity of persons, either to create or to save. In fact, as Aquinas explains here, to know God as Trinity is precisely to know that He created out of love, not out of necessity.

Thus, if the point of the modern 'isolationism' critique is to claim that Aquinas's God is not necessarily or primarily creator or savior—that is, that his God does not exist chiefly 'for us'—then Aquinas is guilty as charged. He makes clear that whereas every creature absolutely depends on God to be and to be what it is, God, whose essence is to be to-be, depends on no creature either to be or to be who He is (see, e.g., I.44.1 co.; I.2.3 co.; I.3.4 co.; I.28.1 ad 3). In other words, if God had never created, He still would have been perfect God. Herbert McCabe puts it this way:

> God is not in himself productive or creative. Sure he takes time to throw off creation, to make something, to achieve something. But the

real interior life of the Godhead is not in creation, it is in the life of love which is the Trinity, the procession of Son from Father and of the Spirit from this exchange. God is not first of all our creator or any kind of maker. He is love.

(McCabe 2002: 75)

Let us turn now to some of the particulars of Aquinas's mature teaching on this life of perfect divine love.

PROCESSIONS, RELATIONS, PERSONS: HOW GOD IS NOT, REVISITED

Aquinas begins his treatment of the Trinity in the *ST* by noting that, because the divine persons are distinguished by relations of origin, the proper "order of teaching" (*ordo doctrinae*) demands consideration of origin or procession first, relations second, and persons third (I.27 prol.). On the face of it, this order of presentation contrasts with that of the *ScG*, where Aquinas begins by setting out what Scripture teaches about the Trinity before engaging various arguments against the doctrine (*ScG* IV.2–26). But to imagine, on this basis, that Aquinas's mature treatment is not deeply informed by Scripture would be a mistake. In fact, the purpose of Aquinas's extended meditation on processions, relations, and persons (qq. 27–29) is precisely, in the words of Gilles Emery, "to bring into relief the deep meaning of biblical revelation" (Emery 2004: 51–52). Similarly, Herwi Rikhof has noted that a key pedagogical principle determines Aquinas's "order of teaching" here, namely that the student must begin by acquiring the conceptual tools that are necessary for making sense of what Scripture reveals concerning the divine threeness. The modern critique outlined above rests, it seems, on an interpretation that fails to recognize his pedagogical approach. Rikhof explains the potential for misunderstanding:

> If one is not aware of Aquinas' procedure, one might think that his primary interest is in the more technical and conceptual issues, since he starts with those. If one does not take his way of ordering into account, one might easily misconstrue Aquinas' theology of the Trinity as an abstract and theoretical game. If, however, one keeps in

mind his pedagogic principle, then those discussions are the introductions ... to the meaning of the terms used in Scripture and to the meaning of the missions. From this perspective, Aquinas' theology of the Trinity is profoundly scriptural and geared toward the history of salvation.

(Rikhof 2005: 40–41)

The deeply scriptural nature of Aquinas's trinitarian theology is evident throughout, from start to finish. He begins with a consideration of the procession of the divine persons (q. 27). Whereas procession, which signifies "outward motion," would seem to violate God's nature as unmoved, simple, and the first principle (I.27.1 objs. 1–3), Aquinas introduces the very words of the Incarnate Son Himself, *I proceeded from God* [*the Father*] (Jn 8:42), as the primary authority to the contrary (I.27.1 s.c.). In this same verse from John's Gospel, Christ continues, *For I came not from myself, but He sent* [misit] *me* (Jn 8:42). Although Aquinas does not cite these latter words in his final question on the mission (*missio*) of the divine persons (q. 43), Christ's encounter with the Pharisees in Jn 8 concerning His true identity is determinative of the Dominican's approach to the Trinity. Indeed, the first authority invoked by Aquinas in q. 43 is the Son's affirmation in Jn 8:16, *I am not alone, but I and He who sent* [misit] *me, the Father.* Can it justifiably be claimed, then, that Aquinas's Trinitarian theology is based on abstract, philosophical concepts rather than the straightforward language of Scripture? It would appear not, as this is a false and anachronistic dichotomy. Aquinas shows throughout his treatment that the concepts he aims to explicate (procession, mission, etc.) come directly from Scripture.

When, for example, he asks whether there is any procession in God (I.27.1), Aquinas opens his response thus: "It must be said that, with regard to the divine reality, divinely inspired Scripture uses language related to procession" (co.). But how precisely is this language to be understood? Is procession in God like any kind of procession in creatures? In Aquinas's view, some prominent early Christian thinkers fell into grave error because they considered divine procession as essentially similar to creaturely procession, that is, as an "outward motion." Arius understood procession in God in terms of an effect proceeding externally from a cause, and thus took the Son to be the first creature who came forth from the Father. Similarly, Sabellius understood it in terms of a cause proceeding externally to an effect, and so assumed that the Son and Holy Spirit were merely different names given to the Father in His diverse roles as savior and sanctifier, respectively (I.27.1 co.). Although every procession entails some action, this act need not be outward. Some actions remain in the agent, and so procession can be internal. As we have seen in Chapter 3, Aquinas understands knowledge and will as the chief acts or operations that remain in the rational operator (I.14 prol.). It should come as no surprise, then, that Aquinas proposes the analogy, inherited from Augustine, of knowing and loving for the two processions in God. He affirms:

It must be carefully considered that in God there is no procession except according to an action that does not tend to something external, but remains in the agent itself. An action of this sort in an intellectual nature is the action of the intellect and the action of the will. The procession of a [mental] word is according to an intelligible action. Moreover, according to the operation of the will there is found in us another procession, namely the procession of love, according to which the beloved is in the lover, just as by the conception of a word, the thing spoken of or understood is in the one who understands. And so, besides the procession of the Word, there is another procession in God, namely the procession of love.

(*ST* I.27.3 co.)

Our reflecting on what happens within us when we understand and love provides an apt analogy for how the Word and Holy Spirit proceed from the Father eternally. That Aquinas offers this analogy indicates his awareness that the Trinity is a deep, inexhaustible mystery at which the human mind cannot naturally arrive. Once this supernatural truth has been revealed, we need some analogue among created realities, which are more well-known to us, to aid our apprehension of it. We should not imagine that Aquinas here seeks to provide a philosophical defense of this article of faith, nor even that "he begins from a human philosophical concept of knowledge and love" (Rahner 1970: 19). On the contrary, he begins where he must: with divine revelation. Christ's twofold teaching that the Holy Spirit proceeds from the

Father (Jn 15:26) and that this Spirit is distinct from the Son (Jn 14:16) provides the authoritative jumping-off point for Aquinas's explication of the two divine processions (I.27.3 s.c.). Furthermore, Aquinas is always careful to emphasize how *dissimilar* divine realities are from their creaturely analogues. Creaturely analogues or counterparts—processions, relations, persons—tell us *not* how God is, but how God is *not*. The theological misstep of Arius and Sabellius, after all, was that they understood procession in God according to the mode of the lowest creatures—as it is "in bodies, or by local motion, or by the action of some cause in relation to an external effect"—rather than according to the similitude of the highest creatures, namely intellectual substances (I.27.1 co.).

And even where an intelligible and volitional emanation internal to humans serves as the analogue, we must bear in mind what Aquinas has taught earlier in the *Prima pars*, namely that God's knowing and willing are quite different from our own. Given divine simplicity, for instance, to understand and to be are identical for God; therefore, the Word that is conceived and generated by the Father is of the very same nature as the Father (I.27.2 co.; I.14.4). Likewise, to will and to be are identical for God, so the Holy Spirit that proceeds by way of love from the Father and the Son is also true God (I.19.1 co.; I.27.4 co.). In short, in treating the divine processions, Aquinas necessarily reminds us of God's simple existence, His unique mode of being: "It must be said that everything that exists in God is one with the divine nature" (I.27.4 ad 1). This example illustrates well how Aquinas's Trinitarian theology is radically dependent on and intricately entwined with what pertains to the unity of the divine essence.

It is equally clear from his consideration of relations in God (q. 28) that Aquinas does not segregate what pertains to the divine threeness from what pertains to God's essential unity. In fact, Aquinas notes at the outset the necessary link between the processions within the *common* divine nature and the real relations that, in the "order of teaching" and human understanding, follow from them:

> When something proceeds from a principle of the same nature, it is necessary that both, namely the one proceeding and that from which it proceeds, agree in the same order; and thus it is necessary that

they have real relations to each another. Since, therefore, the processions in God are in the identity of nature, as has been shown [I.27.2,
4], it is necessary that the relations that are grasped according to the
divine processions are real relations.

(*ST* I.28.1 co.)

In creatures, a relation, according to Aristotle's *Categories*, is an
accidental quality signifying reference or regard to another. A
relation does not subsist or exist on its own apart from the substance in which it inheres accidentally. For example, inhering in
the substance of William Harkins, my father, is his real relation to
me, namely that of paternity. If William—that is, his substance—
did not exist, neither would his relation of paternity. Substance
denotes a thing's essential nature, literally what 'stands under' (*sub*
+ *stare*) the particular constellation of accidents that inhere in it. A
thing's substance (*substantia*) or essence (*essentia*) is what is required
for that thing to be (*esse*). What it takes for me to be is a human
nature, constituted of an animal body animated by a rational soul.
Particular features that are accidental to me—such as my being six
feet tall, having brown hair, or being seated and typing these
words—are not essential for me to be. I existed as a human being
before I was six feet tall and before I had any hair at all, and
I would exist as human even if I were standing and not typing.
Likewise, William would still have been, and would have been
what he is essentially, if he had never been my father. His being
the substance that he is does not depend on the particular accident
of paternity in relation to me. These examples make clear that
what it means to have accidental properties is to be in potential in
some way: accidents point to what is but might not have been, or,
conversely, what might have been but is not (McCabe 2002: 41;
ST I.3.6 co.). I might not have typed these words, and you might
not have read them just now, but, in fact, I did type them and you
did read them. I might have been seven feet tall, but this potentiality was never reduced to actuality in me. Conversely, William
might not have been my father, but his having the accidental
quality of a relation of paternity to me indicates that his being in
potency to fatherhood vis-à-vis me was, in fact, actualized.

Although accidental, my father's relation of paternity to me is
nevertheless real, as is my relation of filiation to him. What

constitutes a *real* relation is that it is, in Aquinas's words, "in the very nature of things" (I.28.1 co.). That is, two things that have real relations to one another—my father and I, for instance—are ordered to each other according to their own natures. A rational or logical relation, by contrast, signifies not an ordering of one thing to another by nature, but rather reference to another merely "in the apprehension of reason comparing one thing to another" (I.28.1 co.). When, for example, I compare my dog, a Lakeland Terrier named Chloe, to my neighbor's dog, an Australian Cobberdog named Molly, the relation of one to the other is only in my mind. It is neither in Chloe nor in Molly, as they are not naturally ordered—or really related—to one another.

Based on Christian doctrine and history, Aquinas knows—or rather, believes—that the Trinitarian relations in God are real and are not merely in our minds. If God *really is*, as Christian faith holds, Father, Son, and Holy Spirit, and not simply thought of or called such, then the processions must point to real relations in God, namely paternity, filiation, spiration, and procession (I.28.1 s.c., a. 4 co.). Sabellianism, a form of Modalistic Monarchianism, jumped the tracks of orthodoxy in imagining the divine relations as purely logical: it maintained that in reality God is one, but in our heads He is known and named according to three economic modes and operations (I.28.1 s.c.). Alternatively, the primary obstacle to locating real relations in God is divine simplicity, as Aquinas is well aware. God's simple nature means that He has no accidents, including relations. How, then, is this theological conundrum to be resolved?

Aquinas settles the question by carefully considering how relations in God are, at the same time, different from and similar to relations in creatures. In other words, relations in creatures tell us at least as much about how relations in God are *not* as how they are. At the heart of Aquinas's deliberation stands a crucial distinction: that between the existence or to-be (*esse*) of accidents such as relations, on the one hand, and their proper notion (*ratio propria*), on the other. First, as our example of human paternity illustrates, the *esse* or to-be of relations in creatures is "to-be in a subject" (*inesse subiecto*): that is, they exist only insofar as they inhere in their proper subject or substance. And because such inherence is accidental to this subject, the relation's existence is an "accidental to-be" (*esse accidentale*) (I.28.2 co.). Second, the *ratio propria* or proper notion of a relation is determined not according to that in which it inheres, but rather according to its reference to another (*ad aliquid*). Whereas *esse* represents a point of radical dissimilarity between relations in creatures and relations in God, *ratio propria* marks a juncture of greater correspondence between the two.

Specifically, concerning *esse*, Aquinas teaches that whereas creaturely relations have an "accidental to-be" (*esse accidentale*), divine relations have a "substantial to-be" (*esse substantiale*). This is so because there are no accidental qualities in God; rather, whatever exists in God is His essence or substance (I.28.2 co.; I.3.6 co.; I.2.3 co.). And there can be no accidental qualities in God because there can be no potentiality in Him. He is pure actuality (I.3.1 co.; I.3.6 co.). In other words, there is nothing in God that is but might not have been, and nothing that might have been but is not (McCabe 2002: 40–41). We cannot affirm of God what we must affirm of William Harkins, namely that H/he would be and would be who H/he is essentially if H/he were not F/father. Rather, paternity is essential to God, as are His other real relations. Thus, Aquinas affirms, "A relation really existing in God has the to-be [*esse*] of the divine essence" (I.28.2 co.). Furthermore, the heart of the doctrine of divine simplicity, as we have seen in Chapter 3, is that the divine essence (*essentia*) is identical with the divine to-be (*esse*) (I.3.4 co.). Thus, just as to be God is to be to-be, so too to be a real relation in God is to be to-be. Clearly, neither of these affirmations is true of any creature. To be me, for instance, is definitely *not* to be to-be, and to be the filiation in me is in no way to be to-be!

Whereas the *esse* of divine relations differs fundamentally from that of creaturely relations, this cannot be said of their *ratio propria*. This is so because the proper notion of any relation, whether in creatures or in God, is its reference to another. Aquinas explains: "Certainly, insofar as reference to another [*ad aliquid*] is designated [by a relation], some disposition [*habitudo*] with respect to the essence is not signified, but rather [a disposition] with respect to its opposite" (I.28.2 co.). Indeed, the very notion (*ratio*) of a relation entails relative opposition, and the very notion (*ratio*) of relative opposition includes distinction (I.28.3 co.). Because there is real relation in God, then, Aquinas concludes: "It is necessary that in God there is real distinction, not, indeed, according to what is absolute—which is the essence, in which there is the greatest unity and simplicity—but according to what is relative" (I.28.3 co.). And what is relative in God is variously signified by the divine processions, relations, and persons.

In enumerating the four real relations in God—paternity, filiation, spiration, and procession—Aquinas returns to the processions. Real relations in God must be based on action (as opposed to quantity, which God does not have), and this action must be internal to God rather than outside Him, since the relations of God to creatures are not real in Him (I.28.4 co.). Thus, the real relations in God can be understood only in terms of the immanent processions. Two opposite relations—namely, that of the one proceeding from the principle and that of the principle itself—arise from each of the two processions within God. From the intellectual procession of the Word arise, on the one hand, paternity, the relation of the principle of generation (viz., the Father) to the one generated (the Son), and, on the other, filiation, the relation of the Son, who is generated, to the Father, the generative principle. Likewise from the volitional procession of Love arise, on the one hand, spiration, the relation of the principle (the Father and Son) to what proceeds from it (the Holy Spirit), and, on the other, procession, the relation of what proceeds from the principle (I.28.4 co.).

Aquinas's consideration of divine processions and relations leads him finally, in the "order of teaching," to the persons in God. Significantly, Giles Emery has claimed that his notion of a divine person as a 'subsistent relation' constitutes "the keystone of Aquinas's Trinitarian doctrine" by virtue of the fact that it accounts for both the essential unity and the plurality in God (Emery 2012: 421). Developing Emery's apt metaphor, we might note that, like the wedge-shaped building block at the crown of an arch, person actually locks together in mutual support the divine oneness and threeness that some modern readers have imagined as wholly disconnected in the *Prima pars*. Aquinas does not, however, apply the term 'person' to God too quickly or easily. As we have seen in Chapter 3, Aquinas flatly denies what many philosophers and theologians today take for granted, namely that God is a person of a certain character, like you and me, only bigger, more powerful, and less visible. "It must be said," Aquinas declares, "that it is impossible to predicate anything univocally of God and creatures"

(I.13.5 co.; I.29.4 ad 4). Thus, person must be said of God in a way that is analogous to its creaturely predication. In other words, knowing what a human person is tells us as much, if not more, about what God is *not* than about what God is.

If, as I have suggested, Aquinas's Trinitarian theology aims at an explication of scriptural revelation, it would seem that the term 'person' should not be applied to God since it is not used in this way in Scripture, either Old or New Testament. Interestingly, Aquinas anticipates this objection (I.29.3 obj. 1). He responds by noting that although Scripture nowhere describes God using the word 'person,' it does variously affirm of God what the word signifies, namely that "He is supremely existing per se and understanding most perfectly [*est maxime per se ens, et perfectissime intelligens*]" (ad 1). Notice that, unlike some published translations, I have not rendered Aquinas's *ens* here using the English noun "being," nor have I added this noun to the end of the second phrase such that Aquinas calls God "the most perfectly intelligent being" (cf. translation of Lawrence Shapcote, OP). Consequently, my rendering appears less clear and more enigmatic. But I hope it is also more accurate and thought-provoking, inviting us deeper into Aquinas's apophaticism, into a recognition that the name 'God,' properly understood, functions more like a verb than a noun. Indeed, Aquinas is profoundly aware that God is *not* 'a being' among beings, but rather is the pure act of existing itself, that is, "supremely existing per se" (*ST* I.29.3 ad 1). In Aquinas's view, the words of Scripture truthfully signify the mystery of God, but sacred doctrine, in explicating and handing on the faith concerning this mystery, must also make use of terms not explicitly set forth in Scripture itself. Aquinas explains:

> If it were necessary to speak about God using only the expressions that Sacred Scripture hands on concerning God, it would follow that no one could ever speak about God in any language other than those in which Old or New Testament Scripture was first written. The necessity of disputing with heretics, however, forced [ancient Christians] to find new words [*nova nomina*] to signify the ancient faith [*antiquam fidem*] concerning God. Nor should this novelty be shunned, since it is not profane, as it is not at variance with the sense [*sensu*] of the Scriptures.
>
> (*ST* I.29.3 ad 1)

If theologians, philosophers, and ordinary people were required to use only the exact words of the canonical Scriptures as originally transmitted, Aquinas could have said nothing whatsoever about God, since he wrote in Latin, of course. Likewise, we could say nothing in English or any other of the approximately 6,500 languages spoken throughout the world today (Hebrew, Greek, and Aramaic excepted).

Aquinas knows well, however, that the Church, under the threat of ancient Christological heresies such as Nestorianism, officially introduced the terms 'person' (πρόσωπον) and 'hypostasis' (ὑπόστασις) at the Councils of Ephesus (431) and Chalcedon (451)—and continues to use them—to signify God relatively and in the plural (I.29.4 co.; III.2.2, 3; Emery 2007: 104). The basic definition of 'person' that Aquinas prefers is that proposed by Boethius (c. 477–524), "an individual substance of a rational nature" (I.29.1 obj. 1, co.). A human person is a rational hypostasis or supposit, a particular instantiation of a rational nature that 'stands under' a constellation of accidental properties (I.29.2 co.). Aquinas notes that, whereas a rational soul, flesh, and bone belong to human nature generally, this particular human person is constituted of *this* soul, *this* flesh, and *this* bone (I.29.2 ad 3). In light of the doctrine of divine simplicity, the difficulties of applying the term 'person'—at least according to its human predication—to God should be obvious. The term 'hypostasis,' which is synonymous with 'person,' seems inapplicable to God, as it signifies the subject underlying accidents, which God clearly does not have (I.29.3 obj. 3). Furthermore, God appears not to fit the Boethian definition of person on two grounds. First, He cannot be called an 'individual substance' because the principle of individuation is matter, but God is wholly immaterial; nor can He be identified as a substance, as He is not the subject of accidents. Second, God cannot be said to have a rational nature since reason implies discursive knowledge, which does not apply to God (I.29.3 obj. 4; I.14.7).

The key authority underpinning Aquinas's response to these objections is the profession of the Athanasian Creed: "There is one person [*persona*] of the Father, another of the Son, [and] another of the Holy Spirit" (I.29.3 s.c.). Aquinas invokes what we might call 'the principle of perfection' to argue that the term 'person' is aptly predicated of God:

> It must be said that 'person' signifies what is most perfect in every nature, namely subsisting in a rational nature [*subsistens in rationali natura*]. Hence, since everything that pertains to perfection must be attributed to God on account of the fact that His essence contains within itself every perfection, it is fitting [*conveniens*] that this noun 'person' is said of God—not, however, in the same way that it is said of creatures, but in a more excellent way [*excellentiori modo*].
>
> (*ST* I.29.3 co.)

'Person' is predicated of humans because of the great dignity of subsisting in a rational nature. But because the divine dignity far exceeds any human dignity, the term 'person' is "supremely applicable to God" (I.29.3 ad 2). Returning to Boethius's definition ("an individual substance of a rational nature"), Aquinas further explains what it means that 'person' is predicated of God "in a more excellent way." God can be called "an individual" not in the sense that matter is the principle of individuation in Him, but only insofar as this designation implies incommunicability. Likewise, to speak of God as a "substance" is not to suggest that He is some subject underlying a constellation of accidents, but rather to signify His self-subsistence or existing per se. And to describe God as "of a rational nature" is not to attribute to Him discursive thought, but rather an intellectual nature more generally (I.29.3 ad 4).

Aquinas makes altogether clear, then, that 'person'—like 'procession' and 'relation'—cannot be predicated univocally of God and creatures. "It is one thing to ask about the meaning of this word 'person' in general," he observes, "and another to ask about the meaning of 'divine person'" (I.29.4 co.). 'Divine person,' according to Aquinas, signifies "a relation as subsisting" (*relationem ut subsistentem*), or a subsistent relation. A subsistent relation, Aquinas explains, is a relation in the mode of substance, which is a hypostasis subsisting in the divine nature. And what subsists in the divine nature is not different from the divine nature itself (ibid.). So the real relation of origin in God that is paternity, for instance, is a hypostasis subsisting in the divine nature, namely the hypostasis or person of the Father (ibid.). Whereas this subsistent relation has the to-be (*esse*) of the divine essence (I.28.2 co.), its proper notion (*ratio propria*) is its reference to another, another hypostasis subsisting in the divine nature that proceeds eternally via an intellectual emanation from the Father. This subsistent hypostasis is the person of the Son, which is the real relation of filiation in God and is also no different from the divine nature itself. And from the volitional procession of Love in God arises the real relation of the Holy Spirit to the Father and Son, which relation constitutes the third subsisting hypostasis or person of the Trinity.

In sum, Aquinas's notion of a divine person as a subsistent relation not only crowns his consideration of processions and relations in God. In doing so, it also provides the keystone of his Trinitarian teaching by binding together what pertains to God's unity, on the one hand, and what pertains to His plurality, on the other.

THE MISSION OF THE DIVINE PERSONS

As our foregoing analysis shows, the modern claim that Aquinas separated the One God from the Triune God is misguided. Equally mistaken is the view that in the *ST* Aquinas locks the Trinity within itself, thereby rendering it both uninteresting and irrelevant. Aquinas not only affirms the necessity of knowing the Trinity for thinking rightly about both creation and human salvation, as we have seen (I.32.1 ad 3). He also draws his treatment of the Trinity to a close by considering the mission of the divine persons (I.43), which provides a suitable segue to all that follows in I.44 and beyond concerning the economy of creation and salvation. It has been suggested, in fact, that the rest of the *ST* provides the conclusion to Aquinas's Trinitarian treatise (Emery 2007: 50, 413). If this is so, q. 43 of the *Prima pars* provides the fulcrum on which Aquinas transitions from a detailed study of God in Himself to an extended consideration of creation and redemption as accomplished by the Triune God.

Indeed, the very notion of divine mission (*missio*) is an important Trinitarian hinge—perhaps *the* theological hinge—on which Aquinas's thought in the whole of the *ST* turns. This is so because the idea of mission includes the relation or disposition (*habitudo*) of the one sent to the sender, on the one hand, and the disposition of the one sent to the end to which he is sent, on the other. The mission of a divine person entails both the procession of origin from the sender, which is eternal, and "a new mode of existing in another [*novum modum existendi in aliquo*]" on the part of the one sent, which is necessarily temporal (I.43.1 co.). In the reality of divine mission, then, the eternal processions of God *ad intra* and the temporal processions of God *ad extra* converge. Taking his cue from Gal. 4:4, *When the fullness of time had come, God sent* [misit] *His Son*, Aquinas understands divine mission as essentially temporal, pertaining primarily to a temporal effect, though also entailing eternal procession (I.43.2 s.c., ad 3). Eternally generated by the Father, the Son, for instance, was sent temporally by this same Father such that "He began to exist in the world *visibly* through assumed flesh" (I.43.1 co., emphasis mine). In line with his understanding of mission as entailing a divine person's "new mode of existing," Aquinas notes that the Son was already in the world prior to His being sent *visibly* through the Incarnation (I.43.1 co.). As an astute reader of Scripture, Aquinas here intimates that the Prologue to John's Gospel indicates as much: Jn. 1:10 tells us, *He was in the world, and through Him the world was made*, before Jn. 1:14 declares, *And the Word was made flesh, and dwelt among us* (I.43.1 co.). In his *Commentary on John*, Aquinas explains that the Word was in the world from its beginning "as an efficient and preserving cause," operating in all things from within by creating, that is, by giving them *esse* or existence (*Super Io.*, cap. 1 lect. 5).

As the cause existing in its effects, God is in all creatures according to His essence, power, and presence. This is the "one common mode" according to which God is in all earthly realities (I.43.3 co.). Beyond this common mode, however, God is present in the rational creature in a "special mode," as the object known is in the knower and as the beloved is in the lover. Indeed, the Son and the Holy Spirit, which proceed eternally as the Word and Love, respectively, are sent temporally and invisibly into rational souls according to the gift of sanctifying grace, and thus they begin to exist in the world "in a new mode" (I.43.3 co). The effect of this mission is that the human person, by grace, draws nearer to the Triune God by reflecting His own immanent operations. Aquinas explains:

> And because, by knowing and loving, the rational creature attains to God Himself, according to this special mode God is said not only to exist in the rational creature, but even to dwell therein as in His own temple [cf. 1 Cor 3:16–17, 6:19].

(*ST* I.43.3 co.)

This concise consideration of divine mission highlights two important characteristics of Aquinas's Trinitarian theology generally. First, it intimates how thoroughly scriptural his doctrine of the Trinity is. Second, it shows how readily his Trinitarian teaching opens up onto God's economic operations for us: creation, redemption, and sanctification. Aquinas will concern himself with precisely these themes throughout the remainder of his *Summa*.

5

CREATION

In order to understand Aquinas's mature teaching on creation and evil as set forth in *ST* I.45–49, we must bear in mind all that he has taught us about God in Himself in I.2–43 (Tanner 2016: 142; Davies 2014: 109). If we forget or fail to grasp, for instance, that God is pure actuality and subsistent being itself or a Trinity of subsistent relations, we will have difficulty appreciating what Aquinas says about creation. Particularly, Gilles Emery has rightly observed that "Saint Thomas developed a profoundly trinitarian conception of creation" (Emery 2005: 59). The truth that God is a Trinity is, for Aquinas, intimately connected to the reality of creation. Indeed, to understand that God is three persons subsisting in one nature is to realize that God creates the universe not because of any necessity, but rather simply out of love, namely "the love of His own goodness" (*ST* I.32.1 ad 3). According to Jean-Pierre Torrell, Aquinas follows Scripture in deeming creation "an act of wisdom and of free will, stemming from a gratuitous love that desires only to share its own good" (Torrell 2005: 24).

In the context of divine love and creation, Aquinas is clear that "God needs nothing outside Himself" (I.20.2 obj. 3; I.44.4 obj. 1). In creating, God does not act for the acquisition of an end whereby He might be augmented or perfected somehow. This is how all creatures act, namely in order to achieve the end of their own perfection (I.44.4 co.). But God is most perfect apart from creation, and so would be most perfect if He never created anything. "Since God is subsistent being itself [*ipsum esse subsistens*]," Aquinas explains, "He can lack nothing of the perfection of being" (I.4.2 co.). Furthermore, because God is the first efficient cause of all things, the perfections of all created things must preexist in Him "in a more eminent way" (I.4.2 co.). Thus, all creaturely being and perfection depend on God. Conversely, however, divine being and perfection in no way depend on creation. This results in a radical asymmetry between the real relation of creatures to God, on the one hand, and the merely logical relation of God to creatures, on the other (see I.45.3 ad 1; I.13.7 co.; I.28.1 ad 3; I.28.4 co.). We will return to this relational disparity below.

Aquinas understands the eternal processions in God as constituting the cause or "reasons" (*rationes*) of the temporal production of creatures (I.45.6 co.). As he explains elsewhere, "The coming forth [*exitus*] of the persons in the unity of [the divine] essence is the cause [*causa*] of the coming forth [*exitus*] of creatures in the diversity of essence" (*Scriptum* I d. 2 q. 1 prol.). The immanent action of God is, for Aquinas, the very condition of His transitive or transient action: stated most succinctly, the Trinity creates. More specifically, God's causality concerning creation is located in His own internal processions by virtue of the fact that, as we have seen, He is the cause of all things by His knowledge and will. Just as an artist—such as Michelangelo—is the cause of his art—the sculpture *David*, for example—through his knowledge and approving will, so too God is the cause of creatures through His Word (that is, the Son) and Love (the Holy Spirit) (I.45.6 co.; I.14.8 co.; I.19.4 co.; see Chapter 3). In a radical digest of his deeply trinitarian theology of creation, Aquinas affirms:

> Just as the Father speaks Himself and every creature by the Word which He has begotten, inasmuch as the begotten Word sufficiently expresses [*sufficienter repraesentat*] the Father and every creature, so also He loves Himself and every creature by the Holy Spirit, inasmuch as the Holy Spirit proceeds as the Love of the primal goodness [*amor bonitatis primae*] according to which the Father loves Himself and every creature.
>
> (*ST* I.37.2 ad 3)

The love that brings each creature into being, then, is none other than God's Love of His own "primal goodness." Aquinas is clear about God's loving purpose in creating: "He intends only to communicate His own perfection, which is His goodness" (I.44.4

co.). The divine goodness, therefore, is the end or final cause of all things (I.44.4 co.). Of the four Aristotelian causes—material, formal, efficient, and final—the final cause causes in the highest, most expansive degree (Kerr 2019: 101; Feser 2009: 16–23). Aquinas calls it "the cause of causes, because it is the cause of causality in all causes" (*De princ. nat.*, ch. 4). In short, the divine goodness or love creates all things and causes all causes—material, formal, and efficient—to cause in their own particular ways.

But all of this raises two more basic questions, to which we now turn: 'What is creation?' and 'Who creates?'

A preliminary twofold precaution seems necessary here in order to smooth our path to understanding Aquinas on creation. First, Aquinas treats creation with great philosophical, particularly metaphysical, sophistication and profundity. As David Burrell has suggested, the doctrine demands precisely such an approach:

> [A]n adequate treatment of the unique activity which constitutes creating, as well as the quite ineffable relation between creatures and creator which it initiates, will tax one's philosophical resources to the limit, so more timid theologians prefer to finesse it altogether.
>
> (Burrell 2004: 28)

Aquinas, however, has no desire to evade the doctrine's difficulties, as we will see. To the contrary, he is determined to bring all the resources at his disposal—metaphysical, scriptural, and patristic—to bear on the question of creation. Consequently, Aquinas's consideration exemplifies the scholastic approach, which assumes that all truth, wherever it is to be found, is ultimately one by virtue of its divine source.

Second, readers today may find Aquinas's approach to and conclusions concerning creation challenging, particularly because, in the long wake of Friedrich Nietzsche's proclamation that "God is dead," some philosophers have declared metaphysical inquiry impossible. In certain fundamental ways, Aquinas's thinking seems quite different from, even alien to, our own. Three brief examples should suffice. First, Aquinas clearly teaches that creation is *not* the coming forth of "some particular being [*alicuius entis particularis*]" from a particular agent, but rather "the emanation of all being [*totius entis*] from the universal cause, which is

God" (I.45.1 co.). What does "all being" mean, and what is its relationship to "particular being"? The following discussion should clarify this distinction. Second, and relatedly, whereas we might (wish to) think of ourselves, and perhaps even non-human animals, variously as co-creators with God, Aquinas maintains that *only* God can and does create. Third, Aquinas understands creation not, in Jean-Pierre Torrell's words, "as an isolated act that occurred in a distant past," but rather as a present, ongoing metaphysical reality (Torrell 2005: 24). Furthermore, in contrast to some modern scientists who, equating creation with the beginning of the universe, imagine that the question of creation is moot if the universe is a closed system without a beginning, Aquinas understands that the universe would still require a cause for its existence even if it were eternal (Kerr 2015: 174–179, 189–194). As we have seen in Chapter 3, Aquinas takes God to be the answer to the most basic question raised by the universe, which is a *why* question, not a *when* question: *why* is there anything rather than nothing?

WHAT IS CREATION?

All that Aquinas says about creation flows from his proper definition of the term. Understood as a verb or an action, 'to create' is, according to Aquinas, "to produce being absolutely [*esse absolute*], not this or that [being]" (I.45.5 co.). Note the contrast here. Properly speaking, to produce your particular being (*esse*) or mine or that of my dog, Chloe, is *not* to create. Nor is it to produce this or that type or class of being, such as human being or canine being. Rather, to create is to cause or grant *esse*—that is, being or existence or to-be—simply, without any qualification whatsoever. Thus, understood as a noun or an effect, 'creation' signifies the most universal effect of transitive divine action, namely "being itself [*ipsum esse*]" (I.45.5 co.). Creation, then, is "the proper effect of the first and most universal cause, which is God" (ibid.). It is the production *ad extra* of "being itself [*ipsum esse*]" by "subsistent being itself [*ipsum esse subsistens*]" (I.4.2 co.). We noted above that God, in creating, intends to share or communicate His own goodness outside Himself (I.44.4 co.; I.47.1 co.). Here we see that the divine goodness communicated is "being itself," which is subsistent in God but shared or participated in creatures. Aquinas explains the derived nature of *esse* in creatures thus:

> [A]ll other things apart from God are not their own existence [*suum esse*], but share in existence [*participant esse*]. It is necessary, therefore, that all things that are diversified according to the diverse participation in existence, so as to exist more or less perfectly, are caused by the one First Being [*ab uno primo ente*] that exists most perfectly.
>
> (*ST* I.44.1 co.)

Gaven Kerr has identified this as the central insight of Aquinas's understanding of God, namely that He is the unique subsisting source of existence or being (*esse*) from which all existing things come (Kerr 2019: 15). Aquinas seems to have first arrived at this insight during his student years at Paris (1252–1256), as *On Being and Essence* ch. 4 suggests (Torrell 1996: 47–48). Here, according to Kerr, Aquinas offers his earliest proof for God's existence, which is best classified as a metaphysical proof (Kerr 2015: xii). His demonstration moves from a consideration of created, composite beings, in which there is a real distinction between *esse* and essence, to the existence of God, in whom there is no such distinction. Unlike all created beings, God is pure *esse* or *esse tantum*, "existence alone" (*De ente*, ch. 4; Kerr 2015, esp. 150–172; MacDonald 2002). Aquinas explains the *esse–essentia* distinction among all created realities thus:

> Every essence [*essentia*] or quiddity can be understood without anything about its existence [*esse*] being understood. For I can understand what a human or a phoenix is and still not know whether they have existence [*esse*] in the nature of things.
>
> (*De ente*, ch. 4)

We can know what constitutes human nature or feline nature, for instance, without knowing whether either actually has *esse* (here *esse* is used in the sense of generic or specific existence). Or, I might know *what* my cat, Murray, is essentially, but be ignorant of *whether* he is—if, for example, he left home two weeks ago and has not been seen since (here *esse* is used to denote individual existence; see Kenny 2002: 189–192, who identifies twelve different uses of *esse* in Aquinas's works).

This basic line of metaphysical thought, first proposed in *On Being* ch. 4, undergirds Aquinas's approach to both God and creation. We have encountered it already in Aquinas's Five Ways, particularly the Second Way, which concludes that God is the first efficient cause, and in the doctrine of divine simplicity (see Chapter 3). In treating God as simple, Aquinas makes clear that creatures differ fundamentally from God in that they are caused. No creature can be the sufficient cause of its own existence or being (*esse*), and so the *esse* of every creature is other than its essence (*essentia*) (I.3.4 co.). But because God is the first efficient cause, "[i]t is impossible that in God existence [*esse*] is one thing and His essence [*essentia*] another" (I.3.4 co.). God simply *is* naturally or essentially. He cannot not be. He is His own *esse*, pure *esse*. "God is being itself subsisting per se [*ipsum esse per se subsistens*]," Aquinas teaches (I.44.1 co.). But creatures do not have existence (*esse*) essentially. Because creatures require an external cause of their *esse*, it is true that essentially creatures are nothing (Kerr 2019: 79–81; Davies 2014: 109–111). Gaven Kerr explains:

> Creatures ultimately exist out of dependence on God, Who is *esse tantum*. What creatures are in themselves is precisely nothing unless granted *esse* from God, without which they would not exist. Creatures thus do not naturally exist, but exist only in dependence upon God, from Whom they receive *esse*. *Esse* then is what brings creatures from a state of nothingness to a state of being, such that *esse* is the first act and perfection of the creature.
>
> (Kerr 2015: 171)

Aquinas's notion that creatures do not exist essentially, and so are naturally nothing, may strike us as counterintuitive and even mistaken. After all, when we hear or think the word 'creature,' we are likely to have in mind an animal such as a cat, a giraffe, or perhaps a human. And an animal, by definition, is an animate or living being: it naturally exists. Likewise, 'organisms'—from ordinary, single-celled slime mold to the more complex and exotic dwarf corkscrew croton or Dumbo octopus—are constituted of mutually dependent organs or organelles precisely in order to carry out the activities of natural life. Modern evolutionary biology recognizes not only that organisms naturally exist, but also that their existence is teleological, a direct result of natural selection (Ruse 1989). Whereas Aquinas agrees that all organisms—indeed, all created things whatsoever—are directed toward an end, he understands this end as God, who is both the first efficient cause and the final cause of every creature (*ST* I.65.2 co.; I.44.1, 4). Furthermore, contrary to the modern assumption that to be a creature is to exist naturally and autonomously, Aquinas takes a creature to be something that (1) has been granted *esse* or produced "according to its entire substance [*secundum suam totam substantiam*]" by God alone, with absolutely nothing presupposed, and (2) is continually conserved in being (*esse*) by God (I.65.3 co.; I.104.1 co.). For Aquinas, then, a 'creature' is a being (*ens*) other than God (indeed God, properly speaking, is not 'a being' [*ens*] but rather 'subsistent being itself' [*ipsum esse subsistens*]) that is absolutely dependent on God not only for the initial gift of *esse* but also for its continuous conservation. "For the being [*esse*] of every creature depends on God," Aquinas teaches, "in such a way that it could not subsist for a moment, but would be reduced to nothingness [*in nihilum redigerentur*], unless it were conserved in being [*in esse*] by the operation of divine power" (I.104.1 co.). Without God's operative power and love, every creature would fall back into the natural nothingness whence it came by way of creation.

THE MODE AND THE AGENT OF CREATION

We come, then, to the question of *how* God creates. The answer, according to the Christian doctrinal tradition inherited and developed by Aquinas, is 'from nothing' (*creatio ex nihilo*). Among all existing realities, God alone exists naturally: His nature or essence is *ipsum esse*. Because nothing besides God truly exists, He makes use of nothing in creating (Kerr 2019: 81). That is, the production or emanation of "being itself," "being absolutely," or "all being [*totius entis/totius esse*]" (I.45.5, 1 co.) from God presupposes nothing apart from God. Indeed, given that creation is "the emanation of complete universal being [*emanatio totius entis universalis*]," Aquinas notes that it is impossible that this emanation should presuppose "any particular being [*aliquod ens*]" (I.45.1 co.). If, for instance, the emanation of "complete universal being" presupposed even one existing thing—my dog, Chloe, for instance—it would not, in fact, be the emanation of "complete universal being." Rather, it would be the emanation of 'complete universal being minus Chloe's being.' In this case God would require Chloe's being in order to create. But if this were so, creation would not be creation and Chloe would not be a creature, according to Aquinas. Furthermore, God would not be the creator of all things, since He would not be the first efficient cause of Chloe. But, in fact, Chloe is a creature, whose *esse* is a consequence, not a presupposition, of creation. And so God is creator of all things, including Chloe. It is clear, therefore, that creation, properly understood, *requires* the presupposition of nothing apart from the creator. God must create everything from nothing.

According to Aquinas, then, creation *ex nihilo* has a twofold signification: 'from nothing' means 'from nonbeing,' on the one hand, and 'from nothing presupposed,' on the other. First, as we have seen, God brings all creatures into being (*in esse*) from non-being, from nothingness, which is prior to being in all things whose *esse* and essence are really distinct. This priority of nonbeing to being need not be temporal, however. That the world began in time instead of existing eternally is, according to Aquinas, neither demonstrable nor naturally knowable; rather, it is an article of faith based on divine revelation (e.g., Gen. 1:1, Prov. 8:22; Jn. 17:5; *ST* I.46.1, 2, 3 s.c., co.). But even if the world were eternal, nonbeing would precede being naturally or causally (as opposed to temporally). Gaven Kerr provides the example, taken from Richard Taylor, of the sun and moon imagined as having existed eternally (Kerr 2019: 78–79; Kerr 2015: 176–177; Taylor 1975: 41). If neither sun nor moon had a temporal beginning, and so no duration, the sun would nevertheless cause the moon's surface to be illuminated. The sun would have a causal priority over the moon, which would depend on the sun's light for its own illumination, even though the sun would not be temporally prior to the moon. The darkness of the moon's surface would also be causally prior to its illumination. Similarly, if the world and its creatures existed eternally, God—who is also eternal, of course—would have a causal priority over them. For Aquinas, the question 'Why is there anything rather than nothing?' would still need to be asked, and God would still provide the answer. And just as the moon's darkness would be causally prior to its illumination by the sun, so too the nonbeing of creatures would be causally prior to their being in being by virtue of God's creative action.

Second, creation *ex nihilo* means that God brings all creatures into being from nothing presupposed. There is no being or matter or stuff that God uses or 'works on' to create. Thus, Aquinas carefully distinguishes creating from related realities with which it might readily be confused. Whereas creating presupposes nothing, the actions of making and generating presuppose something. Aquinas explains:

> Indeed, when anyone makes one thing from another, that thing from which he makes it is presupposed to his action and is not produced by the action itself. A craftsman, for instance, works from natural things, such as wood and bronze, which are not caused by the action of [his] craft, but are caused by the action of nature. And nature itself causes natural things as regards form, but presupposes matter. If, therefore, God did not act except from something presupposed, it would follow that the thing presupposed would not be caused by Him.

> (*ST* I.45.2 co.)

In our earlier example, if God somehow manipulated Chloe the dog to produce another being—Chester the cat, let's say—neither Chloe nor Chester would be a creature. Chloe would be a canine presupposed to God's making, and Chester would be a strangely (albeit divinely) manufactured feline! But let's imagine a more likely scenario, namely that Chester is a real cat who was produced by natural generation. Would he not be, then, a creature produced by the natural causation of his feline parents (let's call them Casper and Fluffy)? If so, can Casper and Fluffy rightly be called Chester's creators, or is God alone his creator? Can Casper and Fluffy at least be considered co-creators with God?

CAN CREATURES CREATE?

It certainly seems as if corporeal creatures can and do create. Indeed, Aquinas himself observes that "they make something similar to themselves, for fire generates fire, and a human generates a human" (I.45.5 obj. 1). Aquinas engages two views, common in the thirteenth century, of how creatures do, in fact, cooperate with God in His creative activity (Kerr 2019: 88–96). We will call the first of these, which Aquinas attributes to the Islamic philosopher Avicenna (c. 970–1037), 'gradation theory.' On this view, creatures proceed from God by degrees (*gradatim*): God created the first separated substance or intelligence immediately, after which this substance created the second, which, in turn, created the world and its soul; then the substance of the world created the matter of lower bodies (I.45.5 co.; I.47.1 co.; I.65.3 co.). Here creation is a necessary emanation from God, according to which God shares His creative power by degrees with each successive emanation. God gets the ball rolling, as it were, but then leaves higher creatures to produce lower ones by their own power, received from God gradationally, all the way down the ontological scale. The second view of creaturely co-creation is that of Peter Lombard (c. 1096–1160), which the "Master" intimates in *Sentences* Bk. IV d. 5. We may aptly call it 'instrument theory.' On this view, God communicates the power of creating to creatures in such a way that they create not by their own power (gradationally or hierarchically received), but rather as instruments or ministers of God's proper power (I.45.5 co.). As a saw, which cuts wood by virtue of its own form, is used by a carpenter to produce the form of a bench, so too creatures—by virtue of their own particular forms—are used as instruments of God, the principle creative agent, to generate individuals of their own diverse kinds (I.45.5 co.). God uses fire to generate fire, for instance, and humans to reproduce humans.

Let us observe, if only in passing, that the modern notion of humans as cultural co-creators appears as an interesting variation on these medieval theories. Certain theologies and pastoral psychologies of our time make much of the idea that humans do and should act as God's agents in the ongoing, creative work of transforming the world. In his theology of work, the twentieth-century Dominican Marie-Dominique Chenu boldly asserted: "Man fulfils himself by dominating, through his discoveries, reason, and virtue, that Nature which is his kingdom, and out of which he creates a new world, a human world" (Chenu 1963: 8, quoted in Capps and Carlin 2016: 871). Building on Chenu, Donald Capps and Nathan Carlin claim that a special emphasis of Christianity, beginning with the book of Genesis, is that "God created humans to be creators and that this involves ... drawing out the potentialities that are already inherent in the material world" (Capps and Carlin 2016: 879). Similarly, the Lutheran theologian Philip Hefner maintains that biological evolution has resulted in a highly developed consciousness and complex self-awareness in humans, which enable our unique status as "created co-creator[s]." Hefner explains:

> Being human involves a great deal of creating, imagining new worlds, and constructing those worlds. We know that this imagining and creating are not just something we *do*; it's what we are. Co-creating is not just our doing; it's our *being*.
>
> (Hefner 2012: 305)

Reminiscent of gradation theory, Hefner suggests that creation, and especially human co-creation, are somehow necessary: to be human is necessarily to be a co-creator. Like instrumental theory, modern theologies of work imagine humans as the ministers of God's primary creative activity. And in both instrumental theory and modern work-theology, the (human) creature is presupposed to the putative co-creative activity.

Aquinas rejects both the gradation theory and the instrumental theory of co-creation, concluding that God alone creates. Likewise, he would refuse to grant that any cultural transformation effected by humans constitutes creation or co-creation. For Aquinas, creation, which is the production of the most universal effect—namely, *ipsum esse*—must be "the proper effect of the first and most universal cause, which is God" (I.45.5 co.). Thus, the emanation of a particular effect from a particular cause—the matter of the lower bodies from the substance of the world, for instance—neither constitutes nor pertains to creation (I.45.2 ad 1). What does properly pertain to the causality of the supreme cause, and thus to creation, is the granting of "that which is first spread out as an underlay in all things [*primo substratum in omnibus*]," namely *ipsum esse* (I.65.3 co.). Aquinas explains that the more something provides an underlying substratum, the more directly it proceeds from a higher cause; thus everything that is created or granted *ipsum esse* is produced *immediately* by God (I.65.3 co.). By contrast, because, according to gradation theory, each level of production beneath

God necessarily presupposes something—namely, the particular substance from which the next emanation flows—every such effluence is an instance of mere making (I.45.2 co.). Aquinas disallows instrumental theory on the same grounds. This account also presupposes something, and so the resultant mode of production does not qualify as creation. Aquinas teaches:

> The proper effect of God creating is what is presupposed to all other effects, namely being absolutely [*esse absolute*]. Hence, a particular thing [*aliquid*] is not able to work dispositively and instrumentally to produce this effect, since creation is not from anything presupposed, which can be disposed by the action of the instrumental agent. So, therefore, it is impossible for any creature to create ... instrumentally or ministerially.
>
> (*ST* I.45.5 co.)

In sum, nothing but God creates because creation is from nothing. Every existing creature necessarily presupposes the *esse* that it receives from God: otherwise it would not exist. Thus, nothing created can create, or help to create, *esse absolute*.

What, then, are creatures like humans and cats actually doing when they generate offspring? How might we understand their causal action vis-à-vis God's creative activity? Natural reproduction is, according to Aquinas, a case of making or changing on the part of creaturely parents. In reply to the objection that creatures seem to create in that they produce a likeness to themselves, Aquinas explains that particular beings who possesses a certain nature "make [*facit*] something similar to themselves not, in fact, by producing that nature absolutely [*producendo absolute*], but by applying it to some particular thing [*applicando eam ad aliquid*]" (I.45.5 ad 1). Note well the distinction here between the nature—which is produced *absolute*, "absolutely" or "simply" or "without qualification"—and an *aliquid*, "some particular thing" or individual that instantiates that nature. Just as no creature can cause *esse absolute*, so this or that human being cannot cause human nature absolutely, nor can a particular cat cause feline nature absolutely. If this were possible, I could cause myself, and Chester the cat could cause himself! Every creature, in fact, would possess the quality of aseity or self-origination, thus having need neither of natural parents nor of God. This is clearly not the case, however. We humans require natural generation, just as we require God as first efficient cause. Aquinas makes clear that whereas human parents are not the cause of human nature's being, they are the cause of human nature's being *in the particular human being* whom they generate (I.45.5 ad 1). In other words, they cause their offspring as regards *form*, but they presuppose *matter* (I.45.2 co.). According to the Aristotelian doctrine of hylomorphism, all ordinary corporeal realities, including humans, are composed of form and matter (Feser 2009: 13–16). Form is the definition or essence of a thing, what actualizes the potential of matter, causing it to become a definite thing. Matter, by contrast, is not a definite thing, but rather signifies the potential to be a definite thing, a potential that form actualizes. Recall Aquinas's example of a craftsman who presupposes and utilizes naturally produced matter such as wood and bronze in his own artistic work (I.45.2 co.). Similarly, human parents presuppose matter and manipulate it in such a way as to cause the form of human nature in their particular offspring.

In considering divine government, Aquinas introduces a distinction concerning causality that is critically important here: that between becoming and being. An agent may be a cause of its own effect, Aquinas teaches, "according to becoming only [*secundum fieri tantum*], but not directly according to its being [*secundum esse eius*]" (I.104.1 co.). He offers the example of a builder constructing a house. The builder is the cause of becoming of the house, but he cannot be called the cause of its being. This is because the being (*esse*) of the house follows from its form, which is the "structure and order" that results from "the natural power of certain things" such as cement, stones, and wood (ibid.). Just as a cook prepares a meal by applying (*adhibendo*) the natural active power of fire to certain foodstuffs, so too, Aquinas explains, "the builder makes a house by applying [*facit domum adhibendo*] cement, stones, and wood, which can support and preserve such a structure and order" (ibid.). The *becoming* of the house depends on the action of the builder in bringing these natural materials together in a certain way. The *being* of the house, by contrast, depends on the particular natures and qualities of these materials themselves. It is clear that the builder is not the cause of the form of the house as such, but rather of this form being *in this matter*: he is the cause of *this matter* receiving this form and thus *becoming* this particular house.

In the background of Aquinas's discussion here looms Aristotle's understanding of form or essence as the cause of the being of a substance (*Metaphysics* VII.17; Witt 1989: 112–115). For Aristotle, the question of a composite thing's cause of being is 'What is responsible for its being a determinate, unified substance?' It should not be surprising that Aristotle's two examples are the ones invoked by Aquinas, namely human generation and the construction of a house. When one asks, for instance, 'Why are these bricks and stones a house?', two possible ways of understanding the question arise. It could mean: (1) '*What* made these bricks and stones into a house?'; or (2) '*Why* do these bricks and stones constitute a house?' For Aristotle, question (1) is a question of making or *becoming*, and the answer is the efficient cause of the making, namely the builder. Contrastingly, question (2) is a question of being, and the answer, for Aristotle, is the form or essence of the house itself. These bricks and stones *are* a house because together they constitute a certain type of shelter for humans (Witt 1989: 112–114).

Following Aristotle, Aquinas understands the same rationale to apply to natural things. A particular created agent is not the *per se* cause of a form as such, and so is not the cause of being (*esse*) that results from that form (*ST* I.104.1 co.). For example, human parents, as we have seen, are not *per se* causes of the form of human nature, but only of human nature being in their particular offspring: thus, they are causes of *becoming* only. Human nature is in the offspring in the same way it is in the parents, but neither is the principle of human nature as such, the very cause of the form of human nature. This principle and cause of human *being*—indeed, of all being—is God. Aquinas provides the analogy of the sun and the air it illuminates:

> Every creature is related to God as the air is related to the sun that illuminates it. For the sun is shining by its own nature [*lucens per suam naturam*], but the air is bright by participating [*luminosus participando*] in the light from the sun, though not by participating in the sun's nature. In the same way, God alone is being through His own essence [*ens per essentiam suam*], because His essence is His existence [*suum esse*], whereas every creature is being by participation [*ens participative*], considering that its essence is not its existence.
>
> (I.104.1 co.)

Like the air in this analogy, no creature is by its nature brilliance capable of granting light universally. Thus, no creature can produce "that which is first spread out as an underlay in all things," namely *ipsum esse* (I.65.3 co.). Rather, just as all are illuminated by the sun, so too all receive *esse* according to their entire substance from God and all are conserved in *esse* by God (I.65.3 co.; I.104.1 co.). In the absence of the sun, the air suddenly returns to darkness. So too without God and His conserving action, all living things would fall back into nothingness (I.104.1 co.). All are creatures. Not one is a creator or co-creator.

IS GOD REALLY RELATED TO CREATURES?

As we have seen, the manner of God's creating differs essentially from the making and generating that is common to creatures. Making and generating always presuppose something and entail movement or change. If I were to build a wooden fence around my house, for instance, I would need first to gather the necessary materials (wooden posts, rails, pickets, post caps, concrete, gravel, wood stain, etc.) and tools (measuring wheel, post-hole digger, power drill, tape measure, level, hammer, screwdriver, etc.). These would be presupposed to my act of building. Then I would measure and lay out the fence posts, dig the holes, add concrete and gravel and position the posts, attach the rails to the posts, secure the pickets to the rails, add the post caps, and, finally, stain the wood. All of this would require a great deal of movement on my part (shoveling dirt, placing posts, carrying rails, hammering pickets, etc.), as well as numerous physical changes in me (sweating and growing tired, for example) and in the materials I use to erect the fence. But creating is altogether unlike fence-building and other varieties of making. Creating is from nothing, and it involves no movement or change whatsoever. In creation, "the entire substance of things [*tota substantia rerum*]" is produced (I.45.2 ad 2). It presupposes nothing that is the subject of change. This implies, significantly, that God never manipulates or interferes with any creature, altering it somehow from one state of being to another (Davies 2014: 112). God is not a being among beings, as I am a being among the posts, rails, and pickets whose positions I alter to build my fence. As *ipsum esse subsistens*, God is of an entirely different order from creatures.

Because creation entails no movement or change, it "places" nothing in the creature except "according to relation alone [*secundum relationem tantum*]" (I.45.3 co.). Aquinas makes clear that when movement is removed from any action or passion—in this case, God's action of producing *ipsum esse* in every creature—only relation remains (I.45. 3 co.). As we have seen, the proper nature of a relation concerns a thing's reference to another (*ad aliquid*). If this *ad aliquid* signifies a natural ordering, the relation is said to be real in the one so ordered, as there is a real relation of filiation in a son to his father. If, by contrast, the *ad aliquid* is not in the nature of things, but rather signifies mental comparison, the relation is not real, but merely logical (see Chapter 4). According to Aquinas, creation signifies or "places" nothing in the creature—no movement, change, or transformation—except "a certain relation to the creator, as to the principle of its being [*ad principium sui esse*]" (I.45.3 co.). This relation is obviously a real relation, as every creature is naturally ordered to God, who grants it *esse* and conserves it *in esse*.

On the other hand, God's act of creating "places" nothing whatsoever in Him. No advantage or perfection that is not His eternally accrues to God by virtue of His temporal creating. In other words, God is not creator by nature, and creation adds nothing to His perfect Triune nature. In His act of creating, God acquires no natural ordering to creation. Creation makes no difference to God—it causes no change in Him. Aquinas explains:

> It must be said that creation understood actively signifies the divine action, which is God's essence, with a relation to the creature. But the relation in God to the creature is not real [*non est realis*], but only according to reason [*secundum rationem tantum*]. The relation of the creature to God, however, is a real relation.
>
> (I.45.3 ad 1; see also I.13.7 co.; I.28.1 ad 3; I.28.4 co.)

In one sense, then, creation introduces a radical ontological asymmetry between God and creatures: whereas creatures are naturally ordered to and wholly dependent on God, God is neither naturally ordered to nor determined by creatures.

This Thomistic teaching has been criticized as often as it has been misunderstood by recent scholars. We have already met Karl Rahner's critique of Aquinas's God as "absolutely locked within itself" and "not, in its reality, open to anything distinct from it"—a God "from which we are excluded" (Rahner 1970: 18). Similarly, Catherine LaCugna questions whether Aquinas's God is, in fact, the God of Christianity:

> And who is this God, what kind of God is not necessarily related to the world? Is this portrait of God consistent with the God revealed in the saving history of Covenant, Christ, and Spirit? And is this God recognizable as the God into whose name and reality Christians are baptized and whom they address in prayer?
>
> (LaCugna 1991: 161)

More recently, Clark Pinnock has answered LaCugna's question negatively. With Aquinas's teaching in mind, Pinnock affirms:

> Conventional theology did not leave enough room for relationality in God's essence. ... While the creatures can be relational, God's essence cannot be involved in real relationships with a changing world, lest it change too. Relations can be real on the side of the creature, but not on the side of God, and not in a mutual way, because that would introduce change into him. Thus it is hard for conventional theism to deal with a relational and personal God, with a God really involved in the world, in short, with the God of the Bible.
>
> (Pinnock 2001: 6)

Over against Aquinas and traditional theology, Pinnock and his colleagues have proposed an "open view of God," which regards God as "dependent on the world" and "receptive to new experiences" in it (Pinnock et al. 1994: 16). The life of the God of the Old Testament, as they read it, is both social and dynamic:

> God enters into relationships and genuinely interacts with human beings. He affects them, and they, in turn, have an effect on him. As a result, God's life exhibits transition, development and variation. God experiences the temporal world in a temporal way.
>
> (Pinnock et al. 1994: 22)

In short, as Emilio Brito has observed, "Today the immutable God of Thomas Aquinas has bad press" (Brito 1988: 111; quoted in Dodds 2008: 2).

But such bad press seems to be the consequence of a fundamental failure to understand what Aquinas means in denying a real relation in God to creatures. That God has no real relation to creatures simply means that God is not naturally ordered to, and thus dependent upon, anything He creates. It is an affirmation of God's absolute transcendence. He has no real relation to creatures because, as Aquinas puts it, "God is outside the whole order of creation" (I.13.7 co.; I.28.1 ad 3). God is clearly not a creature, not a being among beings. Nor does God create out of any natural necessity. Rather, the act of creating is a free act of divine love. Perhaps counter-intuitively, then, it is precisely God's existing "outside the whole order of creation" and His freedom with respect to it that enables Him also to be uniquely and intimately present 'inside' creation. Thus, that God has no real relation to creation certainly *does not mean* that God is not genuinely in 'relationship' with creatures, that God has no connection to or affinity for the beings He creates. Aquinas would consider such an interpretation theologically confused and, in fact, ontologically impossible.

As we have seen, God creates out of love, for the sole purpose of sharing His own goodness with others (I.44.4 co.; I.47.1 co.). And the divine goodness shared is *ipsum esse*, which is subsistent in God but participated in creatures. Many readers of Aquinas today assume that a God who is "subsistent being itself" must be distant, indifferent, and not "really involved in the world" (Pinnock 2001: 6). For Aquinas, however, nothing could be further from the truth. In fact, it is precisely the excellence of God's nature as *ipsum esse subsistens*, according to which He is above all created things, that enables Him to be most profoundly present to all creatures (I.8.1 ad 1). Creation is the means by which God freely and lovingly shares His very self with all that is not God. Indeed, creation is the production *ad extra* of *ipsum esse* by *ipsum esse subsistens*. Aquinas explains:

> As long as a thing has being [*esse*], it is necessary that God is present to it, according to its mode of being. Being [*Esse*], however, is what is most intimate in anything whatsoever and what belongs to all things most profoundly ... Hence, it must be that God is in all things, and intimately [*intime*].
>
> (*ST* I.8.1 co.)

For Aquinas, God is not a person who enters into relationship with us 'from without,' as a friend or neighbor might (see Chapter 3). Rather, He is present to all creatures 'from within' by way of *esse* and according to each one's particular mode of being. Far from competing or interfering with the natures and natural operations of creatures, then, God actually enables all creatures to be and thus to act according to nature. Indeed, God acts in every created agent in three ways, according to Aquinas: as its end, as its prime mover, and as the giver of its form and preserver of its being (I.105.5 co.). "He is at the heart of absolutely everything in the world," Herbert McCabe explains, "holding it in existence and bringing about everything it does" (McCabe 2002: 44). More specifically, God's love is the cause of the being and goodness of all creatures. Whereas we humans love things because they are good, the reverse is true where God's love is concerned: things are good because God loves them (I.20.2 co.). As such, in Aquinas's view, no creature has a relationship more real, more intimate, and more necessary than its relationship with God, the very source of its being. But because God is the transcendent cause of all creaturely being, He utterly surpasses the relation (and the 'relationship') that creatures necessarily have to (and with) Him (Emery 2007: 88; Kerr 2015: 154–155). Thus, God *does* have relations that are more real, more intimate, and more essential than His relation to creatures— namely, the subsistent relations that constitute the Triune God Himself. These relations, which really exist in God, necessarily have the *esse* of the divine essence (I.28.2 co.). For Aquinas, then, to affirm a real relation in God to creatures would be to make the gravest of theological mistakes, namely to dissolve the distinction between God and creation.

6

EVIL

GOD'S LOVE, THE GOODNESS OF THINGS, AND EVIL

For Aquinas, all creatures exist and possesses whatever good they have because God produces and preserves *esse* in them (*ST* I.2.3 co.; I.6.4 co.). In love, He freely shares His own goodness with the created order. Thus, unlike human love, which *responds* to the good in another, God's love actually *causes* all creaturely goodness and being (I.20.2 co.). In other words, God does not love things because they are good; rather, things are good because God loves them. "The love of God pours out and creates goodness in things," Aquinas teaches (I.20.2 co.). Following Augustine, then, Aquinas understands being and goodness as coextensive. "It is manifest," Aquinas affirms, "that goodness and being are, in reality, the same" (I.5.1 co.). Simply stated, to be is to be good. There is nothing that exists that possesses no goodness whatsoever because there is nothing that exists that God does not love (Gen. 1:31; Wis. 11:25; *ST* I.20.2 s.c.). This does not mean, however, that God loves all creatures equally, simply speaking. In fact, because God's love *causes* creaturely goodness, the created order itself makes manifest that God loves some things more than others.

Some things in the universe are *better* than others—that is, they possess greater ontological goodness—because God has willed a greater good for them. It is clear to Aquinas that God loves you, for example, more than the rocks in my garden because God has created you with a rational soul whereby you can know and love Him in this life and attain to the beatific vision in the next (I.65.2 co.). Although God loves my garden rocks with the same simple act of the will with which He loves you, He has willed a lesser good for my rocks, instantiations of inanimate solid mineral matter that are incapable of attaining to God by their own operations (I.20.3, 4; I.65.2 co.). According to the same logic, Aquinas holds that God does not love every human equally. Simply speaking, for example, God loves one who is predestined—even if she is a sinner presently—more than one who is foreknown to be damned—even if she is just presently—since God wills a greater good, namely eternal life, for the former (I.20.4 ad 5; *Scriptum* III d. 32 q. 1 a. 5 qc. 1 co.). Likewise, Aquinas teaches that God loves Christ more than the whole human race, and indeed the entire created universe, "not only with respect to His divine nature, but also with respect to His human nature, insofar as He predestined Him to a greater good, namely to union with a divine person" (*Scriptum* III d. 32 q. 1 a. 5 qc. 4 co.; Rom. 1:3–4; *ST* I.20.4 ad 1).

But if God loves all things that He has created (albeit unequally regarding the good willed for them), whence comes evil? Are some creatures essentially evil? To what extent is God, "the first and most universal cause" (I.45.5 co.), responsible for evil? Does God directly cause evil, or does He merely permit it? And why would He do either? Furthermore, can evil in the world be reconciled with the existence of a perfectly good and omnipotent God? Because these questions are as enduring as they are thorny, we stand to learn much from Aquinas's approach, which differs considerably from that of modern thinkers (Davies 2011: 8). Given the broad scope of this book, only a sketch of Aquinas's teaching on evil in *ST* I.48–49 is possible here.

Three major points are central to Aquinas's understanding of evil. First, because all things that exist are good insofar as they possess *esse*, evil is not a certain being or form or nature (I.48.1 co.; I.5.3 co.). Evil is not a creature, and no creature as such is evil. Rather, following Augustine, Aquinas teaches that when we call something evil or bad (*malum*), we signify a privation, absence, or lack of some being or goodness that a thing naturally possesses or should possess (Stump 2012: 401–402).

> It must be said that no being [*nullum ens*] is called evil insofar as it is a being [*ens*], but rather insofar as it lacks a certain to-be [*esse*], just as a human is called evil insofar as he lacks the to-be [*esse*] of virtue, and an eye is called evil insofar as it lacks keenness of sight.
>
> (*ST* I.5.3 ad 2)

A bank robber, for example, is not evil insofar as he is human; to the contrary, in fact, precisely as a human *being*, the robber is good. What is bad about him is his lack of a certain *esse* that he should possess as a human being, namely the *esse* of virtue. Similarly, the very purpose of the eye is to enable sight, so an eye that lacks visual acuity is a bad eye. "Just as every privation is established [*fundatur*] in a subject that is a being [*ens*]," Aquinas maintains, "so too every evil is established in some good" (I.17.4 ad 2; I.48.3). The bank robber's lack of virtue is founded on his being human; if he did not exist as a human and possess certain human perfections (e.g., a rational soul and hands with opposable thumbs), he could not be an armed robber. Giant pangolins and common earthworms rarely rob banks, after all. In short, Aquinas accepts and develops Augustine's seemingly counterintuitive dictum, "Only something good can be evil" (*Ench.* 13; Russell 1990).

Second, Aquinas distinguishes between two basic kinds of evil, which he calls the "evil of punishment" (*malum poenae*) and the "evil of fault" (*malum culpae*) (I.48.5, 6). Some philosophers have identified this same distinction as that between 'natural evil,' 'physical evil,' or 'evil suffered,' on the one hand, and 'moral evil' or 'evil done,' on the other (Davies 2014: 116; Davies 2011: 67–72; Meister and Moser 2017: 2). Both are instances of privation of some good that a thing is expected to possess: the first is a privation of form or integrity, whereas the second is a privation of appropriate activity or operation. Natural evil is characterized by the removal of a being's form or any part that is required for its integrity. Aquinas provides the examples of being blind and lacking a bodily member (I.48.5 co.). Note, however, that the blindness of a blind mole rat does not constitute an evil, since sight is not a good integral to its nature. Similarly, having only two legs would be *malum* for a dog, but obviously not for a human. Moral evil, by contrast, is characterized by the removal or absence of some appropriate operation in rational creatures possessing a will (I.48.5 co.). Such volitionally disordered evils may be acts of commission, such as murder and lying, or acts of omission, such as failing to share food, possessed in abundance, with the homeless and hungry.

When we think of 'evil' today, extremely morally reprehensible acts, like those associated with the Holocaust, or people, like Adolf Hitler, are likely to come to mind first. We associate evil primarily with moral failure, though we also identify natural disasters and natural suffering as evil. Similarly, Aquinas teaches that fault or moral failure has "more of the nature of evil" than physical failure does (I.48.6 co.). This is so, first, because a person actually becomes evil by voluntarily performing actions that are morally disordered or inappropriate. Whereas moral evil is a privation of appropriate action or operation, natural evil removes form or integrity from its subject. As long as this subject remains in being, natural evil cannot corrupt its good entirely; thus, the human or non-human being who is the subject of natural evil does not thereby 'become evil' (I.48.4 co.). Second, fault has "more of the nature of evil" because it is opposed to the perfect good, namely God, and contrary to the fulfillment of the divine will. Natural evil, by contrast, is not *opposed* to the good; it merely *deprives* a creature of some good (I.48.6 co.). Furthermore, because God is the creator of the good that is corrupted by way of privation, Aquinas understands natural evil as actually willed by God.

Third, and relatedly, Aquinas does not—as we might expect—straightforwardly deny that God is the cause of evil. Brian Davies claims that Aquinas, in treating the cause of evil, is "chiefly concerned to deny that God creates evil" (Davies 2014: 114). But this is incorrect, or at least inexact. Aquinas knows well that divine revelation sometimes attributes evil to God (see I.49.2 obj. 1, where he invokes Isa. 45:5, 7, *I am the Lord, and there is no other God … making peace and creating evil*, and Am. 3:6: *Will there be evil in a city that the Lord has not caused?*). Understanding such texts as referring to natural evil, Aquinas plainly teaches: "God is the author [*auctor*] of the evil of punishment" (I.48.6 co.; I.49.2 ad 1). In what sense, though, can God, the Highest Good, be dubbed the originator of evil, which is a privation of good? In brief, Aquinas teaches that God is the efficient or agent cause of natural evil, not directly (*per se*), but only accidentally (*per accidens*) (I.49.1 co.). Of the four Aristotelian causes, evil clearly has neither a *formal* nor a *final* cause. And good is the cause of evil by way of *material* cause, since evil exists only in something good (I.49.1 co.; I.48.3). Concerning *efficient* causality, Aquinas holds that the evil that consists in the corruption of certain things—i.e., natural evil—is reducible to God as to an efficient cause (I.49.2 co.). But God does not cause corruption *per se*; He is not, as Augustine affirms, the direct "cause of tending toward not-to-be [*non esse*]" (I.49.2 s.c.). Rather, Aquinas explains how God causes corruption indirectly:

> It is manifest that the form that God principally intends in created things is the good of the order of the universe. Now the order of the universe requires [*requirit*] ... that there be some things that can, and sometimes do, fail. And so God, by causing in things the good of the order of the universe, consequently and as it were accidentally [*per accidens*] causes the corruption of things, according to what is said in 1 Sam. 2[:6], *The Lord kills and makes alive*. But what is said in Wis. 1 [:13], *God has not made death*, is understood of God's intention *per se*.
> (*ST* I.49.2 co.)

For Aquinas, then, the corruption of certain things in the world happens accidentally, as a consequence or by-product of God intending directly (*per se*) the good of the universal order. The Lord does kill (1 Sam. 2:6), but inadvertently, as it were. He certainly has not made death (Wis. 1:13) directly or deliberately. A tension seems to arise, however, in that Aquinas understands the existence of corruptible creatures, and even their corruption, as 'required' for the good of the universe as a whole. We might say, then, that the evil of corruption is a 'necessary evil,' an essential condition for the universal good. But what does it mean that God, who is omnipotent and creates all things immediately, does something that is 'required' in a merely accidental way? And why would God, the Highest Good, allow corruption and defects, which are contrary to the being and goodness of things? Such significant questions lead us to what modern philosophers of religion call 'the problem of evil.'

'THE PROBLEM OF EVIL': NOT A PROBLEM FOR AQUINAS

Contemporary philosophers situate what is commonly called 'the problem of evil' at the crossroads of the reality of evil or suffering in the world, on the one hand, and belief in the existence of an omniscient, omnipotent, perfectly good God, on the other (Stump 2010: 3–4; Meister and Moser 2017: 1–4). Although variously conceived, the problem of evil is framed explicitly in terms of what

Daniel Speak has called "common theism" (i.e., those commitments shared by the world's principal theistic religions), and it runs thus (Speak 2015: 4–6):

1 God exists;
2 God is omnipotent;
3 God is omniscient;
4 God is omnibenevolent; and yet
5 evil exists.

For many today, philosophical tension arises from the attempt to hold these five propositions together. The fifth one in particular presents a problem for common theism, according to problem-of-evil philosophers. If (1) through (4) are true, we should expect (5) not to be true; conversely, if (5) is true, as almost everyone recognizes it to be, then (1) through (4) seem to be called into question: that is, the existence of evil in the world seems to preclude the existence of God, at least the sort of God in which common theists have traditionally believed (Speak 2015: 6–7).

It must be noted that the problem of evil, thus formulated, is a post-Enlightenment, philosophical conundrum (Stump 2003: 476–478; Kilby 2003). Whereas modern readers of the biblical book of Job, for instance, understand it as "the paradigmatic presentation of the problem of evil" (Stump 2003: 455), no ancient or medieval Christian writer read Job as treating the question of whether or how evil can be reconciled with God's existence (Steinhauser 2017, esp. 70; Harkins and Canty 2017). Although some scholars have understood Aquinas as grappling with the problem of evil in his *Literal Exposition on Job*, others have noted that he is not here concerned with this problem (Harkins 2017: 161nn1–2). Brian Davies extends this claim, moreover, to Aquinas's entire corpus:

> Aquinas has *nothing* to say on the topic. ... [H]e never offers a stand-alone discussion of what contemporary philosophers have come to call the problem of evil. He has no book or essay on it. He offers no full-length treatment starting along the lines 'God is X, Y, Z, etc; yet evil exists; so how can we reconcile evil with God's existence?' In this

> sense, what now passes as the problem of evil goes unmentioned in Aquinas's writings.
>
> (Davies 2011: 6)

While it is true that Aquinas provides no "full-length treatment" of the contemporary problem of evil, this is not the whole story. Aquinas is certainly aware of the basic line of argument, which he sets forth as an objection to divine existence in *ST* I.2.3. If God, whose name signifies "a certain infinite goodness," existed, then no evil would be found in the world, since if one of two contraries is infinite, the other would be completely destroyed (I.2.3 obj. 1). Aquinas responds by maintaining that it pertains to God's infinite goodness to allow evil and to draw good out of it (I.2.3 ad 1).

As intimated here, the fundamental 'problem' that evil raises for Aquinas is *not* that of God's existence, but rather that of God's providence, specifically its nature and mode (Harkins 2017: 161–162). Evil never suggests to Aquinas that there is no God. Contrarily, Aquinas takes the reality of evil as evidence *for* divine existence (see below). Evil does lead Aquinas to wonder, though, how precisely God's providence operates. Are all things subject to divine providence? Perhaps not, since a wise and omnipotent provider like God would, it seems, exclude defect and evil from those in His care (*ST* I.22.2 obj. 2). Aquinas responds by drawing a critical distinction between a particular provider and the universal provider. A particular provider excludes defects from what she cares for as far as she can. Think, for instance, of a tomato farmer who waters her plants evenly during the growing season to ward off cracks in the skin of the fruit, who avoids over-pruning to prevent sunscald and leaf roll, and who rotates her crops to forestall early blight. Contrastingly, because the universal provider, namely God, takes care of "all being [*totius entis*]," He permits certain defects in some things "lest the perfect good of the universe be hindered" (I.22.2 ad 2). Indeed, for Aquinas, the good of the whole necessitates that there be inequality among things, some incorruptible and others corruptible, so that every grade of goodness might be realized (I.48.2 co.). Thus, the perfect "order of the universe requires [*requirit*]" creatures that can be and sometimes are corrupted (I.49.2 co.; I.48.2 co.). "If every evil were prevented, many good things would be absent from the universe," Aquinas explains. "For no lion would live if there were no killing of animals, and there would be no patience of martyrs if there were no persecution by tyrants" (I.22.2 ad 2).

Similarly, in *Summa contra Gentiles* III.70–71, Aquinas makes clear that divine providence does not prevent corruption, defect, and evil among created things. This is a consequence not of any insufficiency in God's power, but rather of "the immensity of His goodness": indeed, God wills to communicate His likeness to things not only insofar as they *are*, but also insofar as they *are causes* of other things. That is, God and evil coexist precisely because God has willed to operate not only through Himself as primary cause, but also through secondary, created causes (*ScG* III.70, 71). Thus, a defect may occur in an effect by virtue of a defect in a secondary cause without there being any defect in the first cause. Furthermore, it would be "contrary to the mode of divine government," according to Aquinas, if God did not allow created things to act according to the mode of their own natures, which action can produce corruption and evil (*ScG* III.71). As noted above, God does not interfere with the creatures He produces. God does not have to create lions, for instance, but given that He freely does so—for the good of the universal order—antelopes, zebras, and giraffes will inevitably be killed by them (Davies 2011: 68). If God absolutely prevented the corruption of such prey, lions could not live and thus contribute to the good of the universe. Likewise, if God precluded all evil, the good of the human would be "greatly diminished" both in terms of knowledge of and desire for the good. Aquinas explains: "For the good is known to a greater extent by comparison with evil; and while we patiently suffer certain evils, we desire good things more eagerly" (*ScG* III.71).

"IF EVIL EXISTS, GOD EXISTS"

It is obvious that Aquinas approaches the reality of evil and suffering in the world rather differently than do contemporary philosophers of religion concerned with the problem of evil. His perspective is clearly not that of 'common theism' or 'character theism,' which tend to treat both God and evil abstractly and generically, detached from any particular religious narrative or theological context (Kilby 2003: 14). Rather, as a Catholic theologian, Aquinas understands evil from within a theological tradition at the heart of which stands redemption through the suffering, death, and resurrection of Christ (Harkins 2017). With salvation through Christ as the paradigmatic example, Aquinas believes that all natural evil, including human pain and suffering, comes from God and is ordered toward the good. The final good toward which the suffering of the saints, such as Job, is ordered is eternal life and union with God (Stump 2012). On Aquinas's reading, Job's words in 19:25–27—*For I know that my Redeemer lives, and on the last day I will rise from the earth* …—bespeak his hope in salvation through Christ, bodily resurrection, and beatific vision (Harkins 2017: 181–190). Whereas modern readers likely see Job as an extreme case of innocent, involuntary, and unjust suffering, Aquinas views the evil that befalls the faithful otherwise. Eleonore Stump explains:

> Aquinas takes a person of faith to be someone who has committed herself to living a life like that of Christ, with the explicit recognition that such a life includes suffering for the sake of greater spiritual good. And so the person of faith has in effect given consent to living a life which includes suffering. Any particular suffering on the part of a person of faith may in fact be involuntary; but, in virtue of the fact that she has voluntarily chosen a course of life in which (involuntary) suffering has a central role, her suffering is not involuntarily *simpliciter.*
>
> (Stump 2012: 405)

Given Aquinas's convictions that God permits evil for the sake of the universal good, and—on Stump's reading—that the faithful have consented to a life entailing suffering for the sake of everlasting union with God, it is hardly surprising that he does not see evil as signaling the nonexistence of God.

Aquinas concludes *ScG* III.71 by noting that the arguments proposed here exclude the error of those who deny God's existence because they observe evil in the world. Moreover, based on the mode of divine government, which is firmly rooted in God's perfect goodness, Aquinas teaches that the contrary argument could be made. Remarking that Boethius, in Bk. I of *Consolation of Philosophy*, introduces a certain philosopher who asks, "If God exists, whence comes evil?," Aquinas maintains:

On the contrary, however, he ought to have argued, 'If evil exists, God exists.' For evil would not exist if the order of good were removed, the privation of which is evil. But this order would not exist if God did not exist.

(*ScG* III.71)

Strikingly, Aquinas turns the basic problem-of-evil argument on its head: evil presupposes and is parasitic on a good order among creatures, and this good order presupposes a good God who both creates and governs all things well. In sum, if there were no God there would be no good, and if there were no good there would be no evil. Furthermore, Aquinas takes the arguments of ch. 71 as a refutation not only of those who, on account of evil, deny God's existence, but also of those who gainsay that divine providence extends to the corruptible things of this world (*ScG* III.71). For Aquinas, then, evil constitutes compelling evidence that God *does* exist, that He lovingly creates complete universal being, and that He serves as its perfect universal provider (I.45.1 co.; I.22.2 ad 2).

THE HUMAN AND THE VIRTUES

THE HUMAN BEING

Among all creatures, the human being is uniquely like God, according to Aquinas. Whereas all created things are like God inasmuch as they exist, and some are more like God inasmuch as they live, humans are most like God in that they know and love (*ST* I.93.1 co., 2 co.). Thus, in irrational creatures—boulders and bluebirds, for instance—is found a likeness to God by way of a vestige or trace, that is, as an effect generally representing its cause. Rational creatures, however, imitate God by way of an image, that is, they "seem in a certain way to attain to a representation of the species" (I.93.6 co.). By virtue of divine simplicity, God is not a species of any genus (I.3.5 co.), of course. Nevertheless, rational creatures resemble God more profoundly than all others by imitating God's own operations of knowing and willing, the very operations by which God creates (see Chapters 3 and 5). For Aquinas, the perfection of the universe, as God has ordained it, *requires* the existence of intellectual creatures, effects who imitate the divine cause precisely according to the operation whereby the cause produces its effects (I.50.1 co.).

Rational creatures are of two types, angelic and human. Unlike angels, which are purely spiritual creatures, humans are composite rational creatures, consisting of a spiritual and corporeal substance (I.50.prol; I.75.prol.). According to Aquinas's hylomorphic anthropology, inherited from Aristotle, the rational or intellectual soul is the form of the human being, that which actualizes the potential of the matter that is the body (I.76.1 co.). The soul (*anima*) is, in Aquinas's words, "the first principle of life" and of operation of any living thing, that which *animates* it and makes it to be the sort of thing it is (I.75.1 co.; Pasnau 2002: 34–40). By "first principle of life," Aquinas means the primary *internal* source of the life of a creature (Pasnau 2002: 28–29). He understands God, of course, as the absolute first and final cause of all creaturely being and life, as we have seen in previous chapters. All animate, corporeal things have souls, according to Aquinas. Plants, like philodendra and rutabaga, have vegetative souls, according to which they acquire being (*esse*) and have the power to feed and nourish themselves (I.78.2 co.). Animals, such as pangolins and capybaras, have sensitive souls, according to which they perceive the world through sight, hearing, smell, taste, and/or touch and have the power of locomotion or self-movement (I.78.3 co.). Animals also possess appetitive power because, as Aristotle observes, whatever has sense also has appetite, that is, it naturally desires various goods that it perceives (I.78.1 co.; Davies 2014: 127). The human is distinct from and excels all other animate beings in that he has a rational soul—also called a mind or intellect—which is the principle of intellectual life (I.75.2 co.; I.93.6 co.). In addition to the vegetative, sensitive, appetitive, and locomotive powers, the human also possesses the intellectual power, that is, the capacity to know or understand (I.78.1 co.). In this capacity, the human being is the image of God (I.93.6 co.).

Aquinas teaches that the rational human soul is incorporeal, subsistent, and incorruptible. Although sensation, which informs human knowing, requires use of particular bodily organs (eyes, nose, ears) to perceive particular material things—this Cabbage Rose, that Lakeland Terrier—the intellect understands by abstracting the intelligible species from such matter (I.86.1 co.; I.85.1 co.). What it means, according to Aquinas, that I know or understand a Lakeland Terrier, for instance, is that I have the nature or substantial form of a Lakeland Terrier within me, not materially (as every individual Lakeland Terrier has it within itself), but rather intentionally, that is, within my own form, my rational soul (I.75.2 co.; Davies 2002: 90–91). Obviously my understanding what a Lakeland Terrier is never results in my actually *becoming* a Lakeland Terrier (fortunately!)—that is, my knowing this kind of dog by having its form in my mind is always a strictly immaterial and incorporeal reality. Aquinas teaches, then, that "it is impossible that the intellectual principle is a body" and equally impossible for it to understand by means of a bodily organ (I.75.2 co.; Davies 2014: 129–31; Pasnau 2002: 52–57). Because the human soul or mind, in contrast to the souls of animals, has an operation *per se* apart from the body, it is a substance, something subsistent (I.75.2, 3 co.). As an intellectual substance, the human soul is also incorruptible; here too it differs from the souls of animals, which are corrupted when their bodies are corrupted (I.75.6 co.).

Although Aquinas understands the human soul to be incorporeal, subsistent, and incorruptible, he does not identify human beings with their souls, as Plato, Hugh of St. Victor, and Descartes do (I.75.4 co.; III.50.4 co.). Aquinas is not a 'substance dualist,' as he is often described (Pasnau 2002: 45–46; Davies 2002: 89–90). He does not imagine that we humans are essentially incorporeal substances attached to, or trapped in, bodies that are somehow really extraneous to us; indeed, he rejects the view of humans as, in Gilbert Ryle's words, "ghosts in machines" (quoted in Davies 2012: 229). Following Aristotle, Aquinas understands that natural things are defined not by form alone, but by form and matter. Thus, he affirms, "It is clear that a human is not only a soul, but is something composed of a soul and a body" (I.75.4 co.). Aquinas knows well that we humans are fundamentally physical beings, necessarily ensouled bodies. But the soul is not established within the body as another 'part' that completes the whole human, in the way that I might add blueberries to my pancake mix to make blueberry pancakes. Rather, as the substantial form of the human, the soul is whole in each part of the body. It is the form and the act of the whole body and of each of its parts such that, when the soul is withdrawn in death, the human being ceases to be and none of her body parts retains its proper action (I.76.8 co.). Strictly speaking, then, in death a human is no longer human, and a body—understood as matter actualized or animated by a soul—is no longer a body, according to Aquinas (I.76.8 co.; Turner 2016: 175–76). As we will see in Chapter 8, this non-dualist understanding of the human is central, according to Aquinas, to the Christian affirmation that Christ truly died (III.50.4 co.).

In short, the careful reader of Aquinas on human nature finds that his nuanced, hylomorphic understanding is not dualistic at all. To the contrary, in fact, it offers an important corrective to our own ordinary (dualistic) speech concerning souls and bodies. Denys Turner explains:

> Does he [Aquinas] ... think it right to say that I *have* a soul? No he does not. For without a soul there is no I to have one, and there is no such thing as a body that either has or does not have soul: 'have' is the wrong word. For where there is no soul there is no body to lack one ... The reason you shouldn't say that bodies 'have' souls is that their being bodies just is their being matter alive in certain typical ways. And what you mean by 'soul' is what accounts for those typical ways in which a body is alive.
>
> (Turner 2016: 175)

Although Aquinas himself regularly speaks of the human or another living thing as what "has a soul" (*habet animam*; e.g., *Scriptum* II d. 32 q. 2 a. 3 obj. 2; *Scriptum* III d. 10 q. 1 a. 1 qc. 1 co.; *ScG* I.98, *ScG* III.46; *ST* I.3.2 obj. 1; *ST* I.76.3 obj. 2; *ST* II–II.26.10 obj. 1; *ST* III.68.10 obj. 3), he does so assuming an Aristotelian, hylomorphic conception of the soul as the form of the human being, that principle by which we live, nourish ourselves, sense the external world, move ourselves, and understand (*ST* I.76.1 co.).

HUMAN HAPPINESS AND HUMAN ACTION

From the opening question of the *ST*, Aquinas makes clear that the human being is ordered to God as a superrational end and that she must know this end in order to direct her thoughts and actions toward it (*ST* I.1.1 co.). When Aquinas comes to a consideration of human nature and actions in *Prima pars* qq. 75–89 and the *Secunda pars*, then, he maintains a focus on this end and its attainment. Indeed, although he takes sacred doctrine to be more speculative than practical (I.1.4 co.), Aquinas gives particular attention to the practical in treating the rational creature generally. As Herbert McCabe puts it, "He is not interested in spinning theories about angels and the points of a pin. He is concerned with human well-being" (McCabe 2016b: 240). For Aquinas, what constitutes human *well-being* is, of course, directly related to the human *being*, that is, to what kind of creature the human is and to the ultimate purpose for which God has created the human as human.

The human being's being like God—that is, her rational capacity to know and love—profoundly shapes Aquinas's judgments about the human being's being happy (Dewan 2008: 72–75).

The subject of the enormous *Secunda pars* of the *ST*, the moral part, may be aptly described as the human being as the created image of God and her operations toward happiness (I-II.prol). We humans differ from irrational animals, according to Aquinas, precisely in that we are masters of our own actions through the use of reason and free will (I-II.1.1 co.). Properly speaking, human actions are those that we perform by virtue of our self-mastery, that is, those actions that are willed on the basis of rational deliberation (I-II.1.1 co.; Williams 2012: 199). But authentic human action is never in competition with divine action. For Aquinas, in contrast to many modern thinkers, our being masters of our own actions never necessitates that God somehow limit Himself (see Chapter 3). To the contrary, if such divine withdrawal or self-limitation were to occur, human action would be utterly impossible. In fact, no human beings—indeed, no creatures whatsoever—would even exist; we would all be "reduced to nothingness" (I.104.1 co.). For Aquinas, then, our self-mastery and authentic human action toward happiness *require* God on several distinct, but closely related, levels: as our creator, who has granted us *esse* according to His own image and continually conserves us *in esse*; as prime mover or first efficient cause, who moves us according to our nature, that is, through our intellect and free will; and as the Highest Good and thus the end or final cause of our every operation (I.105.5 co.).

Aquinas invokes his argument from motion, the First of his Five Ways (I.2.3 co.), to explain that there is one and only one "ultimate end" of human life, a single prime mover of human action (I-II.1.4 co.; I-II.1.5 co.). Because it is impossible to proceed to infinity in a series of essentially ordered causes, there must be one prime mover in order for there to be any movement whatsoever. The prime mover or principle in the order of intention (as opposed to the order of execution) is the human's final goal or ultimate end, that perfect good which he or she desires as supremely fulfilling (I-II.1.5 co., 6 co.). For Aquinas, just as every creature naturally seeks its own perfection (I.62.1 co.), so too every human naturally desires that his own will be satisfied, which constitutes his happiness. But because not everyone knows that in which happiness specifically consists, not all desire it (I-II.5.8 co.). Many imagine that their ultimate fulfillment consists in wealth, honor, fame, power, or pleasure, but Aquinas is clear that human happiness cannot be found in any bodily goods (I-II.2.1–7). Not even physical health and survival constitute the human being's perfect happiness. This may sound audacious to us moderns, who tend to identify happiness with individually determined notions of personal satisfaction or subjective good feelings (Dewan 2008: 72–73; Porter 2016: 182–183). For Aquinas, however, the preservation of our bodily life cannot constitute our happiness precisely because of our metaphysical status as creatures. What it means to be creatures is that we are ordered to another—namely God—as end (I-II.2.5 co.). Aquinas explains by way of analogy:

> A captain does not intend, as the ultimate end, the preservation of the ship entrusted to him, since the ship is ordered to something else as an end, namely to navigating. Now just as the ship is entrusted to the captain for the purpose of guiding it, so the human has been entrusted to [his] will and reason.
>
> (ST I-II.2.5 co.)

Like the captain of a ship, the powers of will and reason guide the human being in the proper course of life to his final destination, God Himself. Only in God, who is "the universal good" and "the universal true," can the human will and intellect find ultimate rest (I-II.2.8 co.).

Because the intellect is the highest power of the human being and because the perfection of any being consists in its actuality (or being in act) according to its nature, the ultimate perfection or happiness of the human consists, according to Aquinas, in her ultimate intellectual act (I-II.3.2 co.; I.12.1 co.). Furthermore, delight or love, an act of the will, is also necessarily conjoined to this intellectual act (I-II.3.4 co.; Porter 2016: 185–186). As divine revelation makes clear, this ultimate act or operation of the intellect is to know or see God as He is (Jn. 17:3; 1 Jn. 3:2; I-II.3.4 s.c., I-II.3.8 s.c.). "It must be said," Aquinas teaches, "that ultimate and perfect happiness [*beatitudo*] consists in nothing except the vision of the divine essence" (I-II.3.8). Such perfect happiness or beatific vision, which is an operation of the speculative intellect, namely contemplation, is possible for ordinary humans (*puri homines*) only in the next life (I-II.3.5 co.; I-II.5.3 co.; I.12.11 co.). "In that state of [perfect] beatitude," Aquinas explains, "the mind of the human will be united to God by a single, continuous, and everlasting operation" (I-II.3.2 ad 4). Although the human—by virtue of her intellectual and volitional faculties—is capable of such an operation, perfect vision of the divine essence surpasses human nature and thus requires "external help" from God Himself (I-II.5.5 co., ad 2; I-II.5.6 co.). Such external assistance takes the form of a supernatural principle of action that God "superadds" in order to perfect our nature, namely grace in this life and glory in the next (I.12.2 co.; I-II.109.1 co.; Porter 2016: 185–86).

GRACE AND THE VIRTUES

Although the perfect happiness of the beatific vision must await heavenly glory, humans can have a share in it even now through the divine gift of grace and the practice of the virtues. For Aquinas, the imperfect happiness that is possible in this life is an anticipation of the vision of God, "a certain beginning of beatitude" whereby humans move toward their ultimate end "through the operations of the virtues" (I-II.69.2 co.; I-II.69.1 co.; I-II.3.2 co.; I-II.3.3 co.; I-II.4.5 co.). Imperfect, earthly happiness is of two general varieties, each of which is attained by a certain type or mode of virtue, according to Aquinas. First, natural (or connatural) happiness is proportionate to human nature and therefore can be obtained through the human's natural powers and acquired virtues (I-II.62.1 co.; I-II.5.5 co.). Second, what we might aptly call 'graced happiness' surpasses the capacity of human nature and the acquired virtues. As the name we have given it suggests, the human can attain 'graced happiness' only by God's 'superadding' grace and the infused virtues, which Aquinas understands as certain principles of human action beyond those with which God has endowed the human naturally (I-II.62.1 co.).

One noteworthy tendency of modern theology is to identify any and every gift given by God to human beings as 'grace.' Karl Rahner, for instance, describes grace as "God's very self in self-communication," which "is really poured out on all humanity and not merely on the few who have been sealed by the sacraments" (Rahner 2000: 9). Rahner and many other contemporary theologians concur with the nineteenth-century Carmelite, St. Thérèse of Lisieux, that "all is grace" (McCosker 2016: 206). Given Aquinas's rich understanding of the myriad divisions and effects of grace (I-II.109–114), we may be tempted to assume that he too would agree that "all is grace" (McCosker 2016: 206). But throughout the treatise on grace (I-II.109–114), Aquinas is always careful to distinguish what is natural to the human from what is supernatural, that is, to differentiate nature from grace. Whereas Aquinas readily admits that all human powers or capacities, habits, and operations are gifts from God—as, indeed, is existence itself—not all of them are supernatural gifts. Some, such as the power to know and to will freely, are natural gifts. For Aquinas, the supernatural gift of grace that God "superadds" does not destroy these natural gifts, but rather perfects them, as do the infused theological virtues of faith and charity (I.1.8 ad 2). Just as God moves the human soul to know, to will, and to act naturally and endows it with acquired virtues (prudence, justice, fortitude, and temperance) that dispose its powers to right action, so too—indeed, "much more," Aquinas says—does God move the human "to pursue the supernatural, eternal good" by infusing "certain supernatural forms or qualities" into the soul (I-II.110.2 co). Grace and the theological virtues of faith, hope, and love are such supernatural qualities. Aquinas distinguishes grace even from the infused virtues, however. Grace is a certain disposition of the soul that is the "principle and root" of the infused virtues, "a participation in the divine nature" from which these virtues are derived and to which they are ordered (I-II.110.3 co., ad 3). In sum, clarity of theological thought demands, in Aquinas's view, distinguishing those authentically human actions of which we are capable by virtue of God's gift of a human nature from those that require the superadded gift of grace. Thus, if he were alive today, Aquinas would surely wish to modify St. Thérèse's dictum slightly, from "all is grace" to "all is gift."

The theological virtues of faith, hope, and love are supernatural principles of human action that God infuses into—literally 'pours into'—the human soul with habitual grace at the moment of justification in order to direct us to supernatural happiness (I-II.62.1 co.; I-II.113.2–4, 7; Wawrykow 2012; Wawrykow 2005b: 56–57).

They are called 'theological,' Aquinas explains, for three reasons: they rightly order us to God as final end, they are infused in us by God alone (i.e., they cannot be acquired through virtuous action), and they are known to us only by divine revelation in Scripture (ibid.). These virtues elevate the human person's powers to a supernatural level and incline her to the acts of believing, hoping, and loving that anticipate the beatific vision even now. The introductory nature of this book will permit a brief sketch of only the first of the theological virtues.

As we have seen (Ch. 2 pref.), the properly theological mode of the human's apprehending divine realities requires divine revelation and aims at belief in what cannot be proven or 'seen' by natural reason. Aquinas understands, based on revelation itself (especially Heb. 11:1, *Faith is the evidence of things unseen*), that the object of faith is always something that the believer does not know demonstratively (*ST* II-II.1.4 s.c., co.). Although the blessed in heaven will see God face to face as He is (1 Cor. 13:12, 1 Jn 3:2), faith enables us to begin to glimpse God even now, albeit through a glass darkly (1 Cor. 13:12; II-II.1.4 obj. 2, ad 2; II-II.1.5 co; II-II.4.2 s.c.). Aquinas defines the virtue of faith, then, as "a habit of the mind whereby eternal life is begun in us, which causes the intellect to assent to things unseen" (II-II.4.1 co.). This definition makes clear that faith is essentially an intellectual virtue, perfecting the natural powers of human apprehension, though it also involves the will of the believer. Aquinas thus sanctions Augustine's understanding of the act of faith as 'to think with assent' (II-II.2.1 s.c., co.), although he further specifies that "to believe is an act of the intellect assenting to the divine truth at the command of the will having been moved by God through grace" (II-II.2.9 co). Aquinas's assumption that grace perfects nature is conspicuous here. Naturally the human will commands the intellect to assent to truths about which it must deliberate, and God is the prime mover of such purely natural thinking (II-II.2.1 co.; I.2.3 co.). Where faith is concerned, grace is the external principle of human action by means of which God moves the will to command the intellect to assent to unseen divine truth. For Aquinas, the difference between natural human knowing and believing is *not* that the latter requires help from God whereas the former does not. Rather, it is between the mode of help that God offers: in the former, God's gifts and movement are in conformity with the human agent's nature; in the latter, His gifts and movement are above the human's nature. Here we should recall Aquinas's teaching concerning divine government in the *Prima pars*: "All things act according to the power of God Himself, and so He is the cause of the actions of every agent" (I.105.5 co.).

The act of faith, an intellectual act moved by the will, can be conceived as threefold, according to Aquinas (II-II.2.2 co.). First, it entails 'believing God' or 'believing in God' (*credere Deum*), the First Truth, as the material object of faith: believing, for example, such articles of faith as Trinity and Incarnation (II-II.1.1 co.; II-II.2.5, 7, 8). Second, faith requires 'believing by God' (*credere Deo*); here God as First Truth is the formal object of faith, the authority on the basis of which believers believe (II-II.1.1 co.). Aquinas offers a mundane pedagogical analogy: "In order for the human to arrive at the perfect vision of beatitude, it first requires that he believe God, just as a student believes the master who is teaching [him]" (II-II.2.3 co.). Because faith is a *good* habit—specifically, a disposition of a person's intellect to act in a way that is fulfilling by believing divine truth—and because it is infused in the human soul by God, who is the First Truth, Aquinas maintains that nothing false can be held by faith (II-II.1.3 co.). Although we commonly use the language of 'faith' and 'believing' rather nebulously of all manner of things ('I believe it might rain today'; 'He lost all faith in the political system'; 'Mia still believes in the Easter Bunny'), Aquinas's understanding of faith as a theological virtue narrows the field of its possible objects dramatically. Only those truths about God revealed by God Himself constitute legitimate objects of faith. Convictions about the weather or the existence of the Easter Bunny are mere opinions, not proper objects of belief (II-II.1.1, 3, 4).

These first two aspects of belief—'believing in God' and 'believing by God'—relate to faith as an act of the intellect, whereas the third, 'believing into God' (*credere in Deum*), has to do with this act as moved by the will (II-II.2.2 co.). Because the end to which the act of faith is ordered is an object of the will, namely God as the ultimate good, and because this end is the object of charity, charity is the form of faith, that which perfects it (II-II.4.3 co.). Aquinas makes clear that formed faith—faith perfected by charity or love—justifies the believer, ordering her rightly toward

God as end, whereas unformed faith—bare intellectual assent that is not moved or perfected by a will directed toward the divine good—does not. Even the demons believe (Jas. 2:19), but not in such a way that orders them in love toward God and ultimate happiness (II-II.5.2 s.c., co.).

8

CHRIST AND HIS SAVING WORK

PLACEMENT AND STRUCTURE OF CHRISTOLOGY IN THE *SUMMA THEOLOGIAE*

Modern readers of the *ST* have sometimes wondered why Aquinas waits until the Third Part to treat Christ and His saving work (McGinn 2014: 69–73; Kerr 2009: 87). Could the Dominican master have forgotten what lay at the very heart of Christianity, only to return to it, as something of an afterthought, at the end of his *magnum opus*? Or is Aquinas's belated consideration of the Incarnation intentional, indicating his devaluing of Christ and the historical economy of salvation as compared to God in Himself, on the one hand, and humans and their powers of operation, on the other (*ST* I-II.prol.; Coakley 2016: 222)? Either way, is the *Tertia pars* an extraneous addition to an otherwise complete theological *summa* (Torrell 2005: 48)?

Fortunately, most contemporary Thomists attribute Aquinas's reserving Christology to the end of the *ST* neither to theological forgetfulness nor to deliberate disregard. Rather, assuming emanation-and-return as the overall plan of the work, they understand Incarnation and salvation as constituting its purposeful climax, the *Summa*'s summit, as it were. Sarah Coakley, for instance, says: "It is intrinsic to the *exitus/reditus* scheme of the whole work that christology be left thus till the last book of the *ST*—precisely as climax, and as the unique means and access of salvific 'return'" (Coakley 2016: 222). Similarly, Jean-Pierre Torrell observes that the Second and Third Parts "are perfectly unified under the sign of the 'return' of the rational creature to God under the leadership of Christ" (Torrell 2005: 49). Likewise, Bernard McGinn affirms: "Thomas clearly thought that the *Tertia Pars* was a culmination, not an afterthought. The immense *Secunda Pars* about attaining the final goal of human living would mean nothing without Christ, who makes it all possible" (McGinn 2014: 73).

I noted in Chapter 1 what I take to be the key limitations of the commonly accepted *exitus-reditus* model of the *Summa*'s structure. We encounter another one here, related to Aquinas's understanding of the principal purpose of the Incarnation. Many readers take Aquinas's description of Christ as He who "showed us in Himself the way [*viam*] of truth whereby we may arrive at the beatitude of eternal life by rising again" (*ST* III.prol.; I.2.prol.) as evidence that he understands Jesus as the 'means' of humankind's Neoplatonic 'return' to God (Chenu 2002: 137–138; Coakley 2016: 222). As Rudi te Velde has noted, however, Aquinas uses the term *via* to describe Christ as "the way" or access to God and immortal life for fallen humankind precisely by means of His saving work. Te Velde affirms: "It must be emphasized that nowhere in the *Summa* is Christ characterized as the means of return to God.... Any association of 'way' with the notion of mediated return is, as far as I know, absent in the *Summa*" (Te Velde 2006: 16). Although the distinction between Aquinas's *via* and our commonly used 'means of return' may seem subtle, it actually suggests two disparate theologies of the Incarnation. Whereas 'means of return' denotes Incarnation as the perfection of creation through the personal union of humankind with God, Aquinas's *via* points to the Incarnation as the salvific remedy for human sin.

Aquinas makes clear at the outset of the *Tertia pars* that it is precisely as "our Savior" who came *to save His people from their sins* (Matt. 1:21) that Christ is "the way" to eternal life (*ST* III.prol.). Significantly, Aquinas uses the terms 'Savior,' 'salvation,' and 'save' seven times in his brief Prologue, whereas he nowhere suggests that Christ is to be understood as the fulfillment of creation. Furthermore, when he inquires after the motive of the Incarnation, Aquinas observes that the reason (*ratio*) offered "everywhere in Sacred Scripture" is human sin (III.1.3 co.). God ordained the Incarnation as a remedy for sin such that "if sin had not existed, there would have been no Incarnation" (III.1.3 co.). Moreover, Aquinas explicitly rejects the view that the Incarnation would have happened regardless of human sin because it aimed at the perfection of the universe by uniting the last creature, the human, to God as first principle (III.1.3 obj. 2; Te Velde 2006: 32n14). For Aquinas, it suffices for the perfection of the universe that every creature be ordained "in a natural way" to God as end; but that a creature is personally united to God in the Incarnation "exceeds the limits of the perfection of nature" (*ST* III.1.3 ad 2; see also I.48.2 co., I.49.2 co., and Chapter 6, this volume). In sum, then, conflating Christ as the post-lapsarian "way" to God with a Neo-platonic 'means of return' risks obfuscating the central conviction of Aquinas's Christology, namely that God freely chose to become human in order to save humans from their sins.

Aquinas's mature consideration of Christ occupies *ST* III.1–59 and is divided into two major sections. The first (qq. 1–26) treats, as Aquinas puts it, "the actual mystery of the Incarnation, accord-ing to which God was made human for our salvation," while the second (qq. 27–59) concerns "those things that were done and suffered by our Savior Himself, that is, God incarnate" (III.prol.). Note how Aquinas's language here emphasizes soteriology, which he always has in view in treating Christ (Wawrykow 2015: 235–236). In the first section, following an introductory question on the "fittingness" of the Incarnation (q. 1), Aquinas takes up the mode of union of the Word Incarnate (qq. 2–15). Here he con-siders the union itself (q. 2), the person assuming (q. 3), and the nature assumed (qq. 4–15). The questions on the assumed nature concern the human nature and its constituent parts (qq. 4–6) as well as the perfections and defects that the Son of God "coas-sumed" (qq. 7–15). Aquinas rounds out this first major section by considering various consequences of the union (qq. 16–26). In the second major section (qq. 27–59), which constitutes an innovation in scholastic theology, Aquinas offers a detailed treatment of the life, actions, and passions of the Incarnate Word whose identity he has probed in qq. 2–26 (Wawrykow 2005a: 233). Aquinas's account is fourfold, considering (1) those things pertaining to Christ's coming into the world (qq. 27–39), (2) those things related to the course of His life in the world (qq. 40–45), (3) His departure from the world (qq. 46–52), and (4) those things pertaining to His exaltation after this life (qq. 53–59; III.27.prol.). Although this second major part generally follows the synoptic Gospel narratives, the Christological portrait that Aquinas paints differs substantially from that of the 'historical Jesus' offered by modern biblical criticism (Kerr 2009: 87–88). This is so because his reading of the Gospels is profoundly incarnational, shaped by an understanding of hypostatic union that is thoroughly indebted to patristic and conciliar teaching on Christ (Wawrykow 2005a: 233; Wawrykow 2015: 237–238; on the ancient Christological tradition, see, e.g.: Anatolios 2015; Ayres 2004; and Louth 2015).

THE PERSON OF CHRIST

THE "FITTINGNESS" AND MODE OF THE INCARNATION

The Incarnation, like the Trinity, is a sacred mystery that far exceeds our rational powers of apprehension. It is superrational, not irrational: that is, it is above reason, but not contrary to it. Aquinas takes the Incarnation, in fact, to be the supremely superrational mystery of Christian faith. "Among the divine works," he declares, "it surpasses reason most of all, for nothing done by God can be thought of as more marvelous than that the true God, the Son of God, became a true human" (*ScG* IV.27). Thus, our apprehending anything of "this marvelous Incarnation" depends entirely on divine revelation (ibid.). As an article of faith, the Incarnation cannot be proven (or disproven), and so it has no logical necessity. Aquinas begins his treatment of Christ in the *ST*, then, not with a rational demonstration of the Incarnation, but rather with an account of its "fittingness" (*convenientia*).

Fittingness arguments, common in medieval scholasticism, constitute a mode of reasoning according to which the theologian accepts a revealed truth and seeks to show how it is 'appropriate' or 'suitable' given other truths about God, literally how it 'comes together with' (*conveniens*, from *cum* + *venio*) them. A staple of the *ST*, fittingness arguments are particularly significant in Aquinas's Christology and soteriology (Barnes 2012: 180, 193–199). They aim to highlight the coherence and beauty of the divine dispensation, the order and wisdom of the particular ways God has acted in time. Corey Barnes offers an artistic analogy:

> The equivalent would be a magnificent painting, which, when viewed as a whole, seems perfectly proportioned and ordered. It gives the

impression that not one brushstroke could have been different. When then studied in detail, it is obvious that any given aspect could have differed in numerous ways from the actual painting and that such changes, though individually unimpeachable, would have diminished the beauty of the whole.

(Barnes 2012: 195)

This analogy captures well the mind of Aquinas, who presents the Incarnation precisely in terms of "the art of the divine wisdom" and "the order of the divine goodness" (*ST* III.1.1 ad 3).

Based on what Aquinas has taught about God and creatures, however, it appears that the Incarnation was not fitting. God, who is "the very essence of goodness," is immutable, for example, and so it would have been best for Him to remain as He had been from eternity, namely without flesh (III.1.1 obj. 1). Relatedly, because things that are infinitely distant are inappropriately conjoined, it is "unfitting" (*inconveniens*) that God, who is "most simple," should have been united to human flesh, which is composite (III.1.1 obj. 2). Furthermore, the human body is susceptible to natural evil; surely God, "the highest goodness," cannot fittingly have assumed evil (III.1.1 obj. 3)!

Aquinas grounds his reply firmly in scriptural and patristic teaching. Citing Rom. 1:20, he observes that it seems "most fitting" (*convenientissimum*) that the invisible things of God should be made known through visible realities. "In fact, the whole world was made for this," Aquinas teaches (III.1.1 s.c.). And, according to John Damascene, the mystery of the Incarnation has revealed to us God's goodness, wisdom, justice, and power (III.1.1 s.c.). Invoking Dionysius and Augustine, Aquinas argues for the fittingness of the Incarnation thus (III.1.1 co.):

1 What is "fitting" (*conveniens*) for anything is what belongs to it by nature.
2 God's nature is goodness—indeed, He is "the highest good" (*summum bonum*).
3 It pertains to the nature of the good to communicate itself to others.
4 It pertains to the nature of the highest good to communicate itself in the highest manner (*summo modo*).

5   God has communicated Himself to the creature in the highest
     manner by joining the creature to Himself hypostatically or
     personally.

Just as God communicates His own goodness to every creature
by conferring *esse* on it and conserving it *in esse*, so too He has
communicated Himself in the greatest, most profound way by
uniting one creature—namely, the human nature of Christ—with
Himself in the person of the Word. Lest any change be attributed
to God in this union, Aquinas carefully notes that the Incarnation
properly represents not God uniting Himself to a creature, but
rather God uniting the creature to Himself. And because every
creature is mutable by nature, it was fitting that the creature, which
had not previously been united to God hypostatically, should be so
united (III.1.1 ad 1). Significantly, Aquinas makes explicit the
connection in this regard between creation and Incarnation. Just as
it was appropriate for God to bring the creature into being when it
had not existed before, so too it was "most fitting" for Him to
bring the creature into hypostatic union with Himself (III.1.1 ad 1,
s.c.). The reader is left to wonder whether those who deny the
fittingness of the Incarnation would also question God's wisdom in
creating and sustaining the universe—including their very selves—
in being.

Additionally, Aquinas emphasizes the Incarnation's soteriological
purpose from the outset. On account of "the infinite excellence of
His goodness," God bridges the vast ontological divide between
Himself and humanity "for human salvation" (III.1.1 ad 2). Against
the objection that God seems to have assumed evil or wickedness
(*malitiam*) in taking up a human body, Aquinas affirms: (1) that the
uncreated, immutable, and incorporeal God produced mutable and
corporeal creatures "on account of His own goodness"; and (2)
that natural evil (*malum poenae*) was established by divine justice for
the glory of God (III.1.1 ad 3). Thus, it could be fitting for God to
assume a human nature that was created, mutable, corporeal, and
subject to natural evil, though not for Him to assume moral evil
(*malum culpae*) (III.1.1 ad 3; see Chapter 6).

The Word's assumption of a human nature was "necessary
[*necessarium*] for the restoration of the human race," according to
Aquinas, precisely in terms of fittingness. That is, the need for

human salvation did not absolutely require God to become Incarnate, in the way that the preservation of human life absolutely necessitates food. "For God, by His omnipotent power, could have restored human nature in many other ways," Aquinas teaches (III.1.2 co.). Rather, the Incarnation was necessary in the sense that it accomplished the goal of human salvation "better and more fittingly [*melius et convenientius*]," as the end of a journey is arrived at more effectively by means of a horse (III.1.2 co.). Given that the end of the journey of human life is the beatific vision of God, which ordinarily requires a person's voluntary movement toward God in faith and away from sin (I-II.113.6 co.), Aquinas explains how the Incarnation "more fittingly" effects this end by facilitating both our promotion in the good and our removal from evil (III.1.2 co.). Central to our removal from evil is Christ's having made satisfaction for us through His passion, thereby freeing us from slavery to sin (III.1.2 co.; III.46.3 co.). Aquinas observes, "Christ made satisfaction not by giving money or something of this sort, but by giving what was the greatest [*maximum*]—Himself—for us" (III.48.4 co.). Christ is "the greatest" both because He is true God and because, by the perfection of grace in the hypostatic union, He uniquely possesses a perfect human nature (III.1.5 obj. 3; 1.6 co.). Following patristic teaching and Anselm's *Cur Deus Homo*, Aquinas declares: "A pure human [*homo purus*] could not have satisfied for the whole human race" (III.1.2 co.).

In considering the mode of the incarnational union (q. 2)—how divinity and humanity are conjoined in Christ—Aquinas draws heavily on the acts and proceedings of such early ecumenical councils as Ephesus (431) and Chalcedon (451), to which he had access in Latin translation while in Italy in the early 1260s (Wawrykow 2015: 237–238; Torrell 1996: 103, 140; Gorman 2017: 1–4). As the *sed contra*s of his opening articles suggest, Aquinas's primary aim in q. 2 is to explicate and defend the teaching of Chalcedon that Jesus Christ is one person subsisting in two natures. The single subject of the Incarnation is the only-begotten, eternally existing Son of God, the second person of the Trinity. At a particular point in time, this person, without loss to His divine nature, assumed a human nature such that He was, in the words of the Chalcedonian formula, "perfect in divinity and perfect in humanity" (Tanner 1990, 1: 86; *ST* III.3.1, 3.2). This union of human and divine natures necessarily took place in the person or hypostasis of the divine Son—hence the hypostatic union. Aquinas teaches:

> Everything that appertains to a particular person, whether it belongs to his nature or not, is united to him in person. If, therefore, human nature is not united to the Word of God in person, it is in no way united to Him. And thus belief in the Incarnation is totally destroyed, which would undermine the whole of Christian faith.
>
> (ST III.2.2 co.)

If the person of the Word is not the principle and term of the assumption of a particular and integral human nature (constituted of a real carnal body, a rational soul, and a human mind), then the Word did not truly become incarnate and so could not have wrought human salvation (III.2.2 ad 3; III.3.1 co.; III.3.2 co.; III.4.4 co.; III.5.1–4).

With the ancient conciliar declarations in hand and the Incarnate Word's soteriological mission in view, Aquinas deftly navigates between the Scylla of Eutychianism (i.e., monophysitism or one-nature Christology) and the Charybdis of Nestorianism (i.e., a two-person Christology). Against Eutychianism, Aquinas explains that the union of human and divine described by Chalcedon—"two natures which undergo no confusion, no change, no division, no separation, the distinction of natures at no point having been taken away by the union"—could not have taken place in the nature (III.2.1 s.c., co.). Given divine immutability and Christ's consubstantiality with both His divine Father and His human mother, it is impossible that, as Eutyches appears to have taught, divinity and humanity were mixed in Christ such that He was somehow from two natures before the union but only in one (divine) nature after it (III.2.1 co.; 2.6 co.). Likewise, Aquinas rejects the view at the opposite extreme, that of Nestorius and Theodore of Mopsuestia, who held that in the Incarnation two different persons or hypostases—the divine "Son of God" and the human "son of man"—were united in various accidental ways, namely by indwelling, mutual disposition, operation, dignity of honor, and the communication of names (III.2.6 co.; III.2.3 co.; III.3.6 co.). For Aquinas, admitting of two hypostases destroys the very reality of divine Incarnation and thus ruins human salvation. "If, therefore, there is another hypostasis in Christ besides the hypostasis of the Word," he asserts, "it follows that those things that pertain to the human—for example, that He was born of a Virgin, suffered, was crucified, and was buried—are shown to be true of someone other than the Word" (III.2.3 co.).

Sarah Coakley has rightly noted that Aquinas's Christology, while committed to traditional conciliar orthodoxy, is "distinctive and daring" both because of the Dominican's keenness in reading Scripture and because of his "fearless acknowledgement of the metaphysical uniqueness" of the Incarnation (Coakley 2016: 223). These two elements of Aquinas's approach go hand in glove, as we will soon see. Aquinas does not, of course, subscribe to the (modern) notion that Scripture and metaphysics are worlds apart, that a truly biblical Christology diverges from an ontological one (White 2015: 6–7). For Aquinas, Scripture and the doctrinal tradition, when read in tandem, clearly teach the metaphysical singularity of Christ. Although the Son of God, as Brian Davies puts it, "became a particular human being whom anyone around him might have bumped into" (Davies 2014: 300), He was a human unlike any other. Indeed, what the hypostatic union means, most basically, is that Jesus Christ is not a *human person* at all. He is fully human by virtue of a complete human nature assumed, but His human nature does not ground its own person or supposit (*suppositum*), understood as the individual that 'underlies' (*supponitur*) and subsists in a particular nature (*ST* III.2.2 co.; 2.3 co.). In ordinary humans like us, human nature, which is the essence of our species, is the principle whereby we subsist and are persons (defined by Boethius as "individual substances of a rational nature"; III.2.2 obj. 3; I.29.1). In us, human nature grounds supposit or person. Christ's humanity, however, is not the principle by virtue of which He subsists or exists *simpliciter* (Gorman 2017: 73–75). Christ's human nature does not ground His person. Rather, the divine nature, which the Word receives eternally through generation from the Father, grounds the person of Christ; indeed, because of divine simplicity, the divine nature does not really differ from the person of the Word (or from the other supposits in God; III.2.2 co.; I.3.3 co.; I.29.4 co.). This does not mean, however, that Christ's humanity is not real, or that it is somehow less effective or less dignified than ours. Aquinas teaches, on the contrary, that Christ's humanity is more perfect, more powerful, and more dignified than ours precisely because it does *not* ground a human person:

> A new hypostasis or person is not constituted from the union of soul and body in Christ, but the union itself comes to an already existing person or hypostasis. Nor does it follow from this that the union of soul and body in Christ is less efficacious than in us. For its being joined to something nobler does not detract from its power and dignity, but increases it.
>
> (*ST* III.2.5 ad 1; III.2.2 ad 2)

TO BE OR NOT TO BE ONE TO-BE: THAT IS THE QUESTION

That the one person of Christ subsists in two natures—and, as such, possesses both divine and human modes of knowing (qq. 9–12), willing (q. 18), operating (q. 19), etc.—raises the question of the unity of Christ's being or to-be (*esse*). Is Christ one or two with regard to *esse*? That is, does Christ have only one existence by virtue of His divine person, or does He have one according to His divine nature and another according to His human nature? If the former, is Christ truly human? If the latter, are divinity and humanity really united hypostatically? How precisely Aquinas answers this seminal question remains a live interpretive issue among Thomists today, just as it was among his earliest readers (Brown 1998; Cross 1996; West 2002; Weinandy 2004: 79–83; Salas 2006; Froula 2014; Gorman 2017: 101–125). Whether to be Christ is to be or not to be one to-be: that is the question! Nearly every time Aquinas treats this question—in the *Scriptum on the Sentences* Bk. III, *Quodlibet IX, Compendium theologiae* ch. 212, and the *Tertia pars* of the *ST*—he seems to assign only one *esse* to Christ, namely that belonging to the person of the Word. In *ST* III.17.2 co., for example, Aquinas teaches:

> It is impossible for that being [*illud esse*] that pertains to the actual hypostasis or person in itself to be multiplied in one hypostasis or person, because it is impossible that there not be one being [*unum esse*] for one thing. ... So, therefore, since the human nature is united

to the Son of God hypostatically or personally ... and not accidentally, it follows that by the human nature no new personal being [*novum esse personale*] accrued to Him.

In the *Disputed Question on the Union of the Incarnate Word* (*De Unione*) a. 4, however, Aquinas explains how we may speak of two beings in Christ:

And therefore, just as Christ is one simply [*simpliciter*] on account of the unity of the supposit and two in a certain respect [*secundum quid*] on account of the two natures, so too He has one being [*esse*] simply on account of the one eternal being [*esse*] of the eternal supposit. But there is also another being [*esse*] of this supposit, not insofar as He is eternal, but insofar as He became human temporally. That is, although it is not accidental being—because 'human' is not pre-dicated accidentally of the Son of God, as was said above—it is nevertheless not the principal being [*esse principale*] of His supposit, but a secondary one [*secundarium*].

Many Thomists read this "secondary *esse*" as a contradiction of, or at least in considerable tension with, Aquinas's one-*esse* account, which they take to represent his true and most commonly taught view. Thus, they explain his teaching in *De Unione* in one of two general ways. They assume either that Aquinas had a momentary mental lapse, for-getting what he had taught elsewhere, or, as Richard Cross imagines, that he engaged in a very brief "flirtation" with an "account [that] has no explanatory value" (Cross 1996: 200–201; Weinandy 2004: 79–80). For his part, Cross reads Aquinas's example, in *ST* III.17.2, of the acci-dental union of hands or feet or eyes to the already-constituted person of Socrates as the Dominican's "explanation of how the incarnation took place" (Cross 1996: 191; Cross 2002: 55–58, 62–64, 246–256). Presuming that Aquinas understands the hypostatic union to be "in all significant respects just like this" union, Cross charges him with pro-pounding "a version of the monophysite heresy" (Cross 1996: 194, 192; Cross 2002: 57–58, 67–68; Colberg 2010: 67–68). For Cross, such a single-*esse*, and indeed single-nature, Christology simply cannot be squared with the double-*esse* view of *De Unione*.

But Cross appears confused on several significant points. First, Aquinas is certainly no monophysite (Weinandy 2004: 80–83,

89n70). He does not understand the human nature of Christ as an accident having accrued temporally to the divine Word. In fact, Aquinas explicitly rejects this view, citing the Incarnation as an exception to the general rule that whatever comes to a "completed being [*esse completum*]" is brought in accidentally. The human nature was, according to Aquinas, "drawn into the communion of that completed being" of the eternal person of the Word of God; it was not "assumed to the one being [*unum esse*] of a nature" (*ST* III.2.6 ad 2; *ScG* IV.41; West 2002: 241–248).

Second, Aquinas's teaching concerning Christ's one *esse* is not ultimately at odds with a secondary *esse*. Aquinas is clear in *ST* III.17.2 co. that Christ has a single, eternal *esse* that belongs to His divine person and that this person's temporal assumption of a human nature fails to add a "new personal being [*novum esse personale*]" to Him. It adds only a "new relation [*nova habitudo*]" of this preexisting personal *esse* to the human nature such that the person of the Word "is now said to subsist not only according to divine nature, but also according to human nature" (III.17.2 co.). Aquinas readily recognizes that the *esse* of the human Christ, which is *esse temporale*, can be distinguished from the *esse* of the divine Son (III.17.2 obj. 2). In the Incarnation, he teaches, "the eternal being [*esse aeternum*] of the Son of God ... becomes the being of the human [*esse hominis*] inasmuch as the human nature is assumed by the Son of God into the unity of person" (III.17.2 ad 2). This *esse aeternum / esse hominis* distinction aligns perfectly, as far as I can tell, with the *esse principale / esse secundarium* distinction of *De Unione* a. 4. *Esse aeternum* or *esse principale* is that act of existence whereby Christ *is* simply or absolutely, that principle according to which the second trinitarian person exists unqualifiedly, as subsisting in the divine nature. *Esse hominis* or *esse secundarium*, by contrast, is that act of existence whereby Christ *is* in a certain respect, that principle according to which the second trinitarian person exists qualifiedly, as subsisting in human nature. Whereas Christ, as a single person, can and does have only one principal *esse*, which is eternal and uncreated, He can and does also have a temporal and created secondary *esse* insofar as He is human (Froula 2014; Gorman 2017: 112–115; Weinandy 2004: 79–83).

Thirdly, when Cross maintains that "Aquinas uses the example of the advent of a hand to a human being as an explanation of how the incarnation took place" and that Aquinas takes the hypostatic union to be "in all significant respects just like this" (Cross 1996: 191, 194), he infelicitously mistakes an inadequate analogy for a full explanation. For Aquinas, as we have seen, the Incarnation is the supremely superrational mystery of faith, surpassing reason most of all (*ScG* IV.27). Although certain basic truths concerning hypostatic union have been revealed by God and, as such, can constitute a subject of theological reflection, the precise mode of the union evades all rational explanation and linguistic description. "In a certain ineffable way," Aquinas teaches, "a person of God joined human nature to Himself according to the unity of hypostasis" (*De Unione* a. 2 ad 15). Because divine power far exceeds the goodness found among creatures, God can produce "new modes of goodness and being unknown to us," as He has done in the hypostatic union. Consequently, Aquinas acknowledges, "no adequate analogy [*nullum sufficiens exemplum*] for this [union] can be found among creatures" (*De Unione* a. 1 co.).

Thus, all of the analogies that Aquinas provides are, by his own admission, necessarily *insufficient*. Imagining hands, feet, or eyes accruing to the already constituted person of Socrates offers neither an "explanation" (Cross) nor an "adequate analogy" (Aquinas) for the incarnational union (III.17.2 co.). Rather, Aquinas's purpose in using this example is simply to establish that no new personal *esse* would come to Socrates under such conditions, just as no new personal *esse* came to the Word when He assumed human nature. The points of dissimilarity between this imagined union of body parts with Socrates and the incarnational union are obviously far more numerous and far more profound than the points of similarity.

This is equally true of analogies that are most central to Aquinas's Christology. Elsewhere, for instance, he compares Christ's human nature to God as a "proper and conjoined instrument," as the hand is compared to the soul (*ScG* IV.41). Unlike a pickaxe, which is a separated and common instrument, the human hand is joined to the soul personally in order to carry out the soul's own operations. So too with the human nature hypostatically united to the divine Word, according to Aquinas:

> The human nature in Christ was assumed so that it might instrumentally [*instrumentaliter*] perform works that are operations proper to God

> alone, such as cleansing from sins, enlightening minds through grace, and leading [humans] into the perfection of eternal life.
>
> (ScG IV.41; Tschipke 2003; Wawrykow 2015: 235)

A significant point of dissimilarity between this analogue and the analogate, however, is that the hand belongs to the specific nature that constitutes the person whose hand it is, whereas the human nature that becomes conjoined to the Word of God does not belong to the Word's divine nature (though, once conjoined, it does belong to the person of the Word). To highlight this point of dissimilarity, Aquinas compares the human nature in the incarnate Word to "a sixth finger or something of this sort" (ScG IV.41; Colberg 2010). Does Aquinas imagine that the Incarnation is *just like* human polydactyly, or that polydactyly somehow *explains* this otherwise inscrutable mystery? Of course not. "Perfect likenesses must not be sought in the analogies set forth above," Aquinas concludes. "Indeed, we must understand that the Word of God was able to be united to human nature in a much more sublime and intimate way than the soul [can be united] to any kind of proper instrument whatsoever" (ScG IV.41).

FULL OF GRACE AND TRUTH (JN. 1:14): CHRIST'S BEATIFIC VISION

In the Incarnation, the divine Word came to instantiate human nature not only by assuming the essential elements of human nature, a rational soul and a body. The second trinitarian person also "coassumed" certain perfections and defects that are not constitutive of human nature but that variously qualify Christ's concrete humanity (ST III.7–15; Gondreau 2009: 166–181). In considering coassumed perfections—such as the plenitude of grace and knowledge (III.7.9, 10, 12; III.9–12)—and defects of the body and soul—such as death, hunger, thirst, sorrow, fear, and anger (III.14.1; III.15.6, 7, 9)—Aquinas leans heavily on Scripture, patristic teaching, and what is most fitting for Christ in light of His salvific mission (Harkins 2021; Wawrykow 2005b: 76–77). Although it is perhaps the most controversial of his Christological teachings, Aquinas's doctrine of Christ's beatific knowledge provides a clear example of his approach to the *coassumpta*.

According to Aquinas, Jesus was unique among humans in that He knew God fully and enjoyed the beatific vision in His human soul during His earthly life (*ST* III.9.2; III.10). Indeed, from the moment of conception Christ was graced such that He saw the divine essence more clearly than any other creature (III.34.1, 4; III.10.1, 4). As I have shown elsewhere, Aquinas understands Scripture, particularly Jn. 1:14 (*... and we have seen His glory, ... full of grace and truth*), as clearly attributing such plenitude of grace and knowledge to Christ (Harkins 2021). Furthermore, Christ is *full of grace and truth* precisely for the sake of His saving work. For Aquinas, if Christ's humanity is to lead humans to the perfect vision of God in heaven, that same humanity must already possess the fullness of the ultimate end. "It was necessary," he explains, "that the very knowledge consisting in the vision of God should belong to the human Christ in the most excellent way, because the cause should always be superior to what is caused" (III.9.2 co.). Just as any mover must be "in act" with respect to X in order to reduce what is "in potential" with respect to X to actuality, as we saw in Aquinas's First Way (*ST* I.2.3 co.; see Chapter 3), so too Christ's humanity must be "in act" with respect to beatific knowledge in order to reduce the potential of ordinary humans for such knowledge to actuality (*ST* III.9.2 co.).

For Aquinas, Christ's saving work necessitated a certain balance, as it were, between coassumed perfections and defects. Christ could not have fittingly assumed those defects, such as ignorance, that would have disallowed or obstructed His plenitude of knowledge (III.14.4 co.; III.15.3 co.). But other defects—such as death, hunger, and thirst—were, like the perfection of knowledge and grace, "required" in order for Christ to make satisfaction for human sin (III.14.4 co.). Whereas these defects are ordinarily contracted by humans through Original Sin, Christ, who "took up human nature without sin," assumed them voluntarily (III.14.3 co.). Aquinas follows John Damascene, then, in teaching that Christ assumed all "natural and nondetractible passions [*naturales et indetractibiles passiones*]," that is, those that are consequent upon human nature in common but do not detract from the perfection of His particular instantiation of human nature (III.14.4 co.; Harkins 2021).

In considering the human nature in Christ, Aquinas carefully distinguishes between what it is by reason of its species, on the one hand, and what it possesses from its union with the divine hypostasis, on the other (*ST* III.15.3 co.). Whereas it is a *true* human nature on account of what was assumed (namely, a rational soul and body), it is a *perfect* human nature on account of the hypostatic union itself, "by means of which the soul of Christ was filled with grace and truth beyond all others" (*Comp. theol.* ch. 214). By virtue of the incarnational union and its unique graces, then, Christ is similar to ordinary humans "in nature, but not in power [*in natura, sed non in virtute*]" (*ST* III.53.2 ad 1). Thus, as Brian Davies observes, according to Aquinas, "Christ, even as human, was seriously different from your average human being" (Davies 2014: 316).

Since the mid-20th century, some prominent Catholic theologians have sharply critiqued Aquinas on this point, maintaining that his doctrine of Christ's beatific vision effectively denies the true humanity of Jesus and fails to remain faithful to the New Testament. Avery Dulles, for instance, asserts: "Nothing in scripture indicates that Christ continuously had the beatific vision" (Dulles 2001: 278). Gerald O'Collins and Daniel Kendall have noted that for many modern people Aquinas's teaching concerning Christ's beatific knowledge "would seem to inject a strong element of make-believe into the whole of his life story and cast doubt on his authentic humanity" (O'Collins and Kendall 1992: 409). Several decades earlier, Karl Rahner maintained that this doctrine sounds "almost mythological today," and seems "contrary to the real humanity and historical nature of Our Lord" as disclosed in Scripture (Rahner 1966: 194–195). Jon follows suit, claiming that Aquinas's teaching typifies traditional "mythical thinking about Jesus … that abstractly avows the 'humanity' of Jesus without getting at the roots of his existence as a human being" (Sobrino 1978: 80).

These theologians assume not only that the traditional Christian affirmation of Jesus' true humanity must mean that He could not have differed from ordinary humans in any substantive way whatsoever, but also that historical investigation of the New Testament bears out this interpretation. Indeed, Rahner affirms: "[O]ne almost gets the impression [from reading the Gospels] that the only original thing about Our Lord is himself together with the unique combination of environmental influences which, of course, are to be found in every human being" (Rahner 1966: 195). Relatedly, the modern search for the historical Jesus has turned up little evidence of beatific knowledge in Christ's human soul (Ziegler 2015). In fact, James Mackey describes the Savior's knowledge of God, according to Scripture, in strikingly quotidian terms: "The man Jesus … had no more 'information' about God than could be gleaned from the birds of the air, the farmers in their fields, kings in their castles, and merchants in the market-place" (Mackey 1979: 171). Even scholars who are generally amenable to Aquinas's teaching question its scriptural foundation. Simon Gaine, for instance, offers a persuasive systematic-theological defense of the doctrine, but concedes that "nothing in Scripture seems to inform us in any straightforward way that Christ enjoyed heavenly knowledge in his humanity" (Gaine 2015: 39; Barnes 2012: 2).

Aquinas would surely be baffled by these critiques and the flat-footed approach to Christological understanding that bolsters them. On the one hand, Aquinas *does* understand such scriptural texts as Jn. 1:14, Jn. 8:55, Col. 2:3, Heb. 5:8, and Eph. 1:20–21 as explicitly teaching the human Christ's plenitude of knowledge (III.9.2 s.c.; 9.3 s.c.; 9.4 s.c.; 10.4 s.c., co.; Harkins 2021). On the other hand, he reads such Scriptures not as a modern historical-Jesus quester who considers ecclesial dogma a foreign accretion, but rather as a medieval practitioner of sacred doctrine who assumes that patristic and conciliar teaching faithfully embodies and transmits divinely revealed Christological truth (Kerr 2009: 87–88; Prügl 2005: 386; Wawrykow 2005a: 234; Chapter 2, this volume). In Aquinas's view, then, what Scripture teaches about Christ can be understood properly only when it is read through the lens of the dogmatic tradition that clarifies and illuminates it. Indeed, as Paul Gondreau has observed, "For Aquinas, … the authoritative witness of Scripture, defined Church teaching, and the patristic writings combine to make up the lifeblood of any genuine Christological speculation" (Gondreau 2005: 254).

CHRIST'S SAVING WORK

At the heart of Aquinas's soteriology stands the patristic notion, consequent upon the hypostatic union, that Christ's work is theandric or divinely human (*divinamhumanam*) (III.19.1 ad 1). The human nature is, in Aquinas's view, the proper and conjoined instrument of the divinity. Thus, Christ's human actions are instrumental causes vis-à-vis God's principal agency:

> The operation of the human nature in Christ, inasmuch as it is the instrument of the divinity, is not different from the operation of the divinity, for the salvation by which the humanity of Christ saves is not different from that by which His divinity saves. Nevertheless, the human nature in Christ, inasmuch as it is a certain nature, has a certain proper operation besides the divine.
>
> (ST III.19.1 ad 2)

The Incarnate Word's divine operation utilizes His human operation, and His human operation shares in the power of the divine (III.19.1 ad 1). Although the divine Son was perfect from eternity and had no need of a temporal nativity, for instance, He was born—which belongs to human nature—"for us and for our salvation" (III.35.2 ad 2). But, as a divine person, He was born "supernaturally" (III.19.1 ad 1; III.35.4–6). According to Aquinas, the Father and the Holy Spirit mercifully willed Christ to do and suffer human things (III.19.1 ad 1), and Christ also willed such human things for Himself.

Christ's free will and voluntary choices have pride of place in Aquinas's soteriology, as we will see. But did Christ *really* will His own birth? Aquinas teaches that Christ, unlike the rest of us, willingly chose His own birth and all of its particulars:

> There is this difference between Christ and other humans: whereas other humans are born subject to the inevitability of time, Christ, as the Lord and Maker of all times, chose for Himself a time at which to be born, just as He also chose a mother and a birthplace.
>
> (ST III.35.8 co.)

The subject of such choices is the single person of the Word, who always chooses most fittingly. Although it might seem that Christ, who is the Light of the world, should have been born in the summer, when the days are longer, Aquinas observes, "He chose the harshness of winter for His nativity in order that from that time He might endure the suffering of the flesh for us" (III.35.8 ad 3).

This example illustrates two points that are significant for Aquinas's Christology more broadly. First, he understands Christ as having voluntarily chosen all the things that He suffered, including passions that are naturally or ordinarily involuntary, such as birth. Second, Aquinas assumes that everything that Christ experienced as human carries deep salvific significance (Torrell 2011: 91–100). "Because truly the humanity of Christ is the instrument of the divinity," he explains, "… all of Christ's actions and passions operate instrumentally, according to the power of divinity, for human salvation" (III.48.6 co.).

Aquinas rounds out his Christology by offering a substantive treatment of Christ's saving work—including His passion, death, burial, descent into hell, resurrection, and ascension into heaven—in qq. 46–59 of the *Tertia pars*. For our present purposes it will suffice to sketch some of the prominent features of Aquinas's understanding of Christ's passion and death, infernal descent, and resurrection. We will focus particularly on Jesus' passion and death due to the complex and controversial nature of Aquinas's teaching here.

PASSION AND DEATH

With regard to the passion, Aquinas is especially concerned with the who-question, which is twofold: who suffered the passion (the passive who), on the one hand, and who effected it or caused this one to suffer (the active who), on the other? In line with his account of the hypostatic union, Aquinas is clear that the one who suffered the passion (the passive who) is the very Son of God, the second trinitarian person. Aquinas does not, however, share the view of Jürgen Moltmann that "[t]he Christ event on the cross is a God event" in which God "has acted in himself and has gone on to suffer in himself" (Moltmann 1974: 205). For Aquinas, Moltmann's locating the cross "at the heart of the trinitarian being of God" (Moltmann 1974: 207) is ontologically impossible given divine impassibility. Aquinas explains:

> The passion is to be attributed to a supposit of the divine nature, not by reason of the divine nature, which is impassible, but by reason of the human nature. … Therefore, Christ's passion pertains to a

> supposit of the divine nature by reason of the passible nature
> assumed, but not by reason of the impassible divine nature.
>
> (*ST* III.46.12 co.)

The supposit of the Word took up a human nature precisely in order to do and suffer human things for human salvation.

The question of who caused the Incarnate Word to suffer and die (the active who) is somewhat more complicated. For Aquinas, the causes are three, and each cause acted differently. First, Christ's human persecutors acted *directly* to cause His suffering and death. Second, Christ Himself acted *indirectly* as a cause of His own passion in that He did not prevent it (III.47.1 co.). For Aquinas, however, Christ's indirect causality cannot be reduced to what Gerald O'Collins describes as a passive "acceptance of his own victimhood" (O'Collins 2008: 153). In Aquinas's view, Christ was not an ordinary human (*purus homo*) who ran afoul of the religious authorities of His day because of "his particular conception of God" (Sobrino 1978: 205) and simply acquiesced to the penalty of crucifixion (III.2.11 co.; III.17.1 obj. 3; III.41.4 ad 1). Rather, Christ was the *cause* of His own passion and death insofar as He failed to prevent it in two ways, outwardly and inwardly. Christ could have restrained His enemies from without, such that they would have been unwilling or unable to kill Him. Additionally, because Christ's human soul was hypostatically united to the divine Word, it had the power, from within, to preserve His body from the injury inflicted on it; but, instead of repelling this injury, His soul willed that His body should suffer it. This is precisely what it means, according to Aquinas, that Christ laid down His soul (*animam*) and died voluntarily (Jn. 10:15, 17–18; III.47.1 co.). The violence outwardly inflicted on Christ prevailed over His body "only insofar as He Himself willed it" (III.47.1 ad 3).

The third cause of Christ's suffering and death is, for Aquinas, the principal cause, namely God. In general, modern Catholic theology has recoiled from the traditional notion that God willed His Son's death for the sake of human redemption (Van Nieuwenhove 2005: 277–278). In Jon Sobrino's view, God's plan that Jesus should be crucified for human salvation appears "purely arbitrary and cruel" (Sobrino 1978: 189). It is, according to Edward Schillebeeckx, "a sadistic and bloody myth" divorced from

Jesus' life and message (Schillebeeckx 1993: 120). On Schille-beeckx's reading of the biblical and historical evidence, the Jewish and Roman authorities "played the dirty trick" of murdering Jesus because His "proclamation and career" proved too threatening. Thus, Schillebeeckx insists: "God ... did not put Jesus on the cross. Humans did that" (Schillebeeckx 1993: 120). For Aquinas, how-ever, God is the first and final cause of all actions in the universe. Furthermore, God's primary causality does not preclude secondary, voluntary causes from acting voluntarily; rather, it is precisely what enables their voluntary actions (I.83.1 ad 3; see also Chapter 3). Thus, affirming that 'humans put Jesus on the cross'—whether the Jewish authorities, Roman persecutors, Christ Himself, or all of the above—fails, for Aquinas, to account *fully* for the crucifixion. Whereas Christ, according to Aquinas, suffered on account of neither an absolute natural necessity nor a necessity of compulsion, His passion was necessary "from the presupposition of an end" (III.46.1 co.). The end presupposed, or the final cause, was God's eternal knowledge and will that Christ should suffer for human redemption. Aquinas explains:

> Simply and absolutely speaking, therefore, it was possible for God to deliver humankind in another way than by the passion of Christ .... But from a certain presupposition having been made, it was impos-sible. Because it is impossible for God's foreknowledge to be deceived and His will or arrangement to be destroyed, if God's fore-knowledge and foreordaining of Christ's passion is presupposed, it is not simultaneously possible that Christ would not suffer and that humankind would be delivered in another way than by His passion.
>
> (*ST* III.46.2 co.)

Although Christ's passion was known and willed eternally by God, and thus was necessary from this end presupposed, it was also a contingent event from the perspective of its secondary causes, including Christ's persecutors and His own human will (I.14.13 co.). And Aquinas teaches that it was "most fitting" that Christ, as human, should suffer out of obedience to the eternal will of His Father (III.47.2 co., ad 1). Because Christ suffered voluntarily out of obedience (Phil. 2:8), it is truly said that God handed His Son over for human salvation (Rom. 8:32). God the Father handed

Him over to suffering and death in three ways, according to Aquinas. First, by His own eternal will, the Father foreordained Christ's passion for human deliverance. Second, by the outpouring of charity, the Father inspired Christ's human will to suffer for humankind. And third, the Father handed Christ over "by not protecting Him from the passion, but by exposing Him to [His] persecutors" (III.47.3 co.).

Given Aquinas's understanding of the hypostatic union and the metaphysics of voluntary human action, he sees no contradiction between the divine Father's having exposed Christ and Christ's having exposed Himself. He affirms:

> It must be said that Christ, as God, handed Himself over to death by the same will and action by which the Father also handed Him over. But as human, He handed Himself over by a will inspired by the Father. Hence, there is no contrariety in the Father handing Christ over and in Christ handing Himself over.
>
> (ST III.47.3 ad 2)

Aquinas concedes, as Sobrino claims, that it would indeed be "wicked and cruel" for someone to hand an innocent person over to suffering and death against his will. But God the Father did not hand Christ over in this way, Aquinas observes; rather, the Father inspired His only-begotton Son with the will, insofar as He is human, to suffer "for us" (III.47.3 ad 1). For Aquinas, as Rik Van Nieuwenhove rightly notes, "the divine plan does not impose any necessity on genuinely contingent, historical events, and this also applies to the life and death of Christ" (Van Nieuwenhove 2005: 279).

Furthermore, Christ's enduring the passion voluntarily in order to deliver humankind from sin contributed, according to Aquinas, to His having experienced the greatest sensible pain and sadness possible in this life. "He assumed as great a quantity of pain as would be proportionate to the magnitude of the fruit that followed from it," Aquinas teaches (III.46.6 co.). The sources of Christ's pain—both external (e.g., the piercing of His hands and feet) and internal (e.g., all the sins of humankind)—also played a key role in His experiencing the greatest of all suffering, as did the extraordinary sensitivity of the sufferer's body and soul (III.46.6 co.). Because Christ's body was "perfectly constituted" by virtue of the fact that it was formed miraculously by the working of the Holy Spirit, His sense of touch was particularly acute. Similarly, because of its unique perfection, the soul of Christ "apprehended all the causes of sadness most efficaciously" (III.46.6 co.).

Over against the modern critique that Aquinas's Christology casts doubt on Jesus' authentic humanity, the Dominican master is clear that Christ's status as a divine person in no way renders Him less human. To the contrary, the unique circumstances of the Word's becoming incarnate account for His being *perfectly* human. For Aquinas, Christ did not suffer less than the common criminals crucified on either side of Him; in fact, by virtue of the hypostatic union and the voluntary nature of His salvific suffering, Christ experienced far more pain and sadness. Aquinas follows John Damascene in teaching that Christ's divinity permitted His flesh to suffer what is proper to it (III.46.8 s.c.). Likewise, the suffering of Christ's body and the lower powers of His soul did not prevent Him from simultaneously enjoying the beatific vision, the proper act of His soul's higher part (III.46.8 co.; III.46.7 co.; White 2015: 328–339; Lamb 2004: 231–232). Although taking Christ's divinity seriously has led many theologians down the road to docetism, Aquinas shows that a proper understanding of the Incarnation steers Christology in a decidedly anti-docetist direction.

In treating Christ's death in itself, Aquinas maintains his focus both on the Lord's true humanity, on the one hand, and on his identity as a divine person, on the other. He teaches that it was "fitting" for Christ to die, among other reasons, in order display the reality of the human nature assumed (III.50.1 co.). Although Christ is "the principle and font of all life" as God, He died precisely as human and not as God (contra Moltmann); for Aquinas, then, His death presented no logical or theological contradiction (III.50.1 obj. 1, ad 1). The Apostles' Creed—which predicates suffering, death, burial, and descent into hell of the Son of God—serves as a determinative authority for Aquinas's understanding of the who and the what of these sacred mysteries (III.50.2 s.c.; III.50.3 s.c.; III.52.1 s.c.). What it means that the divine Son died is that His human soul was separated from His body, as happens in the death of any "pure human" person, but that neither soul nor body was separated from the second trinitarian person, who cannot die. Because grace is lost only through fault and because Christ was utterly sinless, the unique grace of union was never lost, and so the union of the human nature to the divine Word was never dissolved. "And therefore," Aquinas explains, "just as before death the flesh of Christ was united personally and hypostatically to the Word of God, so too it remained united after death, such that the hypostasis of the Word of God was not different from that of the flesh of Christ after death" (III.50.2 co.).

Aquinas is insistent that the indissolubility of the incarnational union should not be understood in any way to undermine the truth of Christ's death, which is an article of faith (III.50.4 co.). Christ really died—that is, He truly ceased to be human—when His soul, which perfects human nature, was separated from His body. Thus, over against Hugh of St. Victor and Peter Lombard, Aquinas teaches that Christ was not a human "simply and absolutely speaking" during the three days of His death (III.50.4 co.). Though it cannot be affirmed that He was a human, since His soul was not animating His body, Christ can be said to have been a "dead human" during that first triduum (III.50.4 co.). For Aquinas, then, those who looked upon the dead Christ on the cross and those who prepared His body for burial (Jn. 19:26–27, 32–35, 38–42) did *not* see and bury a human; rather, they saw and buried a divine person, the very Son of God, to whom assumed flesh remained hypostatically united. Furthermore, this flesh, although dead, continued to serve as the conjoined instrument of the Son's divinity, by the power of which it was able to conduce to human salvation (III.50.6 co., ad 3). Although this perspective on Christ's death may strike us as completely counterintuitive, it exemplifies Aquinas's careful consideration of and profound insight into what Christian faith professes.

DESCENT INTO HELL

Because the Apostles' Creed also attributes the infernal descent to the Son of God, Aquinas teaches that death could not have severed Christ's human soul, whereby He descended into hell, from the hypostasis of the second trinitarian person (III.50.3 co.; 52.1 co.). Christ's infernal descent was a "fitting" complement to His passion and death, according to Aquinas. Indeed, just as Christ fittingly died in order to redeem us from death, so too it was appropriate that He descended into hell to liberate us from the penalty of descending there (III.52.1 co.). To the objection that Christ's having gone down to hell seems salvifically superfluous since His passion delivered us from both guilt and penalty, Aquinas responds that the Savior's infernal descent functioned as a sort of sacrament for the dead:

> It must be said that the passion of Christ was a certain universal cause of human salvation, as much for the living as for the dead. But a universal cause is applied to singular effects by means of some particular thing. Hence, just as the power of Christ's passion is applied to the living through the sacraments, which configure us to Christ's passion, so too it was applied to the dead through Christ's descent into hell.
>
> (*ST* III.52.1 ad 2)

The singular effects to which the 'sacrament' of Christ's descent applied the saving fruits of His passion were the holy fathers, those pre-Christian saints who were detained in the limbo of the fathers by the penalty of Original Sin. Although these ancient saints were, in life, united to Christ's passion by faith formed by charity, their "access to the life of glory" and the beatific vision was barred prior to Christ's actual suffering, which paid the price of humankind's redemption (III.52.5 co., ad 2). Neither the damned, nor the children who died in a state of Original Sin (i.e., without baptism), nor those in purgatory were liberated by Christ, according to Aquinas (III.52.6–8). Whereas Christ was variously present "through His effect" in each level or region of hell (the hell of the damned, the limbo of the children, the limbo of the fathers, and purgatory), He was present "through His essence" only in the fathers' limbo. Here, Aquinas teaches, even as Christ's soul visited the just in a place, His divinity visited them interiorly by grace (III.52.2 co.; Goris 2018: 94–98). His doctrine makes clear that the hypostatic union persisted in spite of the separation of body and soul that constituted Christ's death. Because the soul, still personally conjoined to the Son of God, descended to the underworld, it was truly "the whole Christ" (*totus Christus*) who was in hell, just as "the whole Christ" simultaneously lay in the tomb by virtue of the body's union with the second trinitarian person (III.52.3 co.).

The whole human nature, however, was in neither place, as Christ was no longer a human (III.50.4 co.; III.52.3 ad 2).

RESURRECTION

Finally, Aquinas continues to emphasize the hypostatic union in considering Christ's resurrection (qq. 53–56). He teaches that the resurrection was "necessary," among other reasons, "for the instruction of our faith," which perforce concerns both Christ's divinity and humanity (III.53.1 co.; III.53.2 co.). Hell and death did not detain Christ (Acts 2:24), as if He were some ordinary human. Rather, Aquinas makes clear that Christ remained in death for three days "by His own will, as long as He judged it to be necessary for the instruction of our faith" (III.53.2 ad 2). In order to teach us that He was truly human and really died, Christ did not rise too soon; on the other hand, in order to confirm our faith in His divinity, He did not tarry in the tomb too long (III.53.2 co.). Whereas some people were miraculously rescued from actual death by the Old-Testament prophets Elijah and Elisha and even by Christ Himself prior to the passion, Christ was the first human to be freed from the necessity—indeed the very possibility—of dying. Thus, He was the first human to experience "a true and perfect resurrection" and so to arrive at "a life utterly immortal" and "conformed to God" (III.53.3 co., obj. 1; III.55.2 co.).

But Christ did not raise Himself as human, that is, by the power of His created nature. Human nature, even the perfect human nature possessed by Christ, is utterly powerless to reunite body and soul after death. Only divinity can do this, as Christ Himself makes clear when he says of His soul, *I lay it down and I take it up again* (Jn. 10:18). The one who speaks here, according to Aquinas, is a *divine person* and He speaks of the revivifying power of His divine nature (III.53.4 s.c., co.). "Therefore, by the power of the divinity united to it, the body again took up the soul, which it had laid down, and the soul again took up the body, which it had abandoned," Aquinas teaches (III.53.4 co., ad 3). Thus, Christ, as God, raised Himself to immortal life by the same divine power whereby God the Father raised Him (Acts 2:24; Rom. 8:11; III.53.4 obj. 1, ad 1).

In His resurrection, the same body that Christ had prior to His death was again united with the same soul, which is its form. Thus,

His resurrected body was a true and whole human body, consisting of "flesh and bones and blood and other such things" and even bearing the scars of His passion (III.54.3 co.; III.54.4 s.c., co.; III.54.1 co.). But the mode or state of Christ's resurrected body was different: now it was a glorious or glorified body, which could enter through closed doors (Jn. 20:26) and vanish instantly (Lk. 24:31) (III.54.1 obj. 1, 2, co.). Additionally, it was "utterly immortal," incorruptible, and with no possibility of dying (III.53.3 co). The divine Word bestowed immortal life upon the body hypostatically united to Him and, through Christ's resurrected body, the Word will work the resurrection of all other bodies (III.56.1 co.). Furthermore, Christ's resurrection is the cause of the resurrection of our souls also, as Aquinas explains:

> It is from God that the soul lives through grace and that the body lives by the soul. And therefore the resurrection of Christ instrumentally possesses an effective power not only with respect to the resurrection of bodies, but also with respect to the resurrection of souls.
>
> (*ST* III.56.2 co.)

The reality of Christ's glorified body returns us full circle to the supremely superrational mystery of the Incarnation and the unique graces bestowed upon Christ therein. According to Aquinas, although Christ's soul was glorified from the moment of His conception by the fullness of grace such that He saw the very essence of God (III.34.4 co.), the divine will prevented the glory of His soul from naturally flowing down into His body so that, for the sake of human redemption, His passible flesh might suffer what was fitting for it (III.14.1 ad 2; III.45.2 co.; III.54.2 co.). But, Aquinas teaches, "when the mystery of Christ's passion and death had been completed, the soul of Christ immediately diverted His glory, having been taken up again in the resurrection, into the body" (III.54.2 co.). Thus, the exemplarity of Christ makes clear that, in Aquinas's view, the body, though it does not contribute to the essence of beatitude, is nevertheless indispensable for perfect human happiness (Leget 2005: 376–377).

9

THE SACRAMENTS

We humans, constituted of an intellectual soul and an animal body, are the sort of creatures who are led by corporeal and sensible things to spiritual and intelligible realities. It is natural to us to use sensible signs whose meaning is known to us to arrive at things previously unknown (*ST* III.61.1 co.; III.60.2 co.). As you are reading this book, for example, you are making use of its words to arrive at a basic understanding of Aquinas's theology (I hope!). And prior to your reading it, I, as the book's author, composed its words in an effort to signify for you various things about Aquinas's thought. Given that both you and I are humans, it is altogether natural, according to Aquinas, that I should have written and that you should be reading this book, consisting of visible signs. Aquinas also teaches that the external worship of God or divine cult (*cultus divinus*)—using words, material objects, bodily gestures, etc.—is a natural obligation of all humans (Holtz 2012: 448–449). That is, natural law dictates that humans should sacrifice to God, from whom they need help and guidance, by way of their natural mode. Aquinas explains:

> Now the mode fitting (*conveniens*) for the human is that he should use sensible signs to express anything, because he acquires knowledge from sensible things. And therefore it proceeds from natural reason that the human should make use of certain sensible things, offering them to God, as a sign of the subjection and honor due [to Him], like those who present some offering to their lord in recognition of his dominion.
>
> (*ST* II-II.85.1 co.)

The sacramental signs that humans should offer to God in worship have been instituted by God Himself, in fact, for the sake of human sanctification. In Aquinas's view, then, a complementary relationship necessarily exists between the divine cult, which concerns humans in relation to God, on the one hand, and human sanctification, which pertains to God in relation to humans, on the other (III.60.5 co.). And, with regard to 'divine determination,' there is an important parallel between Scripture and the sacraments. Specifically, just as God determined the similitudes in Sacred Scripture that would signify spiritual realities, so too did divine institution alone establish what material things are to be used to sanctify in each particular sacrament (e.g., water in Baptism, bread and wine in the Eucharist; III.60.5 ad 1).

Aquinas defines a sacrament, most basically, as "a sign of a sacred thing insofar as it makes humans holy" (III.60.2 co.). It is an efficacious sign of a sacred reality, a sign that effects the sanctification that it signifies. The seven sacraments of the Church—Baptism, Confirmation, Eucharist, Penance, Extreme Unction, Holy Orders, and Matrimony—are, according to Aquinas, extensions throughout space and time of Christ's work for human salvation. Indeed, the words with which his treatment of the sacraments in the *ST* III.60–90 opens make clear the causal connection between the life, death, and resurrection of Christ, on the one hand, and the sacraments, on the other: "After considering those things that pertain to the mysteries of the incarnate Word, we must consider the sacraments of the Church, which have their efficacy from the incarnate Word Himself" (III.60.prol.). We will consider the nature of sacramental efficacy—that is, what the sacraments effect or bring about in the people who receive them—in greater detail below. For now, though, suffice it to note Aquinas's view that the sacraments are "certain remedies by means of which the benefit of Christ's death may in a certain way be conjoined" to individual Christians in and through Christ's mystical body, the Church (*ScG* IV.56). The sacramental remedies are necessary, according to Aquinas, insofar as the death of Christ, the universal cause of human salvation, must be, like any universal cause, applied to each of its effects somehow (*ScG* IV.56). But how exactly?

SEPARATED INSTRUMENTS OF THE DIVINITY

For Aquinas, Christ's death is applied to or 'brought into contact' with particular humans *instrumentally*, that is, in the manner of an instrument (*per modum instrumenti*). As we have seen in Chapter 8, the saving death of Christ itself was accomplished instrumentally, insofar as the human nature that the divine Word assumed in order to suffer and die was itself an instrument conjoined to His divinity. In the Incarnation, Christ's humanity was conjoined to God and carried out His will in the world in the same way that in ordinary humans the hand is conjoined personally to the soul or mind and acts outwardly according to its command (*ST* III.62.5 co.). Aquinas extends this analogy—and indeed Christ's saving work—by noting that there is also a second kind of instrument, namely one that is separated from the person who uses it. Just as a stick or a hammer is not conjoined to the person whose instrument it is, but rather is moved by the hand, which is personally conjoined, so too the sacraments are not personally united to the Word, but are 'moved,' as it were, by the human nature of Christ, which is hypostatically united to the divine Word (III.62.5 co.). As a hammer's ability to move and accomplish its purpose comes from the soul through the hand of the carpenter who uses it, so also, according to Aquinas, "the saving power in the sacraments themselves is derived from the divinity of Christ through His humanity" (III.62.5 co.).

This analogy sheds light on Aquinas's teaching that it is "necessary" that the remedies of human salvation be conferred under visible signs. The Dominican master offers three reasons (*ScG* IV.56), the first two of which are noteworthy here. First, God provides for the human, as is true for all creatures, according to his nature. And because the human naturally is led to apprehend spiritual and intelligible realities through sensible things, it is appropriate that healing remedies be given under sensible signs. Specific words (*signa*) determined by Christ and ecclesiastical tradition are also added to each material thing or element (*res*), as the form that determines it as a sacrament ("This is my body..." for the Eucharist, for example; *ST* III.60.7 co.). This union of matter and form is fitting as a sign of sanctification for the human, who is composed of body and soul: the material thing (*res*) touches the body, and the soul believes the sacrament by means of the word (III.60.6 co.). Second, the visible mediation of sanctification is suitable because instruments should be proportionate to the first cause, which is, in the case of salvation, the divine Word who became incarnate and thus visible. "And it is not unfitting [*inconveniens*]," Aquinas explains, "that spiritual salvation is supplied by means of visible and corporeal things, because visible things of this kind are certain instruments, as it were, of a God who became incarnate and suffered" (*ScG* IV.56). Here too, with regard to the divine cause of sanctification, the addition of sacramental words is appropriate: "the word is added to the sensible sign," Aquinas affirms, "just as in the mystery of the Incarnation the Word of God was united to sensible flesh" (*ST* III.60.6 co.). In sum, the proper instrument for salvation—constituted of determinate matter and form—should be proportionate both to its primary cause (the incarnate Word) and to its effects, that is, those individuals in whom it is effective (humans).

The sacraments are effective primarily in that they cause grace in the souls of those humans who receive them (*ST* III.62). But how can natural, corporeal signs—like water, bread, and wine—actually cause grace, which is a supernatural and spiritual reality, in the human soul or mind, which is itself spiritual? And how can what is proper to God—to cause grace—be attributed to created things? The 'occasionalist' explanation of the sacraments, held by some of Aquinas's contemporaries, offered one response to these difficult questions. On this account, the sacraments do not cause grace by their own operation; rather, God Himself works grace in the human soul at the same time as the sacraments are celebrated. Here the sacraments do not actually cause the grace that they signify; they merely provide the occasion for God alone to cause it (*ST* III.61.1 co.; Holtz 2012: 452–453). Aquinas rejects this occasionalist view on the grounds that Scripture and many saints teach that the sacraments of the New Law—that is, those of the Christian Church—both signify and somehow cause grace. But again, how?

Invoking the Aristotelian distinction between a principal efficient cause and an instrumental efficient cause, Aquinas argues that the sacraments are instrumental causes of grace. A principal efficient cause operates by the power of its own form, and makes its effect similar to itself—as, for instance, fire makes something hot by its own heat. Only God can cause grace in this way, according to Aquinas, "because grace is nothing other than a certain participated likeness of the divine nature, according to 2 Pet. 1[:4], *He has given us great and precious promises so that we might be sharers of the divine nature*" (III.61.1 co.). An instrumental efficient cause, by contrast, does not operate by the power of its own form, but only by the movement of the principal agent. As a result, the effect is not made similar to the instrument, but rather to the principal agent. To use Aquinas's own example, a bed is not similar to the ax by which it is made, but rather to the art (of woodworking) in the mind of the artist. The sacraments cause grace in this way, in Aquinas's view, "for they are employed according to divine ordination for the purpose of causing grace" (III.61.1 co.). Just as a woodworker makes use of the proper action of an ax (namely to cut wood) when she uses it as an artistic instrument to build a bed, so too in the sacraments God makes use of the proper actions of visible signs such as water and bread and wine (namely to wash and to nourish the body, respectively) to effect instrumental operations (namely washing and nourishing) in incorporeal souls (III.61.1 ad 2). Thus, God can produce supernatural, spiritual effects through natural, material objects.

Postmodern theology of the last several decades, influenced by the German philosopher Martin Heidegger, is characterized by an insistence on the cultural and linguistic mediation of all doctrine and by the rejection of classical metaphysics. Postmodern theologians have critiqued what they have dubbed the "ontotheology" of the Church Fathers and scholastic theologians for, among other failures, having reduced the mystery of God to a being or first cause and for having interpreted the sacraments according to an impersonal model of mechanistic production (Blankenhorn 2006: 255–256). The French sacramental theologian Louis-Marie Chauvet has criticized Aquinas's understanding of the sacraments as instrumental causes of grace precisely on these grounds. For Chauvet, the fundamental problem is that Aquinas depersonalizes and objectifies sacred liturgical signs, representing "the relation of humans to God in the sacraments … according to the technical and productionist scheme of instrumentality and causality" (Chauvet 1995: 44; Holtz 2012: 453–454). According to this scheme, which is—in Chauvet's view—foreign to the order of love, the sacraments, acting as instrumental causes, produce grace. Grace, then is necessarily understood as a *product*, an impersonal object of value. For Chauvet, however, God's grace defies the logic of objective production and the marketplace: indeed, divine graciousness is a "non-value" (Chauvet 1995: 45; Blankenhorn 2006: 258). Finally, Chauvet critiques Aquinas's understanding that the power of the sacraments, as separated instruments, flows from the hypostatic union and from God's salvific operation through the conjoined instrument of the Word's human nature. Indeed, Chauvet denies that such a metaphysical sacramental theology can be "inserted into the movement of concrete history" (Chauvet 1995: 456; Blankenhorn 2006: 259).

But does Chauvet properly capture Aquinas's understanding of sacramental causality and its connection to the Incarnation? Let's take a closer look. To the objection that the power of causing grace cannot be in the sacraments because a spiritual power cannot be in a body, Aquinas offers an *interpersonal* example of how a body can, in fact, be moved instrumentally by a spiritual substance in order to produce a particular spiritual effect. "In the sensible voice itself," he explains, "there is a certain spiritual power, inasmuch as it proceeds from a mental concept, for arousing the understanding of a human [hearer]" (III.62.4 ad 1). Just as God has ordained a human speaker's voice to be moved by her own mind for the sake of causing understanding in the mind of her hearer, so too has God ordained the sacraments as instruments of various spiritual effects in their recipients. In neither of these cases is the spiritual power in the body as something perfect and proper to it; only in the principal efficient cause (namely the speaker's mind and God, respectively) does the spiritual power exist in this way. Rather, the spiritual power has being in the sacraments, as in a speaker's voice, instrumentally, that is, in an incomplete way as it passes from one into another (III.62.4 co.; III.62.3 co., ad 1, ad 3). Once uttered, the audible word quickly passes away; but it remains and takes effect in the hearer's mind.

As his analogy of human communication suggests, then, Aquinas understands the instrumental causality of the sacraments not as mechanistic and productional, but rather as essentially and profoundly personal, both *interpersonal* and *intrapersonal*. The sacraments are interpersonal in that they are divine acts whereby God applies the saving work of Christ, the second person of the Trinity, to persons of faith in the Church. They are also intrapersonal in that they realize in the members of Christ's own body, the Church, what is fully realized in its head (Holtz 2012: 454). Indeed, as John Yocum observes, Aquinas understands the sacraments as efficacious signs of Christ's own theandric words and deeds for human salvation:

> The sacraments are means by which the Word himself speaks and acts within and through the ritual actions of his body, just as the incarnate Word spoke and acted within and through the organ of his human nature, to bring human beings to their divinely ordained end of perfect worship.
>
> (Yocum 2004: 159)

EUCHARIST

Aquinas had completed and revised his *Summa contra Gentiles* by the autumn of 1265, just prior to the time he began to write the *ST* (Davies 2016b: 8–9). This means that he set his earlier systematic treatment of the Eucharist—found in *ScG* IV.61–68—to parchment approximately a half century after the Fourth Lateran Council (1215). Under the leadership of Pope Innocent III, Lateran IV aimed at unifying religious belief and practice throughout Christendom. Toward this end, the Council anathematized all heretics and their doctrinal positions once and for all (can. 3), for example, and promulgated a series of canons intended to limit the public presence and sphere of influence of Jews. Jews were to be distinguished from Christians in their dress and prohibited from appearing in public during Holy Week (can. 68), for instance; they were also prevented from holding public office (can. 69) and practicing usury (can. 67), and forbidden to return to the practice of their Jewish faith if they had converted to Christianity (can. 70). Additionally, the bishops at Lateran IV sought to formulate Christian teaching clearly and definitively, as is exemplified by the doctrine of transubstantiation.

Transubstantiation seeks to explain the mode of Christ's true presence in the Eucharist, insofar as this sacred mystery can be understood and explained, of course. It is the medieval Church's answer to the question, 'How is it that Christ truly becomes present in the eucharistic bread and wine?' The basic answer it provides is found in its very name, 'Transubstantiation,' which literally means change in substance or substantial change. What the Church holds by faith is that at the moment of consecration (i.e., when the priest or minister pronounces the words "This is my body ..."), by the power and working of the Holy Spirit, the substance of the eucharistic elements, bread and wine, is changed into the substance of Christ's body and blood, though the accidents of the bread and wine remain unchanged. After the consecration, the elements still look, feel, smell, and taste like ordinary bread and wine, but the real substance that stands beneath these accidental properties has been transformed into Christ's own body and blood. The Church first officially promulgated this doctrine at Lateran IV thus: "[Christ's] body and blood are truly contained in the sacrament of the altar under the appearances [*sub speciebus*] of bread and wine, the bread having been transubstantiated [*transsubstantiatis*] into the body and the wine into blood by divine power" (Tanner 1990, 1: 230).

We must note at the outset that Aquinas takes this teaching—that Christ is really, substantially present in the Eucharist—as an article of faith, a truth revealed by God in Scripture and clarified by the Church's tradition, especially at Lateran IV. Thus, we humans can neither sensibly apprehend this truth nor can we arrive at it by natural reason. Without revelation and faith, both of which Aquinas takes to be supernatural gifts from God, no human could grasp the truth of transubstantiation at all. This is precisely why Aquinas begins his treatment of the Eucharist in *ScG* IV with Sacred Scripture, specifically with Christ's own words in ch. 6 of John's Gospel: "My flesh is meat indeed, and my blood is drink indeed" (Jn. 6:56; *ScG* IV.61). And to make clear his own recognition of the difficulty of Christ's teaching here, Aquinas also notes that some of Jesus' own disciples were troubled and responded, "This is a hard saying, and who can bear it?" (Jn. 6:61; *ScG* IV.62). Whereas Brian Davies (2016: 367) has described Aquinas's treatment of the Eucharist here as "polemical" against "the errors of the infidels," the Dominican master's emphasis on Christ's disciples in Jn. 6 suggests that his teaching in *ScG* IV.61–68 is aimed at 'insiders' striving to understand this hard saying of their Lord and of their Church. "Some are led to disagree on account of the many difficulties that seem to follow this teaching of the Church,"

Aquinas observes (IV.62). Indeed, in commenting on the alternative title of the *ScG, The Book on the Truth of the Catholic Faith against the Errors of Unbelievers*, Joseph Wawrykow (2005b: 146) explains that "infidels" or "unbelievers" (*infideles*) is a rather fluid term for Aquinas: "Unbelief can take different forms, running from those who know or accept little of what falls under the Christian faith, to those who are Christians but who differ from the orthodox on some crucial aspect of the faith." The "unbelievers" Aquinas has in view here are principally of this second sort, and his approach to the Eucharist is that of a theologian or practitioner of wisdom, who engages in the twofold task of proclaiming the truth of faith and defending it against detractors (see *ScG* I.1). He is well aware that because it is an article of faith, the truth of Christ's real presence in the Eucharist, and transubstantiation as its mode, cannot be rationally demonstrated or proven. But neither can it be disproven. In fact, because such a revealed truth is above reason but not contrary to it, Aquinas can employ the tools of reason to answer any objections that reason might raise against this truth and to show that what this article of faith holds is not impossible.

Throughout our introduction to Aquinas, we have focused our attention largely on his mature theological thought as found in the *ST*. But because his treatment of the Eucharist in *ScG* IV exemplifies what Aquinas himself teaches concerning the mode of sacred doctrine and the proper approach of the theologian to arguments proposed against faith—namely that they are difficulties to be answered (*ST* I.1.8 ad 2; *ScG* I.2)—we will conclude our study of the basics of Aquinas's theology with a close, albeit cursory, reading of *ScG* IV.61–68.

PHILOSOPHICAL AND SENSIBLE DIFFICULTIES

Aquinas takes seriously the various philosophical and sensible difficulties that the eucharistic teaching of Christ and the Church might raise in the minds of believers and unbelievers alike. He classifies these difficulties in five general categories:

1 Problems concerning how Christ's body begins to be on the altar.
2 Problems concerning place.

3   Problems concerning perception.
4   Problems concerning actions and passions.
5   Problems concerning fraction.

First, there is the problem of how the true body of Christ begins to be on the altar in a church. Something can begin to be where it previously was not in one of two ways, Aquinas explains: either by local motion (that is, by moving from one place to another), or by being converted or changed from something else. Fire, for example, can either be carried from this place to that, or it can be kindled anew in that particular place (*ScG* IV.62). It seems to human reason, however, that Christ's body becomes present on the altar in neither of these ways. Local motion appears to be excluded, Aquinas acknowledges, because it necessitates a thing's beginning to be in one place in such a way that it is not in another. Thus, if Christ's body moved onto this or that altar on which the Eucharist was being celebrated, it would necessarily move from heaven, where it now remains, according to the Church's profession. Furthermore, if Christ were present on this particular eucharistic altar (in Boston, let us say), He could not also be present on any other eucharistic altar (in London or Los Angeles, for instance) at the same time. "But it is clear that this sacrament is celebrated on different altars simultaneously," Aquinas teaches (IV.62). Just as local motion seems impossible, so too does conversion as an explanation of how Christ's body begins to be on the altar. If something begins to be by conversion, that very same something cannot have existed prior to the conversion. If yesterday a heap of ashes came to exist where my outdoor woodpile had stood for the past three years because a lightning strike set all of my wood aflame, that precise ash heap could not have existed there last week, prior to the process of combustion by which my woodpile was converted into it. If, on the other hand, the ash heap had been there a week ago, it cannot be said that it was a product of a combustive conversion just yesterday. Similarly, because the body of Christ existed from the moment of His conception in the womb of the Blessed Virgin Mary, it seems impossible that these elements of bread and wine could be converted into Christ's body on this or that altar today.

The second class of difficulties pertains to place, and Aquinas describes three such problems. The first is what we will call the problem of 'the separated Savior.' If Christ's body exists "under the appearance [*sub specie*]" of the eucharistic bread and Christ's blood exists "under the appearance" of the wine, it seems as if Christ does not remain whole in the sacrament on account of the fact that what appear to be bread and wine continue to exist in different places. The second difficulty concerning place is what we might dub the problem of 'large body, small bread.' It seems impossible, Aquinas explains, that the true body of Christ be whole and entire where the eucharistic bread appears since Christ's body is of a greater quantity than the bread offered on the altar (IV.62). How can the whole of Christ's rather large body 'fit' under the appearance of relatively small portions of bread? The third problem of place, which we can describe as 'one body, many breads,' is the flip side, as it were, of the second. The difficulty here is that the single, relatively small body of Christ seems unable to exist under the appearance of many portions of bread on many different altars simultaneously. Even if Christ's body were divided into parts (which would return us to the first class of difficulties), it is not sufficiently large to be 'distributed across' all the places where the sacrament is celebrated and all the portions of bread in which He is believed to be present.

The third set of problems has to do with our sensible perception. "For clearly in this sacrament," Aquinas observes, "even after the consecration, we perceive all the accidents of bread and wine, namely color, taste, smell, shape, quantity, and weight" (IV.62). According to Aristotle's understanding, accidents exist only by inhering in their proper subject: they cannot exist in themselves (*per se*), nor can they exist in a subject or substance that is not their own. My particular height—a measure of what Aristotle would call quantity (in this case vertical extension)— cannot exist in my wife or in my son. If my wife or my son were, in fact, the same height as I am, this height would be, in either of them respectively, her or his height. But *my* height is an accidental feature of *me*, and so it must inhere in the particular substance that is me. Similarly, my height cannot exist or subsist *per se*, on its own apart from me. So if you should ever see my height walking to the grocery store or attending an academic conference without me, please let me know immediately! Similarly, the accidents of bread and wine that we perceive after the consecration must inhere in their proper substances, bread and wine respectively. They cannot inhere in the substances of Christ's body and blood, nor can they subsist in themselves without any substance whatsoever. It seems, then, that after the eucharistic consecration, the substances of bread and wine, whose proper accidents we accurately perceive, remain.

Closely related to these problems of perception is the fourth category of difficulties, that pertaining to the actions and passions of the eucharistic elements. Specifically, the consecrated bread and wine seem to do and to suffer no differently than they did and suffered prior to consecration. Concerning their actions, the consecrated bread—if a sufficiently large quantity were ingested—would strengthen and nourish the communicant, and the consecrated wine would warm and intoxicate him. As for their passions, the consecrated bread and wine—if not properly stored or guarded—may suffer rotting, be burned to ashes, or even be consumed by mice! Appearing to recognize the persuasive power of this objection, Aquinas affirms: "[But] none of these [passions] can be fitting for the body of Christ, since faith proclaims that it is impassible. It seems impossible, therefore, that Christ's body is contained substantially in this sacrament" (IV.62). It is noteworthy that this philosophical difficulty is partially built on—and indeed strengthened by—a truth proclaimed by faith, namely the impassibility of Christ's body, resurrected and glorified as it now is. Similarly, as intimated above, the first class of difficulties partially depends on two other articles of faith: the divine Incarnation and Christ's bodily Ascension into heaven. That Aquinas introduces such articles of faith as foundational to objections raised against the Church's eucharistic doctrine strongly suggests that his audience consists of people who intend themselves as Christians, even if they have lapsed into heresy concerning the Eucharist.

The fifth difficulty, akin to the third and fourth, concerns the breaking or fraction of the consecrated bread. This breaking appears sensibly and cannot be without a subject, but it seems absurd to affirm that the subject of this breaking is the substance of Christ's body. It appears, then, that the subject of the fraction is the substance of ordinary bread, and that the body of Christ is not present substantially.

ANSWERING THE DIFFICULTIES

Having briefly described each of these difficulties, Aquinas imme-diately offers a statement of how he will (and will not) proceed to deal with them:

> Although, of course, the divine power operates with a greater sub-limity and secrecy in this sacrament than a human can investigate, nevertheless, lest the Church's teaching concerning this sacrament seem impossible to unbelievers, we must try to exclude every impossibility.
>
> (*ScG* IV.63)

These words align well with what Aquinas says in *ST* I.1.8 con-cerning the theologian's method regarding articles of faith (see Chapter 2). The theologian does not—indeed, cannot—prove the articles by reason; God's secret working in the Eucharist, for instance, is inaccessible to the scrutiny of human reason. This also means, of course, that the opponent or unbeliever cannot demonstrate that what faith teaches is erroneous. She can only propose difficulties for a particular teaching of faith, which diffi-culties the theologian can then attempt to answer. This is precisely what Aquinas aims to do in *ScG* IV.63–67: to answer each of the five classes of difficulties that would seem to render impossible the Church's eucharistic doctrine. Let's look in on the Dominican theologian at work.

In answer to the first difficulty, concerning how Christ's body begins to be on the altar, Aquinas grants the impossibility of local motion. If Christ became present on the altar by moving from a certain place, He would cease to be present in heaven, the Eucharist could be celebrated in only one place at any particular time, and Christ could not become present instantaneously when the minister pronounces the words of institution (IV.63). Again, notice that Aquinas upholds the impossibility of local motion on account of certain truths of faith with which it seems to conflict, namely Christ's Ascension into heaven, His bodily presence at many eucharistic celebrations throughout the world simulta-neously, and the instantaneous presence of His body whenever a proper minister vocalizes the proper words. We see, then, that the objection here is not purely philosophical, but rather is rooted in important teachings of Christian faith. This explains why Aquinas takes this objection so seriously and even agrees with it.

Local motion having been deemed impossible, the only remaining possibility is that Christ begins to be present on the altar by some sort of conversion. For Aquinas, God has revealed infallibly that conversion is indeed the true mode of Christ's coming-to-be in the Eucharist, and that the proper name of this conversion is transubstantiation. His aim here, then, is a rather modest one: to show that this substantial change is not impossible for God. Aquinas assumes, of course, that nothing is impossible for God. Well, almost nothing—to fail to exist would be impossible for God, as would to lie or to commit some other sin. But nothing that requires or manifests real power, rather than a lack of power (such as not existing or lying), is impossible for God. To transubstantiate ordinary bread and wine into Christ's body and blood requires real power and so is possible for God, although such a mysterious divine work easily outstrips the natural capacity of human comprehension. In short, it is beyond reason. "It is clear, however, that God can do more in operation than the intellect can do in apprehension," Aquinas teaches (IV.65).

God can also do more in operation than nature can. Specifically, God can convert one substance (bread) into another substance (Christ's body). But such substantial conversion is not merely beyond nature; indeed, what happens here is the opposite of what occurs in a natural conversion (IV.63). The process of human aging exemplifies what Aquinas calls a natural or formal conversion. To see this for yourself, try to find a photo of yourself as a toddler or young child, 3 or 5 years old perhaps. If you compare your appearance at the present moment—whether you are now 15 years old or 95, or somewhere in between—to that photo, you will likely notice a number of rather dramatic 'accidental' changes: you are now taller, wider, and heavier than you were then; you have more—or perhaps less—hair; your hair may be a different color; your ears and nose are bigger; and you may even have grown facial hair. Although these various accidental qualities of yourself have changed over the years, the substance that is you—which we will call _____-ness (supply your name here)—has remained unchanged. You are the same person with the same substance, _____-ness, whose (very different) accidents were captured in that photo years ago. In the supernatural, substantial conversion called transubstantiation, by contrast, the subject or substance of bread is changed into that of Christ's body, while the accidents of bread remain unchanged, and the substance of wine is changed into that of Christ's blood, while the accidents of wine persist (IV.63). Because every operation of nature presupposes matter, which is the principle of individuation of a substance, nature cannot change one substance (my right index finger, for example) into another (my left big toe). But because matter is subject to divine power, which brings it into being, it is possible by divine power that this individual substance be converted to another that existed prior to the conversion (IV.63). Therefore, although the substance of Christ's body came into being in Mary's womb over 2,000 years before a celebration of the Eucharist that takes place at St. Joseph Church in Kalamazoo Michigan today, God—who is Lord over all matter and all substances—can change the bread on the altar at St. Joseph into this selfsame body of Christ.

We might rightly ask why, once the substances of bread and wine have been converted to those of body and blood, the accidents of bread and wine should persist. Why doesn't God also convert the accidents of bread and wine into those of Christ's body and blood, such that Christ would appear on the altar according to His ordinary mode of being (as is depicted in Robert Campin's *The Mass of St. Gregory*)? It seems, after all, that this minor adjustment in divine operation would bear much fruit among humans in facilitating greater understanding of and inculcating deeper faith in Christ's real presence in the Eucharist. Aquinas's profoundly theological vantage point, however, enables him to see this issue differently than we might. That Christ's body remains hidden under the accidents of bread respects the nature of faith, whose object is always something unseen (cf. Heb. 11:1). The invisibility of Christ's body also promotes the merit of faith in the sacrament (*ScG* IV.63; *ST* III.75.5 co.). Furthermore, Aquinas suggests that something from before the conversion should remain afterwards— namely the accidents of bread and wine—so that believers might understand that a substantial conversion has occurred and that the body of Christ now occupies, through the mediation of the bread's dimensions, the place once filled by the bread (*ScG* IV.63). Finally, it is "more suitable" and "more honorable" that the faithful should receive Christ's body and blood under the appearance of bread and wine, common food and drink, than under their own appearances. It would be horrible for communicants and an abomination to onlookers, Aquinas declares, if Christ's flesh and blood were consumed under their proper accidents (*ScG* IV.63; *ST* III.75.5 co.)!

When Aquinas comes to the second class of difficulties, those pertaining to place, he draws a critically important distinction that enables him easily to answer the problem of 'the separated Savior.' The distinction is between what is in the sacrament "by the power of the conversion [*ex vi conversionis*]," on the one hand, and what is in the sacrament "by natural concomitance [*ex naturali concomitantia*]" (*ScG* IV.64). What is in the Eucharist by the power of the conversion is that in which the conversion directly terminates, namely Christ's body under the appearance of bread (hence the words of consecration, "This is my body") and Christ's blood under the appearance of wine (hence, "This is the chalice of my blood"). In the Eucharist by natural concomitance are those things in which the conversion does not terminate directly, but which are "really conjoined" to that in which it does terminate directly. For example, the conversion of the bread directly terminates in Christ's body, which is therefore present under the appearance of bread by the force of the conversion, but Christ's blood, soul, and divinity are also present under the appearance of bread by natural concomitance because they are truly conjoined to Christ's body by the hypostatic union (and again by the resurrection after the three days of death). Now Christ's blood, soul, and divinity always naturally exist together with or accompany His body. Likewise, the conversion of the wine directly terminates in Christ's blood, but Christ's body, soul, and divinity are also present under the appearance of wine by natural concomitance. With this distinction in hand, Aquinas shows that although the appearance of the bread remains separate from that of the wine, the whole Christ—body, blood, soul, and divinity—is present under each species.

This distinction between power of conversion and natural concomitance, together with that between substance and accidents, also enables Aquinas to answer the second and third problems of place, which we have called 'large body, small bread' and 'one body, many breads,' respectively. To the first of these, Aquinas responds that the dimensions of Christ's body are in this sacrament by natural concomitance and not by the power of the conversion, since the dimensions that remain after consecration are those of the bread. Indeed, what it means to affirm that Christ is substantially present under the species of bread is, in part, that His body is mediated by the dimensions of the bread offered on the altar, however small those dimensions might be, and not by its own (relatively large) dimensions (IV.64). This point also enables Aquinas to resolve the 'one body, many breads' problem. The body of Christ exists in only one place with its own proper dimensions mediating: heaven. With the dimensions of bread mediating, however, Christ's body exists wholly under the species of every portion of consecrated bread on every altar in every church throughout the world where the Eucharist is properly celebrated (IV.64). It is estimated that in our time more than 350,000 Masses are celebrated each day on planet earth! This, of course, makes for innumerable 'accidental manifestations' of bread, beneath each of which the one Christ is hidden from view.

Aquinas answers the third class of difficulties, concerning our perception of what appears to be ordinary bread and wine after the consecration, by emphasizing the supernatural power of divine operation in the Eucharist. Although, as we have seen, God is the Prime Mover or primary cause of all effects in the universe, He ordinarily acts by means of natural, secondary causes. Customarily, for example, God operates as the primary cause of a new human being through the secondary causality of the reproductive union of a mature male and female human. Similarly, God acts to heal an infection in the human body through the body's own natural immune response, by a fever, for instance. That God works through secondary causes is not, for Aquinas, a sign of divine weakness, as if God somehow needs such created causes in order to carry out His tasks in the world. Rather it is a manifestation of "the immensity of His goodness, through which He has willed to communicate His own likeness to [created] things, not only inasmuch as they are but also inasmuch as they are causes of other things" (ScG III.70). This is precisely what it means to call natural causes 'secondary,' namely that God gives them their power to act (IV.65). Although God has chosen ordinarily to work through such secondary causes, however, He is by no means bound by them. "Divine power can produce the effects of any secondary causes whatsoever without the secondary causes themselves," Aquinas teaches (IV.65). In the Eucharist, for example, God can conserve the accidents of bread and wine in being without the presence of the proper subjects, the substances of bread and wine, in which these accidents naturally inhere. This is schematized in Table 9.1.

Although God does more in this eucharistic conversion than the human observer can do in apprehension, Aquinas's aim is to show that such divine action is not, in fact, impossible. He does this by identifying two comparable examples of God's extraordinary, supernatural operation: "He was able to form a human without seed, and to heal a fever without the operation of nature" (IV.65). Aquinas says nothing more about either of these examples, and so the reader may be left wondering, 'When did God do these things, and how are we to know that He did them?' The reader familiar with Scripture, however, will recall that Adam and Eve and the human Christ were formed without human seed (Gen. 2:7, 21–23; Lk. 1:26–35). And each of the four Gospels recounts how Christ miraculously healed those suffering from fever (Mt. 8:14–15; Mk. 1:30–31; Lk. 4:38–39; Jn. 4:46–53). In all of these cases, the ordinary secondary cause is not operative; and so these divine acts are necessarily beyond sensible apprehension and natural reason. That Aquinas would offer such miraculous divine acts as evidence supporting the possibility of God's secret operation in the Eucharist may, at first glance, seem strange. They are not rational demonstrations, of course. Rather, they are answers based on the authority of divine revelation to an objection brought against faith (*ST* I.1.8).

Aquinas's response to the fourth category of difficulties, concerning how the consecrated elements act and suffer, is an extension of his answer to the third. On account of the fact that the accidents of bread and wine persist after consecration, Aquinas

Table 9.1 God's supernatural operation in the eucharist

	Primary cause	Secondary cause	Effect
Before consecration	GOD	Substances of bread and wine	Accidents of bread and wine
After consecration	GOD		Accidents of bread and wine

explains, it seems "sufficiently fitting" that the actions and passions of bread and wine would also remain. This is so, in particular, because the sensible qualities of bread and wine, which are the principles of their actions and passions, are among the persisting accidents (*ScG* IV.66, 63). Although he certainly recognizes the miraculous nature of accidents persisting without their proper substance, Aquinas also seeks to show that this reality can be considered philosophically. Because dimensional quantity is the accident that inheres most closely to its proper substance, the qualities of that substance that are the principles of its actions and passions are received into the subject with quantity mediating. Thus, according to Aquinas, one should hold that quantity is the only accident that, properly speaking, persists without a substance or subject after the eucharistic conversion on account of the fact that all the qualities "are established on it as if on a subject" (IV.63, 66). Aquinas's explanation here intends to convince readers that transubstantiation is not impossible. After such attempts at philosophical insight into this sacred mystery, however, Aquinas closes by having recourse to divine miracle:

> [J]ust as the substance of bread is miraculously converted into the body of Christ, so too it is miraculously conferred on the accidents that they subsist, which is proper to substance, and that they can do and suffer all the things that the substance could do and suffer if the substance were present.
>
> (*ScG* IV.66)

Aquinas provides a brief answer to the fifth and final difficulty, that of the breaking of the consecrated bread, by drawing on the previously established notion that dimensional quantity is the primary accident, which uniquely subsists without a subject. He affirms:

> It is clear, moreover, according to what has been said, that we can identify the subject of the breaking as the dimensions subsisting in themselves (*per se*). Nevertheless, when the dimensions of this sort are broken, the substance of Christ's body is not broken, because the whole body of Christ remains under every portion [of the bread].
>
> (*ScG* IV.67)

To aid his reader's understanding, Aquinas offers two ordinary examples illustrating how, if some substance is whole in something whole, this same substance is also whole in each part of the whole. Because the whole nature or substance of water is in water—the whole Atlantic Ocean, for instance—this same substance will be in every portion or drop of water that might be taken from the Atlantic. Similarly, because the whole rational soul is in the whole human body, the whole soul is also in every part of the (living) body (IV.67). In the Eucharist, then, just as the whole substance of bread is in the bread and in every portion of the bread prior to consecration, so too after the conversion the whole substance of Christ's body is under the dimensional quantity of the bread and, after fraction, under the dimensions of every portion, however small. Thus, the breaking of the consecrated bread or the division of the consecrated wine never "reaches to" Christ's body and blood, Aquinas explains, because the dimensions of bread and wine always remain the subject of this breaking or division (IV.67).

Having answered the five classes of difficulties proposed against transubstantiation, Aquinas closes with this summary statement: "Therefore, with these difficulties removed, it is clear that what ecclesiastical tradition holds concerning the sacrament of the altar contains nothing impossible for God, who can do all things" (IV.68). We might observe, in concluding our own consideration of the basics of Aquinas's theology, that the Dominican master's words here reach well beyond the Eucharist and provide an apt summary of his understanding of sacred doctrine generally and of the articles of faith specifically. Although preambles of faith— God's existence and oneness, for example—can be demonstrated by natural reason, the articles of faith—such as Trinity, creation, and Incarnation—cannot be apprehended by humans without divine revelation and the gift of faith. That the articles are beyond natural reason means, on the one hand, that they cannot be proven; it also means, on the other hand, that they cannot be disproven. Against unbelievers who may raise objections to what the articles affirm, the best the theologian can do is to answer the objections in the hopes of showing that what ecclesiastical tradition holds contains nothing impossible for God.

GLOSSARY OF KEY TERMS

Anthropomorphism   Understanding or interpreting what is not human or personal in terms of human or personal characteristics. Many modern theologians, philosophers of religion, and ordinary believers understand God in more or less anthropomorphic terms, as an all-powerful, incorporeal, and invisible person. Aquinas rejects all such anthropomorphic notions of God, claiming that God is neither a person with certain characteristics nor a being among or alongside beings in the universe. God is of a completely different order than every creature. See also: apophaticism; character-theism; simplicity.

Apophaticism   Negative theology, in contradistinction to kataphaticism or positive theology; a way of coming to know God by understanding what He is not. Aquinas's approach to God is thoroughly apophatic and inferential. According to Aquinas, we humans do not and cannot naturally have any positive idea of what God is. We can naturally come to know something of God only by denying that God is composed in any of the ways that creatures are composed and thus positively known. See also: kataphaticism; simplicity.

Arianism   The Christological teaching, first proposed by the Alexandrian presbyter Arius in the fourth century, that the Son of God is not eternally begotten of the Father and therefore of the same substance as the Father, but rather was begotten in time and is thus a creature who is subordinate to God the Father. In 325 the Council of Nicaea, the first ecumenical council, condemned Arianism as heresy and affirmed that the Son is homoousios ("of the same substance" or "one in being") with the Father. In Aquinas's view, Arius's fundamental theological mistake was assuming that procession in God is, like creaturely procession, an outward motion and that, as such, the Son was an effect proceeding externally and temporally from His cause, the divine Father (*ST* I.27.1).

Articles of faith   One of two types of truth that constitute sacred doctrine, according to Aquinas (the other being preambles of faith). Articles of faith are those truths about God—such as the Trinity, Incarnation, and bodily resurrection—that exceed the capacity of human reason. They cannot be proved demonstratively, nor can they be disproved. They are above reason (suprarational), but not contrary to it (not irrational). Because humans cannot arrive at them by natural reason, they must be revealed by God in order to be apprehended at all. Apprehension of the articles also requires the supernatural gift of faith, the first of the theological virtues, which elevates the human's rational capacity beyond its nature such that it is able grasp these unseen realities. See also: preambles of faith; sacred doctrine.

Aseity   The quality or state, traditionally attributed to God, of being originated or derived "from oneself" (*a se*). Because God exists simply and eternally, without any cause whatsoever, divine aseity is generally taken to mean not that God is an effect caused by or from Himself. Rather, aseity signifies that God is entirely self-sufficient and self-existent, lacking dependence on anything other than Himself. In this way God is radically different from all creatures, which necessarily depend on God for their being, life, and natural operations. See also: esse.

Beatific vision   The final goal or ultimate end for which God has created and ordained human beings, according to Aquinas. Having been created uniquely in the image of God—with a rational soul whereby they can know and love—humans are ordered to the supernatural end of knowing or seeing God as He is (Jn. 17:3; 1 Jn. 3:2). Their perfect happiness or beatitude, then, consists in this vision of the divine essence, which is possible for ordinary or pure humans only in heavenly glory (*ST* I-II.3.8; I.12.11). Furthermore, it is possible for pure humans in the next life only because Jesus Christ, who was no ordinary human, enjoyed the beatific vision in His human soul from the moment of conception and throughout His earthly life. See also: happiness; pure human.

Character-theism   Belief in the existence of God as a person, more or less like human persons, who possesses certain character traits, such as power, knowledge, goodness, creativity, love, and mercy. In conceiving of God, many modern theologians, philosophers, and ordinary believers begin with such character traits in humans and then envisage God as the being who possesses these attributes in the highest degree. Aquinas, by contrast, teaches that humans can naturally have no positive idea of what God is; rather, we can only know what God is not. See also: kataphaticism.

Christology   The area of theology concerned with the person and work of Jesus Christ. Aquinas sets forth his mature Christology in *ST* III.1–59, which he divides into two major sections: qq. 1–26 treat the mystery of the Incarnation, whereby God was made human for our salvation, whereas qq. 27–59 concern those things that the Word incarnate did and suffered for human redemption. As this basic twofold division suggests, Aquinas is always and everywhere concerned, when treating Christ, with His role and work as Savior of humankind; in order words, Aquinas's Christology has a profoundly soteriological orientation. See also: soteriology.

Dominican Order   Also known as the Order of Preachers, the Dominican Order is a Catholic mendicant ("begging") religious order founded by St. Dominic of Guzman in 1215 in southern France with the purpose of saving souls through learned preaching. In the spring of 1244 Aquinas joined the Dominican Order, whose educational mission he served for the rest of his life by teaching theology in Cologne, Paris, Naples, Orvieto, and Rome.

Esse   Aptly rendered as "being" or "to-be," this Latin term is used by Aquinas to denote a thing's act of existence or being. According to Aquinas, God is *ipsum esse subsistens*, "subsistent being itself"—thus, God necessarily exists; He cannot not be. What it means to be God is to be *esse*, that is, to be to-be or existence itself. God's essence, then, is His existence. In every creature, by contrast, essence and *esse* are distinct. Because creatures, in Aquinas's view, do not have *esse* essentially, they require God to grant them being (*esse*) and to conserve them in being (*in esse*) at every moment. See also: aseity; essence.

Essence   The nature or "whatness" of a being or thing, by which it is the type of being or thing it is. For example, human nature, constituted of a body animated by a rational soul, is the essence of all pure or ordinary human beings. Aquinas teaches that in all creatures there is a real distinction between essence (*essentia*) and existence or to-be (*esse*). In God, by contrast, *essentia* is identical to *esse*. To be God is to be existence itself. For Aquinas, this basic truth underlies the doctrines of divine simplicity and creation. See also: esse; quiddity; simplicity.

Eutychianism A monophysite or one-nature Christology that takes its name from the ancient Constantinopolitan presbyter Eutyches and was condemned as heretical by the Council of Chalcedon in 451. Eutyches appears to have taught that divinity and humanity were mixed in Christ such that He was somehow of or from two natures before the union but in only one (divine) nature after it. Emphasizing the unity of Christ's nature over against the Christological teaching of Nestorius, Eutyches imagined that the divine nature overwhelmed or consumed the human nature such that Jesus was of the same substance as the Father but not of the same substance as humanity. See also: hypostatic union; Nestorianism.

Exitus-reditus the Neoplatonic scheme of creaturely emanation from and return to God that, according to Marie-Dominique Chenu, constitutes the architectonic plan of Aquinas's *ST*. Although *exitus-reditus* has gained nearly unanimous acceptance among Thomists today as the organizing principle underlying the basic tripartite division of the *ST*, a few scholars have identified fundamental problems with *exitus-reditus* and suggested alternate schemes.

Faith an infused intellectual virtue that perfects and elevates the natural powers of human apprehension, causing the intellect to assent to truths about God that are unseen or unknowable by natural reason alone. For Aquinas, faith is thus an anticipation of the beatific vision and the beginning of eternal life in the believer even now. It is the first of the theological virtues (the others being hope and charity), supernatural principles of human action that God pours into the human soul with habitual grace in order to direct humans to perfect happiness. See also: beatific vision; happiness.

Fittingness (convenientia) a mode of reasoning common in scholastic theology according to which the theologian accepts a particular supernatural truth revealed by God—that God is a Trinity of persons or that God became incarnate, for instance—and seeks to show how it is 'appropriate' or 'suitable' given other truths about God. Common throughout the *ST*, fittingness arguments are of central significance in Aquinas's Christology and soteriology. They aim to highlight the order, wisdom, and beauty of the divine dispensation.

Five Ways Aquinas sets forth his famous Five Ways (*quinque viae*) or proofs for the existence of God in *ST* I.2.3. The Five Ways are: (1) the proof from motion; (2) the proof from efficient causality; (3) the proof from contingency and necessity; (4) the proof from gradation of being; and (5) the proof from the governance of things. Although modern readers often mistake the Five Ways as (unconvincing) scientific proofs, Aquinas intends them as meta-scientific or meta-physical demonstrations of divine existence.

Happiness   The ultimate perfection or happiness (*beatitudo*) of human beings consists, in Aquinas's view, in their ultimate intellectual act, namely seeing or knowing God as He is (Jn. 17:3; 1 Jn. 3:2). This beatific vision, an operation of the speculative intellect, is above human nature and is possible for ordinary humans (*puri homines*) only in the next life. As such, its attainment requires that God perfect human nature by 'superadding' grace in this life and glory in the next. Through the divine gift of grace and the practice of the virtues in this life, humans can have some share in the perfect happiness of the beatific vision even now.

Human actions   those actions, according to Aquinas, that humans perform by virtue of their self-mastery—that is, those actions that are willed on the basis of rational deliberation—and that lead humans to happiness. For Aquinas, in contrast to many modern thinkers, such authentic human actions are never in competition with divine action. On the contrary, that human beings perform voluntary actions rooted in rational thought requires God on several levels, namely as creator and providential governor, as prime mover or first efficient cause, and as the Highest Good or final cause.

Hylomorphism   the Aristotelian doctrine that all corporeal beings are constituted of form and matter. Form is the definition or essence of a thing, what actualizes the potential of matter, causing it to become a definite thing. Matter, by contrast, signifies the potential to be a definite thing, a potential that form actualizes. According to Aquinas, the rational or intellectual soul is the form of the human being, that which actualizes the potential of the matter that is the body.

Hypostatic union   the union of the divine and human natures of Christ in a single hypostasis or person, namely the divine Son or Word, the second person of the Trinity. Although Aquinas takes the Incarnation to be the supremely superrational mystery of Christian faith, he also understands hypostatic union as providing the classical, orthodox account of the truth of the Incarnation. Thus, in his mature treatment of the mode of the incarnational union (*ST* III.2), Aquinas aims primarily to explicate and defend the teaching of the Council of Chalcedon (451) that Jesus Christ is one person subsisting in two natures. See also: Christology; Eutychianism; Nestorianism.

Image   According to Aquinas and classical Christian theology more generally, whereas irrational creatures are like God by way of a vestige or trace (most basically inasmuch as they exist or have *esse*), the human being, a rational creature, resembles God more profoundly. Indeed, in humans is found a likeness to God by way of an image. That we humans have been created according to the image of God (Gen. 1:26–27) means that we imitate God's own operations of knowing and willing, the very operations whereby God creates.

Impassibility   The inability to suffer or to experience pain. In line with classical theology and in contradistinction to modern theologians such as Jürgen Moltmann, Aquinas attributes impassibility to God in Himself. The Dominican master teaches that although, simply speaking, God is wholly unable to suffer, the divine Word, the second person of the Trinity, did suffer and die according to the human nature He assumed for the sake of human salvation.

Kataphaticism   positive theology, as opposed to apophatic or negative theology; a way of coming to know God by understanding and affirming what He is. Character-theism is a contemporary manifestation of kataphatic theology. Aquinas, by contrast, teaches that because God is not a being among or alongside the universe of beings, we cannot naturally have any positive idea of what God is. Rather, we can only know God apophatically and inferentially, by knowing what God is not. See also: apophaticism; character-theism; simplicity.

Metaphysics   According to Aristotle, Aquinas, and other ancient and medieval thinkers, metaphysics is the highest philosophical 'science,' also called "first philosophy," "wisdom," "divine science," and "theology." It is called metaphysics because it studies what is beyond the physical: its subject matter is 'being (*esse*) as such' or 'being *qua* being.' Thus, it treats what is most universal, most immaterial, and most causal. For Aquinas, this subject is God, who is "subsistent being itself [*ipsum esse subsistens*]" (e.g., *ST* I.4.2 co.; I.11.4 co.).

Neothomism   The sustained and global revival of the study of the philosophy of Thomas Aquinas, particularly in Roman Catholic seminaries and universities, from the late-nineteenth to the mid-twentieth century. The impetus for the Neothomist revival was *Aeterni Patris*, the encyclical issued by Pope Leo XIII on August 4, 1879, whose goal was to aid and advance the restoration of Christian philosophy, particularly that of the Angelic Doctor, in the face of modernism, rationalism, and secularism.

Nestorianism   a two-person Christology that takes its name from the ancient Patriarch of Constantinople, Nestorius, and was condemned as heretical by the Council of Ephesus in 431. Nestorius appears to have held that in the Incarnation two different persons or hypostases—the divine Son of God and the human son of man—were united in various accidental ways, namely by indwelling, mutual disposition, operation, dignity of honor, and the communication of names (*ST* III.2.6; III.2.3; III.3.6). See also: Eutychianism; hypostatic union.

Ontological argument   the famous argument for the existence of God set forth by Anselm of Canterbury in chapter 2 of the *Proslogion*. It is an *a priori* argument according to which, if one understands what God is, it is evident that God exists. Anselm's basic line of argument runs thus: (1) God is "a certain thing than which nothing greater can be thought"; (2) This "certain thing than which nothing greater can be thought" exists in the mind or intellect of all who think of 'God,' even of those who, like the "fool" of the Psalms, say "There is no God" (Ps. 13:1; 52:1); (3) God must exist in reality as well as in the human mind if He is, in fact, "a certain thing than which nothing greater can be thought," because it is greater, ontologically speaking, to exist in reality than in the mind alone.

Preambles of faith   one of the two types of truth that constitute the science of sacred doctrine; they are presupposed by the articles of faith (the other type of truth in sacred doctrine) and, in terms of our human mode of knowing, 'walk before' (*pre* + *ambulo*) them. Although, like the articles of faith, they have been revealed by God, the preambles of faith are those sacred truths that can be arrived at by natural reason; for Aquinas, they include God's existence, God's oneness, God's goodness, and the incorruptibility of the human soul. See also: articles of faith.

Predestination   the doctrine that God has determined or destined some human beings for eternal salvation 'beforehand,' that is, eternally, 'before' humans themselves did anything good or bad that might have influenced the divine will. According to the commonly received Calvinist understanding, the eternal God actively and inscrutably wills either salvation or reprobation for each human from before all time and supervenes upon human freedom such that each one is ineluctably moved by divine imperative toward unending beatitude (and the grace such movement requires), on the one hand, or everlasting damnation (and the grave sin it demands), on the other. Given his understanding of God's eternal knowing and willing and his profound metaphysics of human action, Aquinas's doctrine of predestination looks rather different from this popular Calvinist version. The eternal, singular will of God regarding salvation 'takes into account' and even causes the contingencies of human freedom and action that play a necessary role in each human's attainment of his or her final end.

Problem of evil a post-Enlightenment, philosophical conundrum according to which evil and suffering in the world threaten belief in the existence of an omnipotent, omniscient, and omnibenevolent God. For Aquinas, in contrast to modern 'problem of evil' philosophers, evil never poses a 'problem' for God's existence. To the contrary, in fact, Aquinas takes the reality of evil as evidence for divine existence, noting that one can legitimately argue, "If evil exists, God exists" (*ScG* III.71).

Pure human (homo purus) an ordinary human being or human person like you and me, possessing a human nature constituted of a rational soul and a corruptible, animal body. Although Jesus Christ is fully human, possessing a complete human nature, He is not, according to Aquinas, a pure human. In fact, Christ is not a human person at all. Rather, Christ is a divine person, the eternally-existing second person of the Trinity; His divine nature is what grounds His person, the principle by which He exists simply. See also: beatific vision; supposit.

Quiddity From the Latin *quid*, meaning "what," quiddity is the "whatness" or essence of a thing. Aquinas teaches that, although we can naturally know that God is, we cannot know what God is (*quid est*). Instead of having a positive notion of God's quiddity, we come to know God by knowing what God is not. See also: apophaticism; essence; simplicity.

Relation according to Aristotle's *Categories*, an accident or accidental quality of a thing that signifies reference or regard to another. A relation, such as paternity or filiation, does not subsist or exist apart from the substance in which it inheres accidentally. Aquinas distinguishes between real relations, according to which one thing is ordered to another by nature, and rational or logical relations, according to which one thing is ordered to another merely "in the apprehension of reason comparing one thing to another" (*ST* III.28.1 co.). The notion of relation plays a significant role both in Aquinas's Trinitarian theology, according to which the divine persons constitute subsistent relations in the Godhead, and in his doctrine of creation, according to which all creatures are really related to God but, contrastingly, there is no real relation in God to creatures.

Sabellianism named for Sabellius, who may have been a presbyter in Rome in the third century, this heresy was a form of Modalistic Monarchianism, which held that God was really one (a divine monarchy or monad) but appeared in three modes or played three different roles in history: as Father in creation, as Son in redemption, and as Holy Spirit in sanctification. Father, Son, and Holy Spirit, then, are not distinct persons in the Godhead, but rather mere modes or manifestations of the one God. Pope Calixtus (r. c. 218-c. 222) condemned Sabellianism and excommunicated Sabellius himself. The Church rejected Sabellianism in favor of the doctrine of the Trinity, according to which God is three distinct, coequal, and coeternal persons: Father, Son, and Holy Spirit. In his mature treatment of the Trinity, Aquinas notes that Sabellius wrongly understood procession in God in terms of a cause (namely, the Father) proceeding externally to effects (the Son and Holy Spirit) rather than in terms of the internal processions of knowledge and love in an intellectual nature (*ST* I.27.1).

Sacred doctrine (sacra doctrina) the 'holy teaching' concerning God that, according to Aquinas, proceeds by way of divine revelation and is, on account of the "defect of philosophy" regarding the knowledge of God (*Scriptum* q. 1 a. 1 s.c. 2), necessary for human salvation. In terms of content, sacred doctrine includes the articles of faith, which cannot be known by natural reason, as well as the preambles of faith, to which reason can attain. As *ST* I.1 makes clear, Aquinas understands sacred doctrine as a single science (in the Aristotelian sense) that is principally speculative, that is nobler than all other sciences, and that proceeds principally by way of arguments from authority based on divine revelation, though it also makes use of philosophy and natural reason. See also: articles of faith; preambles of faith.

Scholasticism The system of education and modes of discourse characteristic of the European universities in the High and Late Middle Ages (13th–16th c.). Central to the scholastic method was ordering and reconciling the ever-growing body of knowledge in the medieval West, resultant particularly from the new translations of Aristotle's into Latin in the mid-twelfth century. The greatest works of scholastic theology—Peter Lombard's *Sentences* and Aquinas's *Summa theologiae*, for example—applied dialectic (i.e., logic or reason) to the numerous, scattered, and inchoate statements of Scripture, the

Church Fathers, and ecumenical councils on a wide range of questions concerning faith and doctrine.

Simplicity The traditional Christian doctrine of divine simplicity affirms that God is fundamentally different from all creatures. Whereas creatures are composed in various ways—in terms of body and soul, matter and form, potency and act, nature and supposit, essence and existence, genus and species, and substance and accidents—God is entirely simple, being composed in none of these ways. God has no 'parts,' whether spatial, temporal, or metaphysical. And because God utterly transcends every mode of composition according to which we understand creatures, we cannot naturally know what God is. The doctrine of divine simplicity is central to Aquinas's apophaticism and to his theology in general. See also: apophaticism.

Socius The Latin term meaning associate or companion. Reginald of Piperno, often described by modern scholars as Aquinas's "secretary," was his *socius* in the Dominican Order and his confessor from c. 1265. Reginald began teaching with Aquinas in Naples in 1272, and he produced written reports of several of Aquinas's works, which he heard via lecture or direct dictation. He also collected all the works of Aquinas.

Soteriology The area of theology concerned with salvation, particularly as effected by Jesus Christ. Although Aquinas has human salvation in view throughout the *ST*, beginning with the opening question on sacred doctrine, he treats soteriology in particular in the *Tertia pars*. See also: Christology.

Substance the essential nature of a thing, as distinct from its accidental qualities. A thing's substance is literally what 'stands under' (*substare*) the particular constellation of accidents that inhere in it. A thing's substance or essence is what is required for it to be and to be what it is. Following patristic tradition, Aquinas teaches that God differs from all created things in His simplicity: that is, He is not composed of substance and accidents (or of body and soul, matter and form, potency and act, nature and supposit, essence and existence, genus and species). Furthermore, the Aristotelian categories of substance and accidents figure prominently in Aquinas's eucharistic theology, particularly in *ScG* IV.61–68, where he seeks to answer various philosophical difficulties proposed against the doctrine of transubstantiation. See also: essence; simplicity; transubstantiation.

Supposit an individual that underlies (*supponitur*), subsists in, and instantiates a particular nature (*ST* III.2.2, 3). An individual instantiation of a human nature is a human supposit, also known as a human person. In ordinary humans like you and me, human nature is the principle whereby we subsist and are supposits or persons; in us, in other words, human nature is supposit-grounding. Aquinas teaches that Christ's human nature, by contrast, is not supposit-grounding. Rather, the divine nature, whereby the Word of God exists eternally, grounds the supposit or person of Christ. The theological upshot is that the one Christ, according to Aquinas, is a divine person, not a human person, though He is fully human by virtue of the perfect human nature assumed by the person of the Word.

Transubstantiation   the Catholic doctrine concerning Christ's real presence in the Eucharist, first officially promulgated by the bishops convened at the Fourth Lateran Council in 1215. Drawing on the Aristotelian distinction between substance and accidents, the Church believes and teaches that at the moment of eucharistic consecration, by the power and working of the Holy Spirit, the substance of the sacramental elements of bread and wine is changed into the substance of Christ's body and blood, though the accidents of bread and wine remain unchanged. In his treatment of the Eucharist in *ScG* IV.61–68, Aquinas sets forth and answers five major classes of philosophical and sensible difficulties with the doctrine of transubstantiation, which he takes to be an article of faith revealed in Scripture and clarified by ecclesial tradition.

Trinity   the Christian doctrine that the one God is three coeternal, coequal, and consubstantial persons, Father, Son, and Holy Spirit. Although some modern readers have criticized Aquinas for marginalizing the Trinity and isolating it from such theological topics as creation and Incarnation, in fact the doctrine is absolutely central to the Dominican's theology and to his understanding of the whole of Christian faith and life. According to Aquinas, the Trinity is an article of faith that surpasses the capacity of human reason; in order for this profound mystery to be grasped at all, then, it is necessary that it has been revealed by God Himself and that it be apprehended by faith. See also: articles of faith.

Vestige   A trace, track, or footprint (Latin *vestigium*). According to Aquinas (and other premodern theologians), in all irrational creatures is found a likeness to God by way of a vestige, that is, as an effect that generally represents its cause (by existing and living, for example). Most basically, the *esse* or being of creatures reflects and points to God, the Creator, who is subsistent being itself (*ipsum esse subsistens*) and grants *esse* to all created effects. Although different irrational creatures resemble God to varying degrees based on each one's mode of existence, none imitates God as profoundly as rational creatures, in whom is found a likeness to God by way of an image. See also: *esse*; image.

BIBLIOGRAPHY

Anatolios, Khaled (2015). "Christology in the Fourth Century," in *The Oxford Handbook of Christology*, ed. Francesca Aran Murphy, assisted by Troy A. Stefano, pp. 105–120. Oxford. Oxford University Press.

Ayres, Lewis (2004). *Nicaea and its Legacy: An Approach to Fourth-Century Trinitarian Theology*. Oxford: Oxford University Press.

Baglow, Christopher T. (2004). "Sacred Scripture and Sacred Doctrine in Saint Thomas Aquinas," in *Aquinas on Doctrine: A Critical Introduction*, ed. Thomas Weinandy, Daniel Keating, and John Yocum, pp. 1–25. London: T&T Clark.

Barnes, Corey L. (2012). *Christ's Two Wills in Scholastic Thought: The Christology of Aquinas and Its Historical Contexts*. Toronto: Pontifical Institute of Mediaeval Studies.

Bauerschmidt, Frederick Christian (2005). *Holy Teaching: Introducing the Summa Theologiae of St. Thomas Aquinas*. Grand Rapids, MI: Brazos Press.

Blankenhorn, Bernard, O.P. (2006). "The Instrumental Causality of the Sacraments: Thomas Aquinas and Louis-Marie Chauvet," *Nova et Vetera* 4/2: 255–294.

Boyle, Leonard E., O.P. (1982). *The Setting of the Summa theologiae of Saint Thomas*. Toronto: Pontifical Institute of Mediaeval Studies.

Brito, Emilio (1988). "Dieu en mouvement: Thomas d'Aquin et Hegel," *Revue des sciences religieuses* 62: 111–136.

Brown, Stephen F. (1998). "Thomas Aquinas and His Contemporaries on the Unique Existence in Christ," in *Christ among the Medieval Dominicans: Representations of Christ in the Texts and Images of the Order of Preachers*, ed. Kent Emery, Jr. and Joseph Wawrykow, pp. 220–237.

Burrell, David B., C.S.C. (1979). *Aquinas, God and Action*. Notre Dame, IN: University of Notre Dame Press.

Burrell, David B., C.S.C. (2004). "Act of Creation with its Theological Consequences," in *Aquinas on Doctrine: A Critical Introduction*, ed. Thomas Weinandy, Daniel Keating, and John Yocum, pp. 27–44. London: T&T Clark.

Capps, Donald, and Nathan Carlin (2016). "Releasing Life's Potential: A Pastoral Theology of Work," *Pastoral Psychology* 65: 863–883.

Chauvet, Louis-Marie (1995). *Symbol and Sacrament: A Sacramental Reinterpretation of Christian Existence*, trans. Patrick Madigan, S.J., and Madeleine Beaumont. Collegeville, MN: Liturgical Press.

Chenu, Marie-Dominique, O.P. (1939). "Le plan de la Somme théologique de S. Thomas," *Revue thomiste* 45: 93–107.

Chenu, Marie-Dominique, O.P. (1963). *The Theology of Work: An Exploration*, trans. L. Soiron. Dublin: M. H. Gill & Son.

Chenu, Marie-Dominique, O.P. (2002). *Aquinas and His Role in Theology*, trans. Paul Philibert, O.P. Collegeville, MN: Liturgical Press.

Coakley, Sarah (2016). "Person of Christ," in *The Cambridge Companion to the Summa Theologiae*, ed. Philip McCosker and Denys Turner, pp. 222–239. Cambridge: Cambridge University Press.

Colberg, Shawn (2010). "Accrued Eyes and Sixth Digits: Thomas Aquinas and Cardinal Cajetan on Christ's Single Esse and the Union of Natures," *Nova et Vetera*, English edition, 8/1: 55–87.

Copleston, F. C. (1955). *Aquinas: An Introduction to the Life and Work of the Great Medieval Thinker*. London: Penguin Books (repr. 1991).

Cross, Richard (1996). "Aquinas on Nature, Hypostasis, and the Metaphysics of the Incarnation," *The Thomist* 60/2: 171–202.

Cross, Richard (2002). *The Metaphysics of the Incarnation: Thomas Aquinas to Duns Scotus*. Oxford: Oxford University Press.

Davies, Brian, O.P. (2002). *Aquinas*. London: Continuum.

Davies, Brian, O.P. (2011). *Thomas Aquinas on God and Evil*. Oxford: Oxford University Press.

Davies, Brian, O.P. (2012). "Happiness," in *The Oxford Handbook of Aquinas*, ed. Brian Davies and Eleonore Stump, pp. 227–237. Oxford: Oxford University Press.

Davies, Brian, O.P. (2014). *Thomas Aquinas's Summa Theologiae: A Guide and Commentary*. Oxford: Oxford University Press.

Davies, Brian, O.P. (2016a). "God," in *The Cambridge Companion to the Summa Theologiae*, ed. Philip McCosker and Denys Turner, pp. 85–101. Cambridge: Cambridge University Press.

Davies, Brian, O.P. (2016b). *Thomas Aquinas's Summa Contra Gentiles: A Guide and Commentary*. Oxford: Oxford University Press.

Dawkins, Richard (2006). *The God Delusion*. Boston, MA: Houghton Mifflin.

Dawkins, Richard (2019). *Outgrowing God: A Beginner's Guide*. New York: Random House.

Dewan, Lawrence, O.P. (2008). *Wisdom, Law, and Virtue: Essays in Thomistic Ethics*. New York: Fordham University Press.

Dodds, Michael J., O.P. (2008). *The Unchanging God of Love: Thomas Aquinas and Contemporary Theology on Divine Immutability*, 2nd edition. Washington, DC: Catholic University of America Press.

Dulles, Avery (2001). "Jesus and Faith," in *The Convergence of Theology: A Festschrift Honoring Gerald O'Collins, S.J.*, ed. Daniel Kendall, S.J. and Stephen T. Davis, pp. 273–284. New York: Paulist Press.

Emery, Gilles (2004). "The Doctrine of the Trinity in St Thomas Aquinas," in *Aquinas on Doctrine: A Critical Introduction*, ed. Thomas Weinandy, Daniel Keating, and John Yocum, pp. 45–65. London: T&T Clark.

Emery, Gilles (2005). "Trinity and Creation," in *The Theology of Thomas Aquinas*, ed. Rik Van Nieuwenhove and Joseph Wawrykow, pp. 58–76. Notre Dame, IN: University of Notre Dame Press.

Emery, Gilles (2007). *The Trinitarian Theology of Saint Thomas Aquinas*, trans. Francesca Aran Murphy. Oxford: Oxford University Press.

Emery, Gilles (2012). "The Trinity," in *The Oxford Handbook of Aquinas*, ed. Brian Davies and Eleonore Stump, pp. 418–427. Oxford: Oxford University Press.

Feser, Edward (2009). *Aquinas: A Beginner's Guide*. London: Oneworld.

Froula, John (2014). "Esse secundarium: An Analogical Term Meaning That by Which Christ is Human," *The Thomist* 78: 557–580.

Gaine, Simon Francis (2015). *Did the Saviour See the Father? Christ, Salvation and the Vision of God*. London: Bloomsbury.

Gilson, Etienne (1994). *The Christian Philosophy of St. Thomas Aquinas*, with a Catalogue of St. Thomas's Works by I. T. Eschmann, O.P., trans. L. K. Shook, C.S.B. Notre Dame, IN: University of Notre Dame Press.

Gondreau, Paul (2005). "The Humanity of Christ, the Incarnate Word," in *The Theology of Thomas Aquinas*, ed. Rik Van Nieuwenhove and Joseph Wawrykow, pp. 252–276. Notre Dame, IN: University of Notre Dame Press.

Gondreau, Paul (2009). *The Passions of Christ's Soul in the Theology of St. Thomas Aquinas*. Scranton, TX: University of Scranton Press.

Goris, Harm J. M. J. (2018). "Thomas Aquinas on Christ's Descent into Hell," in *The Apostles' Creed: 'He Descended into Hell'*, ed. Marcel Sarot and Archibald L. H. M. van Wieringen, pp. 93–114. Leiden: Brill.

Gorman, Michael (2017). *Aquinas on the Metaphysics of the Hypostatic Union*. Cambridge: Cambridge University Press.

Griffin, David Ray (1976). *God, Power, and Evil: A Process Theodicy*. Philadelphia, PA: Westminster Press.

Harkins, Franklin T. (2014a). "The Early Aquinas on the Question of Universal Salvation, or How a Knight May Choose Not to Ride His Horse," *New Blackfriars* 95: 208–217.

Harkins, Franklin T. (2014b). "Contingency and Causality in Predestination: 1 Tim. 2:4 in the Sentences Commentaries of Albert the Great, Thomas Aquinas, and John Duns Scotus," *Archa Verbi* 11: 35–72.

Harkins, Franklin T. (2017). "Christ and the Eternal Extent of Divine Providence in the *Expositio super Iob ad litteram* of Thomas Aquinas," in *A Companion to Job in the Middle Ages*, ed. Franklin T. Harkins and Aaron Canty, pp. 161–200. Leiden: Brill.

Harkins, Franklin T., trans. (2019). *St. Albert the Great On Job*, volume 1. The Fathers of the Church Mediaeval Continuation 19. Washington, DC: Catholic University of America Press.

Harkins, Franklin T. (2021). "Christ's Perfect Grace and Beatific Knowledge in Aquinas: The Influence of John Damascene," in *Reading the Church Fathers with St. Thomas Aquinas: Historical and Systematic Perspectives*, ed. Piotr Roszak and Jörgen Vijgen, pp. 335–68. Turnhout: Brepols.

Harkins, Franklin T. and Aaron Canty, eds. (2017). *A Companion to Job in the Middle Ages*. Leiden: Brill.

Hart, David Bentley (2013). *The Experience of God: Being, Consciousness, Bliss*. New Haven, CT: Yale University Press.

Hefner, Philip (2012). "A Fuller Concept of Evolution—Big Bang to Spirit," *Zygon: Journal of Religion and Science* 47/2: 298–307.

Holtz, Dominic, O.P. (2012). "Sacraments," in *The Oxford Handbook of Aquinas*, ed. Brian Davies and Eleonore Stump, pp. 448–457. Oxford: Oxford University Press.

Johnstone, Brian V. (2002). "The Debate on the Structure of the Summa Theologiae of St. Thomas Aquinas: from Chenu (1939) to Metz (1998)," in *Aquinas as Authority: A Collection of Studies Presented at the Second Conference of the Thomas Instituut te Utrecht, December 14–16, 2000*, ed. Paul van Geest, Harm Goris, and C. J. W. Leget, pp. 187–200. Leuven: Peeters.

Jordan, Mark D. (2016). "Structure," in *The Cambridge Companion to the Summa Theologiae*, ed. Philip McCosker and Denys Turner, pp. 34–47. Cambridge: Cambridge University Press.

Kenny, Anthony (1969). *The Five Ways: Saint Thomas Aquinas' Proofs of God's Existence*. London: Routledge & Kegan Paul (repr. 1980, University of Notre Dame Press).

Kenny, Anthony (2002). *Aquinas on Being*. Oxford: Clarendon Press.

Kerr, Fergus (2009). *Thomas Aquinas: A Very Short Introduction*. Oxford: Oxford University Press.

Kerr, Gaven (2015). *Aquinas's Way to God: The Proof in De Ente et Essentia*. Oxford: Oxford University Press.

Kerr, Gaven (2019). *Aquinas and the Metaphysics of Creation*. Oxford: Oxford University Press.

Kilby, Karen (2003). "Evil and the Limits of Theology," *New Blackfriars* 84: 13–29.

LaCugna, Catherine Mowry (1985). "The Relational God: Aquinas and Beyond," *Theological Studies* 46: 647–663.

LaCugna, Catherine Mowry (1991). *God For Us: The Trinity and Christian Life.* New York: HarperCollins.

Lamb, Matthew L. (2004). "The Eschatology of St Thomas Aquinas," in *Aquinas on Doctrine: A Critical Introduction*, ed. Thomas Weinandy, Daniel Keating, and John Yocum, pp. 225–240. London: T&T Clark.

Leget, Carlo (2005). "Eschatology," in *The Theology of Thomas Aquinas*, ed. Rik Van Nieuwenhove and Joseph Wawrykow, pp. 365–385. Notre Dame, IN: University of Notre Dame Press.

Levy, Ian Christopher (2018). *Introducing Medieval Biblical Interpretation: The Senses of Scripture in Premodern Exegesis.* Grand Rapids, MI: Baker Academic.

Louth, Andrew (2015). "Christology in the East from the Council of Chalcedon to John Damascene," in *The Oxford Handbook of Christology*, ed. Francesca Aran Murphy, assisted by Troy A. Stefano, pp. 139–153. Oxford: Oxford University Press.

MacDonald, Scott (2002). "The *Esse/Essentia* Argument in Aquinas's *De ente et essentia*," in *Thomas Aquinas: Contemporary Philosophical Perspectives*, ed. Brian Davies, pp. 141–157. Oxford: Oxford University Press.

Mackey, James P. (1979). *Jesus, the Man and the Myth: A Contemporary Christology.* London: SCM Press.

Marenbon, John (2016). "Method," in *The Cambridge Companion to the Summa Theologiae*, ed. Philip McCosker and Denys Turner, pp. 74–82. Cambridge: Cambridge University Press.

Marenbon, John (2017). "Why We Shouldn't Study Aquinas." Unpublished paper. Retrieved from www.academia.edu/32902867/Why_we_shouldnt_study_Aquinas.

Marshall, Bruce D. (2005). "*Quod Scit Una Uetula*: Aquinas on the Nature of Theology," in *The Theology of Thomas Aquinas*, ed. Rik Van Nieuwenhove and Joseph Wawrykow, pp. 1–35. Notre Dame, IN: University of Notre Dame Press.

McCabe, Herbert (2000). "A Modern Cosmological Argument," in *Philosophy of Religion: A Guide and Anthology*, ed. Brian Davies, pp. 196–201. Oxford: Oxford University Press.

McCabe, Herbert (2002). *God Still Matters*, ed. Brian Davies, O.P. London: Continuum.

McCabe, Herbert (2016a). "Eternity," in *The Cambridge Companion to the Summa Theologiae*, ed. Philip McCosker and Denys Turner, pp. 102–116. Cambridge: Cambridge University Press.

McCabe, Herbert (2016b). "A Very Short Introduction to Aquinas," in *The McCabe Reader*, ed. Brian Davies and Paul Kucharski, pp. 239–255. London: Bloomsbury.

McCosker, Philip (2016). "Grace," in *The Cambridge Companion to the Summa Theologiae*, ed. Philip McCosker and Denys Turner, pp. 206–221. Cambridge: Cambridge University Press.

McCosker, Philip and Denys Turner (2016). "Introduction," in *The Cambridge Companion to the Summa Theologiae*, ed. Philip McCosker and Denys Turner, pp. 1–5. Cambridge: Cambridge University Press.

McGinn, Bernard (2014). *Thomas Aquinas's Summa theologiae: A Biography*. Princeton: Princeton University Press.

McInerny, Ralph, ed. and trans. (1998). *Thomas Aquinas: Selected Writings*. London: Penguin Books.

Meister, Chad, and Paul K. Moser, eds. (2017). *The Cambridge Companion to the Problem of Evil*. Cambridge: Cambridge University Press.

Moltmann, Jürgen (1974). *The Crucified God: The Cross of Christ as the Foundation and Criticism of Christian Theology*. New York: Harper & Row.

Moonan, Lawrence (2000). "The Responsibility of Theology for the Question of God," *New Blackfriars* 81: 2–15.

Mulchahey, M. Michèle (1998). *"First the Bow is Bent in Study …": Dominican Education before 1350*. Toronto: Pontifical Institute of Mediaeval Studies.

Muller, Earl, S.J. (1995). "Real Relations and the Divine: Issues in Thomas's Understanding of God's Relation to the World," *Theological Studies* 56: 673–695.

Newton, Isaac (1730). *Opticks, or A Treatise of the Reflections, Refractions, Inflections and Colours of Light*, 4th edition. London: Printed for William Innys at the West-End of St. Paul's.

Noone, Timothy B. (2003). "Scholasticism," in *A Companion to Philosophy in the Middle Ages*, ed. Jorge J. E. Gracia and Timothy B. Noone, pp. 55–64. Malden, MA: Blackwell Publishing.

O'Collins, Gerald, S.J. (2008). *Jesus: A Portrait*. Maryknoll, NY: Orbis Books.

O'Collins, Gerald, S.J. and Daniel Kendall, S.J. (1992). "The Faith of Jesus," *Theological Studies* 53: 403–423.

O'Meara, Thomas F., O.P. (1997). *Thomas Aquinas: Theologian*. Notre Dame, IN: University of Notre Dame Press.

Pasnau, Robert (2002). *Thomas Aquinas on Human Nature: A Philosophical Study of Summa theologiae Ia 75–89*. Cambridge: Cambridge University Press.

Patfoort, Albert, O.P. (1963). "L'unité de la Ia Pars et le mouvement interne de la Somme théologique de S. Thomas d'Aquin," *Revue des sciences philosophique et théologiques* 47/4: 513–544.

Pawl, Timothy (2012). "The Five Ways," in *The Oxford Handbook of Aquinas*, ed. Brian Davies and Eleonore Stump, pp. 115–131. Oxford: Oxford University Press.

Pinnock, Clark H. (2001). *Most Moved Mover: A Theology of God's Openness*. Carlisle: Paternoster Press.

Pinnock, Clark H., Richard Rice, John Sanders, William Hasker, and David Basinger (1994). *The Openness of God: A Biblical Challenge to the Traditional Understanding of God*. Downers Grove, IL: InterVarsity Press.

Pope, Stephen J. (2002). "Overview of the Ethics of Thomas Aquinas," in *The Ethics of Aquinas*, ed. Stephen J. Pope, pp. 30–53. Washington, DC: Georgetown University Press.

Porter, Jean (2016). "Happiness," in *The Cambridge Companion to the Summa Theologiae*, ed. Philip McCosker and Denys Turner, pp. 181–193. Cambridge: Cambridge University Press.

Prügl, Thomas (2005). "Thomas Aquinas as Interpreter of Scripture," in *The Theology of Thomas Aquinas*, ed. Rik Van Nieuwenhove and Joseph Wawrykow, pp. 386–415. Notre Dame, IN: University of Notre Dame Press.

Radcliffe, Timothy, O.P. (2016). "Dominican Spirituality," in *The Cambridge Companion to the Summa Theologiae*, ed. Philip McCosker and Denys Turner, pp. 23–33. Cambridge: Cambridge University Press.

Rahner, Karl (1966). "Dogmatic Reflections on the Knowledge and Self-consciousness of Christ," in *Theological Investigations* V, trans. K.-H. Kruger, pp. 193–215. London: Darton, Longman & Todd.

Rahner, Karl (1970). *The Trinity*, trans. Joseph Donceel. New York: Herder and Herder.

Rahner, Karl (2000). "Experiences of a Catholic Theologian," *Theological Studies 61*: 3–15.

Rikhof, Herwi (2005). "Trinity," in *The Theology of Thomas Aquinas*, ed. Rik Van Nieuwenhove and Joseph Wawrykow, pp. 36–57. Notre Dame, IN: University of Notre Dame Press.

Rosemann, Philipp W. (2004). *Peter Lombard*. Oxford: Oxford University Press.

Ruse, Michael (1989). "Do Organisms Exist?" *American Zoologist 29*: 1061–1066.

Russell, Frederick H. (1990). "'Only Something Good Can Be Evil': The Genesis of Augustine's Secular Ambivalence," *Theological Studies* 51: 698–716.

Salas, Victor (2006). "Thomas Aquinas on Christ's Esse," *The Thomist 70*: 577–603.

Schillebeeckx, Edward (1993). *Church: The Human Story of God*. New York: Crossroad.

Sobrino, Jon, S.J. (1978). *Christology at the Crossroads: A Latin American Approach*, trans. John Drury. Maryknoll, NY: Orbis Books.

Speak, Daniel (2015). *The Problem of Evil*. Cambridge: Polity Press.

Steinhauser, Kenneth B. (2017). "Job in Patristic Commentaries and Theological Works," in *A Companion to Job in the Middle Ages*, ed. Franklin T. Harkins and Aaron Canty, pp. 34–70. Leiden: Brill.

Stump, Eleonore (2003). *Aquinas*. London: Routledge.

Stump, Eleonore (2010). *Wandering in Darkness: Narrative and the Problem of Suffering*. Oxford: Clarendon Press.

Stump, Eleonore (2012). "Providence and the Problem of Evil," in *The Oxford Handbook of Aquinas*, ed. Brian Davies and Eleonore Stump, pp. 401–417. Oxford: Oxford University Press.

Swinburne, Richard (1977). *The Coherence of Theism*. Oxford: Clarendon Press.

Tanner, Kathryn (2016). "Creation," in *The Cambridge Companion to the Summa Theologiae*, ed. Philip McCosker and Denys Turner, pp. 142–155. Cambridge: Cambridge University Press.

Tanner, Norman P., S.J. (1990). *Decrees of the Ecumenical Councils*, 2 volumes. London: Sheed & Ward.

Taylor, Richard (1975). "The Metaphysics of Causation," in *Causation and Conditionals*, ed. Ernest Sosa, pp. 39–43. Oxford: Oxford University Press.

Thiel, John E. (2002). *God, Evil, and Innocent Suffering: A Theological Reflection*. New York: Crossroad Publishing Company.

Torrell, Jean-Pierre, O.P. (1996). *Saint Thomas Aquinas. Volume 1: The Person and His Work*, revised edition, trans. Robert Royal. Washington, DC: Catholic University of America Press.

Torrell, Jean-Pierre, O.P. (2005). *Aquinas's Summa: Background, Structure, & Reception*, trans. Benedict M. Guevin, O.S.B. Washington, DC: Catholic University of America Press.

Torrell, Jean-Pierre, O.P. (2011). *Christ and Spirituality in St. Thomas Aquinas*, trans. Bernhard Blankenhorn, O.P. Washington, DC: Catholic University of America Press.

Tschipke, Theophil (2003). *L'humanité du Christ comme instrument de salut de la divinité*. Fribourg: Academic Press.

Tück, Jan-Heiner (2018). *A Gift of Presence: The Theology and Poetry of the Eucharist in Thomas Aquinas*, trans. Scott G. Hefelfinger. Washington, DC: Catholic University of America Press.

Tugwell, Simon, O.P., and Leonard E. Boyle, O.P., trans. and ed. (1988). *Albert & Thomas: Selected Writings*. New York: Paulist Press.

Turner, Denys (2016). "The human person," in *The Cambridge Companion to the Summa Theologiae*, ed. Philip McCosker and Denys Turner, pp. 168–180. Cambridge: Cambridge University Press.

Van Nieuwenhove, Rik (2005). "'Bearing the Marks of Christ's Passion': Aquinas' Soteriology," in *The Theology of Thomas Aquinas*, ed. Rik Van Nieuwenhove and Joseph Wawrykow, pp. 277–302. Notre Dame, IN: University of Notre Dame Press.

Van Nieuwenhove, Rik (2012). *An Introduction to Medieval Theology*. Cambridge: Cambridge University Press.

Velde, Rudi te (2006). *Aquinas on God: The 'Divine Science' of the Summa Theologiae*. Aldershot: Ashgate.

Wallace, W. A. (1956). "Newtonian Antinomies against the Prima Via," *The Thomist* 19/2: 151–192.

Wawrykow, Joseph P. (2005a). "Hypostatic Union," in *The Theology of Thomas Aquinas*, ed. Rik Van Nieuwenhove and Joseph Wawrykow, pp. 222–251. Notre Dame, IN: University of Notre Dame Press.

Wawrykow, Joseph P. (2005b). *The Westminster Handbook to Thomas Aquinas*. Louisville, KY: Westminster John Knox Press.

Wawrykow, Joseph P. (2012). "The Theological Virtues," in *The Oxford Handbook of Aquinas*, ed. Brian Davies and Eleonore Stump, pp. 287–307. Oxford: Oxford University Press.

Wawrykow, Joseph P. (2015). "The Christology of Thomas Aquinas in its Scholastic Context," in *The Oxford Handbook of Christology*, ed. Francesca Aran Murphy, assisted by Troy A. Stefano, pp. 233–249. Oxford: Oxford University Press.

Weinandy, Thomas G. (2004). "Aquinas: God *IS* Man: The Marvel of the Incarnation," in *Aquinas on Doctrine: A Critical Introduction*, ed. Thomas Weinandy, Daniel Keating, and John Yocum, pp. 67–89. London: T&T Clark.

Weisheipl, James A., O.P. (1974). *Friar Thomas d'Aquino: His Life, Thought, and Works*. Garden City, NY: Doubleday.

West, J. L. A. (2002). "Aquinas on the Metaphysics of the Esse in Christ," *The Thomist* 66: 231–250.

White, Thomas Joseph, O.P. (2015). *The Incarnate Lord: A Thomistic Study in Christology*. Washington, DC: Catholic University of America Press.

Wilhelm, Joseph, and Thomas B. Scannell (1909). *A Manual of Catholic Theology based on Scheeben's "Dogmatik"*, vol. 1, 4th ed., revised. London: Kegan Paul, Trench, Trübner & Co.

Williams, Thomas (2012). "Human Freedom and Agency," in *The Oxford Handbook of Aquinas*, ed. Brian Davies and Eleonore Stump, pp. 199–208. Oxford: Oxford University Press.

Wippel, John F. (2000). *The Metaphysical Thought of Thomas Aquinas: From Finite Being to Uncreated Being*. Washington, DC: Catholic University of America Press.

Wippel, John F. (2002). "The Five Ways," in *Thomas Aquinas: Contemporary Philosophical Perspectives*, ed. Brian Davies, pp. 159–225. Oxford: Oxford University Press.

Witt, Charlotte (1989). *Substance and Essence in Aristotle: An Interpretation of Metaphysics VII–IX*. Ithaca, NY: Cornell University Press.

Wolterstorff, Nicholas (1988). "Suffering Love," in *Philosophy and the Christian Faith*, ed. Thomas V. Morris, pp. 196–237. Notre Dame, IN: University of Notre Dame Press.

Yocum, John P. (2004). "Sacraments in Aquinas," in *Aquinas on Doctrine: A Critical Introduction*, ed. Thomas Weinandy, Daniel Keating, and John Yocum, pp. 159–181. London: T&T Clark.

Ziegler, Philip G. (2015). "The Historical Jesus and Christology from David Friedrich Strauss to Käsemann," in *The Oxford Handbook of Christology*, ed. Francesca Aran Murphy, assisted by Troy A. Stefano, pp. 328–344. Oxford: Oxford University Press.

INDEX

Printed in the United States
By Bookmasters